FRENCH ARMIES OF THE THIRTY YEARS' WAR 1618–48

Stéphane Thion

'This is the Century of the Soldier', Fulvio Testi, Poet, 1641

D1716568

HELION &
COMPANY

Helion & Company Limited
Unit 8 Amherst Business Centre
Budbrooke Road
Warwick
CV34 5WE
England
Tel. 01926 499 619
Email: info@helion.co.uk
Website: www.helion.co.uk
Twitter: @helionbooks
Visit our blog http://blog.helion.co.uk/

Published by Helion & Company 2024
Designed and typeset by Mary Woolley, Battlefield Design (www.battlefield-design.co.uk)
Cover designed by Paul Hewitt, Battlefield Design (www.battlefield-design.co.uk)

Text © Stéphane Thion 2024
Photographs and illustrations © as individually credited
Colour artwork by Giorgio Albertini © Helion & Company 2024
Colour flag artwork by Stéphane Thion © Helion & Company 2024
Maps by George Anderson © Helion and Company 2024

ISBN 978-1-804514-48-1

British Library Cataloguing-in-Publication Data.
A catalogue record for this book is available from the British Library.

For details of other military history titles published by Helion & Company Limited
contact the above address or visit our website: http://www.helion.co.uk.

We always welcome receiving book proposals from prospective authors.

Contents

Introduction

The three musketeers, Cyrano de Bergerac, Louis XIII, Richelieu, Condé, Turenne, La Rochelle, Rocroi… these few words sum up the literary and historical representations most people are able to associate with the tumultuous events of the first half of the seventeenth century. We're not complaining – it's a good start!

This book begins in 1617, the year that Louis XIII really took power by distancing the Queen Mother and ordering the assassination of Concini (24 April 1617) and ends in 1648 – five years after the death of Louis XIII – the year of the Westphalia Peace Treaty (24 October 1648). This period was mainly dominated by the personality and works of Richelieu, who entered the King's Council in April 1624. He gave the King an ambition: 'to procure the ruin of the Huguenot party, humble the pride of the great, reduce all subjects to their duty, and elevate your Majesty's name among foreign nations to its rightful reputation.'[1] By the time of his death, on 4 December 1642, this programme had been accomplished.

The first military action of this period, called the 'Drôlerie des Ponts-de-Cé' was the uprising of the nobility who supported the Queen Mother against the King in August 1620. In reality the rebels were roundly defeated by the King's armies, but very few units actually fought. In his memoirs, Richelieu, who at the time was on the Queen's side, gives a detailed analysis of this defeat. In particular, he drew from it principles that he was to follow throughout his life:

> I realised on this occasion that any party composed of many entities that have nothing in common other than their lightness of spirit – which makes them approve the present government constantly, and makes them desire change without knowing why – does not have great subsistence. I also realised that which is held only by a precarious authority does not last long; that those who fight against a legitimate power are already half-defeated by their own imagination; that their thoughts – that not only are they exposed to the risk of losing their life through arms but, what is more, by the paths of justice if they are captured, representing for them the hangman at the same time that they affront the enemy

---

1   Armand du Plessis de Richelieu, *Testament Politique d'Armand du Plessis, Cardinal Duc de Richelieu* (Amsterdam: Henri Desbordes, 1688), p.9.

– renders the contest most unequal, there being few men brave enough to ignore these thoughts as well as if they had never come to their mind.[2]

These political beliefs gave Louis XIII and Richelieu a powerful instrument that was to emerge transformed from the Thirty Years' War.

The army that Marie de Medici left to Henri IV's heir was small and inexperienced, but the Wars of Religion at the beginning of Louis XIII's reign, combined with Richelieu's actions, gave the French Kingdom an increasingly efficient army. Commanded by great captains such as the Duc de Rohan, the Vicomte de Turenne and the Prince de Condé, the army was highly successful, as shown by the long list of French victories, from Île de Rhé in 1626 to Lens in 1648.

Standard-Bearer. Sketch by Ernest Meissonier (1815–1891) (Public Domain)

It is now 15 years since the first edition of *French Armies of the Thirty Years War* was published. This new edition is an updated and expanded version, bringing new resources and materials. For instance, because most of the famous French regiments of this period were raised in the previous era, a new chapter dealing with the transformation of the French Army has been added. This new edition also includes numerous new illustrations. Finally, references have been added in the footnotes, which I hope will be very useful for researchers.

The aim of this book is to understand how the French Army evolved during the first half of the seventeenth century to become a formidable war machine in the hands of Louis XIV. To this end, this book is divided into several chapters. The first chapter sets the historical framework for this transformation, the Thirty Years' War, and presents its main phases in France and Germany. The second chapter summarises the evolution of the French Army in the previous century, to give a better understanding of the origins of these transformations. The third chapter presents the French Army between 1617 and 1634 while the fourth chapter presents this same army after its entry into the war in 1635 up to 1648. The fifth chapter briefly discusses the uniforms and flags of this army. The sixth chapter presents the main actions and

---

2   Armand du Plessis de Richelieu, 'Mémoires du Cardinal de Richelieu,' in *Nouvelle Collection des Mémoires pour servir à l'Histoire de France* (Paris: Michaud et Poujoulat, 1837), deuxième série, tome VII, pp.226–227.

numerous orders of battle of different French armies between 1620 and 1648. The seventh chapter presents accounts and relations of the main battles fought by the French Army of this era. A timeline has been added to this research work and, of course, finally, a bibliography closes the text.

Henri IV, sketch by Ernest Meissonier (1815–1891) (Public Domain)

Chronology

1617   Assassination of Concini (24 April): Louis XIII takes power.

1618   Protestant revolt in Bohemia and Defenestration of Prague (23 May). Archduke Ferdinand II, King of Bohemia, controls the Empire (18 July).

1619   France: rebellion of the Queen Mother. Austria: Ferdinand II is elected Emperor by the Electoral College (28 August). The states of Bohemia pronounce the deposition of Ferdinand II (19 August) and designate the Elector Palatine Frederick V King of Bohemia; coronation on 4 November.

1620   France: rebellion of the nobility resulting in the *Drôlerie des Ponts-de-Cé* (7 August). Bohemia: Battle of the White Mountain (8 November): the Imperial army overwhelms the Protestant army of Christian d'Anhalt.

1621   France: storming of Privas by the Protestants (February). The army of Louis XIII enters the campaign: Siege of Saint Jean d'Angély (June).

1622   Campaign of Saintonge and Languedoc, storming of Nègrepelisse by the Royal Armies (10 June), Siege and Treaty of Montpellier (18 October).

1623   Tilly's victory over Christian of Brunswick at Stadtlohn (6 August).

1624   Richelieu enters the *conseil*. French expedition under François d'Estrées to the Valtelline (October).

1625   France: second Protestant revolt (January). Intervention of Christian IV, King of Denmark in the Thirty Years' War.

1626   English landing on the Île de Rhé (26 July). Defeat of Christian IV of Denmark by Tilly on the 26 August at Lutter-am-Barenberg.

1627   Beginning of the siege of La Rochelle (15 August). Beginning of the succession of Mantua.

1628   Surrender of La Rochelle (28 October). Siege of Stralsund by the Danish navy. The Danish Army is defeated by Wallenstein at Wolgast (September).

1629   *Code Michau* (*Ordonnance* of January 1629). Edict of Grace of Nîmes (28 June). Mantua campaign (1629–30).

1630   Landing of Gustav II Adolph in Pomerania (6 July). Battle of Carignan (6 August); the 'Day of Dupes' (11 November) reinforces Richelieu's powers while Louis XIII sends the Queen Mother into exile.

1631 Italy: Treaty of Cherasco (26 April). Storming and massacre of Magdeburg by Tilly's Imperial Army (20 May). Battle of Breitenfeld (17 September): victory of the Swedes under Gustav II Adolph over Tilly's Imperialists.

1632 France: revolt of the Duc de Montmorency. In May, La Force and Effiat fight a Hispano-Lotharingian army in Mars la Tour. Saxony: Battle of Lützen (16 November); victory of the Swedes under Gustav II Adolph over Wallenstein's Imperialists.

1633 Louis XIII enters Nancy (25 September). The Swedes defeat the Lotharingians at Pfaffenhofen.

1634 Abdication of the Duc de Lorraine Charles IV (19 January) who joins the Imperial army. Battle of Nördlingen (6 September): the Swedes (Bernhard of Saxe-Weimar) are defeated by the Imperialists.

1635 Declaration of war by Louis XIII against Philip IV. Battle of Avins (22 May): victory of Brézé and Châtillon over the Spanish Army of Principe Thomas François de Carignan. Campaign of Henri de Rohan in the Valtelline (Battle of Livigno on 27 June, Battle of Mazo on 29 June and Battle of Morbegon on 10 November).

1636 The Cardinal-Infante launches an offensive in Picardie (2 July): storming of Corbie (15 August) and Siege of Saint Jean-de-Losne, which is lifted on 4 November. Battle of Tornavento (22 June), victory of the Franco-Savoyards under Charles de Créqui and Victor Amedeo of Savoy over the Spanish of the Marquess of Leganés. Battle of Wittstock (4 October), victory of Banér's Swedes over the Imperialists.

1637 Death of Emperor Ferdinand II (15 February), succession of Ferdinand III. Campaign of Bernhard of Saxe-Weimar on the Rhine. Victory of Bernhard over the Imperialists at Breisach (30 July). Flanders campaign (1637–38). In Languedoc: Battle of Leucate (24 September 1637): victory of the French under the Duc d'Halluin against the Spanish under Cerbelloni. Death of Duke Victor Amedeo of Savoy (8 September).

1638 Winter campaign of Bernhard of Saxe-Weimar. Death of the Duc de Rohan at Rheinfelden (February). Storming of Brisach by Bernhard of Saxe-Weimar and Turenne (18 December).

1639 Death of Bernhard of Saxe-Weimar (8 July). Battle of Chenmitz (14 April), victory of Banér's Swedes against the Saxons. Battle of Thionville (7 June 1639), defeat of Châtillon by Piccolomini's Imperialists. In the Piedmont: Battle of La Rota (20 November 1639), victory of Harcourt over the Spanish of Leganez.

1640 Siege and storming of Arras by the French (8 August). Battle of Casale in Piedmont (29 April): victory of Harcourt over the Spanish of Leganez. Battle of Turin (11 July): victory of Harcourt over the Spanish of Leganez.

1641 Battle of Ziegenhaun (25 November), victory of a Weimarian detachment under Rosen against an Imperial force. Battle of Wolfenbüttel (29 June), victory of a french and swedish army under Guébriant and Königsmark against the imperialists. Battle of Sedan

(6 July 1641), defeat of Châtillon by the Imperialists under Lamboy allied with the Comte de Soissons and the Duc de Bouillon (both in rebellion).

1642   Battle of Kempen (17 January), victory of Guébriant at the head of 10,000 Weimarians over Lamboy's Imperialists. Battle of Honnecourt (25 May), defeat of the French under de Guiche by the Spanish of de Melo. Battle of Lleida (7 October), victory of the French of La Mothe-Houdencourt over the Spanish of Leganez. Second battle of Breitenfeld (2 November), victory of the Swedes under Torstensson over the Imperialists of Archduke Leopold. Death of Richelieu on 4 December, he is replaced at the Council by Cardinal Mazarin.

1643   Spain: Olivarès is distanced from power on 16 January. France: death of Louis XIII on 14 May. Battle of Rocroi (19 May): victory of the Duc d'Enghien (16,000 infantry, 7,000 horses) over the Spanish of Don Francisco de Melo (18,000 infantry, 9,000 horses and 18 cannon). Battle of Tuttlingen (24 November): Rantzau's Weimarians are decimated.

1644   Battle of Freiburg in Brisgau (3–9 August), victory of the Duc d'Enghien over Mercy's Bavarians.

1645   Battle of Jankau (6 March), victory of the Swedes under Torstensson over Hatzfeld's Imperialists. Battle of Mergentheim (5 May), victory of Mercy's Bavarians over the French under Turenne. Battle of Alerheim, or Nördlingen, (3 August), victory of the Duc d'Enghien over Mercy's Bavarians. Gaston d'Orléans (with Gassion and Rantzau) completes the conquest of Flanders (July-August). Catalonia: Battle of Lhorens (20 October), victory of Harcourt over the Spanish.

1646   Storming of Courtrai (15 June) and Dunkirk (10 October) by the Duc d'Enghien. Franco-Swedish expedition (Turenne and Wrangel) into Bavaria. Storming of the Isle d'Elbe and Piombino in Italy (16 October) by La Meilleraye. Failure of the Comte d'Harcourt against Lleida (5 October).

1647   Plessis-Praslin victorious over the Marquis of Caracena on the Oglio in Italy (4 July). Failure of the Duc d'Enghien against Lleida (May to August). Mutiny of Turenne's Weimarians (June-July).

1648   Battle of Zusmarchausen (17 May), the Franco-Swedish Army (as well as the Weimarians and the Hessians) of Turenne and Wrangel defeat the Imperialists of Mélander, Montecuccoli and Holzupfel. Battle of Lens, (20 August), the French under the Duc d'Enghien defeat the Spanish under Archduke Leopold. Treaty of Westphalia (24 October).

Winning Game, Ernest Meissonier (1815–1891) (Public Domain)

1

Context: The Thirty Years' War

From the Origins of the War to the End of the Swedish Period

The Thirty Years' War should never have been a French war. It was originally a religious conflict between the Catholics and Protestants of the Habsburg Empire. When France became involved in 1635, the Thirty Years' War was theoretically over... This terrible conflict began in Bohemia, the Czech Republic of today, during 'counter-reformation' operations carried out by the Catholics, at the instigation of the Habsburg Emperor Ferdinand II, who was trying to reconquer lands lost to the Protestant Church. In his *Letter of Majesty for Religious Liberty* published on 9 July 1609, Rudolf II granted his Bohemian subjects the privilege to 'practice freely and fully the religion in which he believes.' The Bohemian Protestants also enjoyed political advantages, as well as special arrangements that meant religious buildings could be used by different faiths. This *Letter of Majesty*, accorded reluctantly by Rudolf II, was a thorn in the side of both the Catholics and the Habsburgs, headed up by the new Emperor, and King of Bohemia, Ferdinand II. The Catholics mobilised all their energy to regain control of Protestant parishes. Whenever possible, Royal (Bohemian) or Imperial (on the lands of the Emperor) power intervened in favour of the Catholics in issues where the two faiths were opposed. It was the brutal resolution of such an issue in favour of the Catholics that resulted in the 'Defenestration of Prague' on 23 May 1618. From 1618 to 1635, Ferdinand II was forced to constantly re-establish Imperial power and the pre-eminence of the Catholic faith within the Empire. To do this, he was obliged to nullify the 'illegal' secularisation of Catholic property by the Protestants wherever possible.

The Bohemian states revolted, and gave the Crown of Bohemia to the Elector Palatine Frederick V. On 7 November 1620, the Imperial army under Tilly defeated the combined armies of Mathias Thurn, von Mansfeld and Christian of Anhalt at the Battle of White Mountain, a few miles outside of Prague. Christian of Brunswick later suffered a total defeat against Tilly at Stadtlohn on 6 August 1623, and the many Imperial successes between 1620 and 1624 began to be of grave concern to the European powers: the United

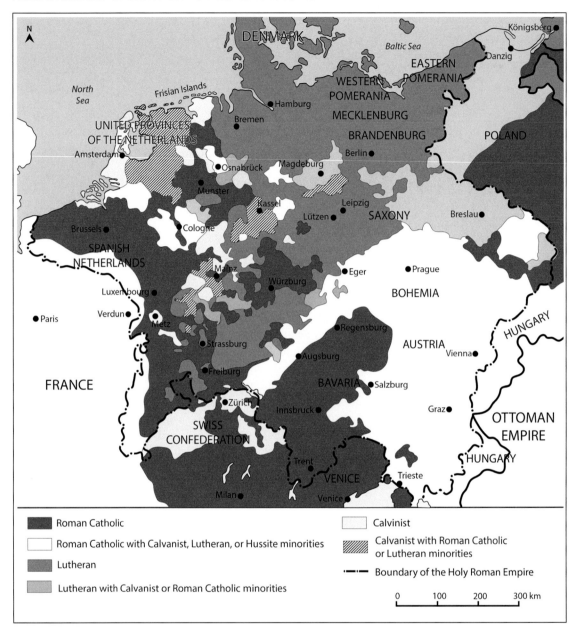

The religious situation in Central Europe *c*.1618

Provinces, the Protestant States of North Germany, England, Denmark and Sweden, but also to France. At this time, the United Provinces were at war with Spain and were unable to intervene; Sweden was at war with Poland; and France was trying to suppress Protestant rebellions. It was therefore Christian IV of Denmark who came to the rescue of the Protestant cause in June 1625, a cause supported in Northern Germany by the Electors of Brandenburg and Saxony. However, on 26 April 1626, Wallenstein – who had entered the service of the Emperor – defeated von Mansfeld at the Battle of Dessau Bridge, and Tilly crushed Christian IV's army at Lutter-am-Barenberg on 26 August of the same year. 1627 and 1628 saw the capture of territory from Christian IV and his allies in Northern Germany, followed by a religious reorganisation of these conquered lands. The peace treaty of 7 June 1629 put an end to the Danish intervention in the Thirty Years' War and Ferdinand II now had his hands free to issue his Edict of Restitution in February 1629, which called into question the abusive secularisation that had taken place since 1555. The period of conflict appeared to have passed – but plotting was at its height. Wallenstein aroused much enmity within the Empire, especially that of Duke Maximilian of Bavaria, and of Count Tilly. Encouraged by his entourage and Richelieu's agents, the Emperor Ferdinand II dismissed Wallenstein on 13 August 1630. Fearing the victory of Ferdinand II, the French contributed to the Emperor losing his right-hand man just before the Swedish intervention.

At the same time, the combination of the success of Ferdinand II, French diplomacy and subsidies encouraged Gustav II Adolph of Sweden to intervene in North Germany, which he did, landing on 6 July 1630. Tilly, fearing the arrival of the Swedish army, ordered an assault on Magdeburg on 20 May 1631, in which the entire population of the town was massacred. Gustav II Adolph's victory over Tilly at Breitenfeld on 17 September 1631 encouraged the Emperor to recall Wallenstein. He abandoned Duke Maximilian's Bavaria, leaving it to be ravaged by Swedish troops, while Tilly died of an injury at the end of April 1632. Gustav II Adolph was defeated by Wallenstein at the walls of *Alte Feste*, a fortress close to Nuremberg, in July 1632, but he in turn defeated Wallenstein at the Battle of Lützen on 16 November 1632. This victory came with a heavy price – the death of the King of Sweden, the 'Lion of the North'. Encouraged by the King of France, Louis XIII, and the Swedish Chancellor Oxenstierna, the Swedish generals Banér, Horn and Torstensson, and the German general, Bernhard of Saxe-Weimar, continued the war, despite the lassitude of the population. Wallenstein defeated the Swedes at Steinau in September 1633, but Bernhard of Saxe-Weimar entered Donauwörth, then Ratisbon on 14 November 1633. The storming of Ratisbon, the town of the Imperial Diet, had a significant impact in that it incited Duke Maximilian of Bavaria to once again plot against Wallenstein. The Duke's hatred of Wallenstein led to the assassination of the Generalissimo during the night of 25/26 February 1634. But this heinous crime did not help the Swedes – on 6 September, Marshal Horn suffered a heavy defeat at Nördlingen. The Swedes abandoned Bavaria and Bernhard of Saxe-Weimar returned to Alsace. On 23 November, the preliminaries for peace were negotiated between Ferdinand II and the Electors of Saxony and

Brandenburg. A peace treaty was signed in Prague on 30 May 1635 between the Elector of Saxony and the Emperor, a treaty which was extended to all German Princes who wished to join, and which was agreed by the Elector of Brandenburg on 6 September.

With the coalition between Gustav II Adolph of Sweden and Richelieu of France severely damaged, Germany was on the point of restoring peace, even if many Protestant princes and free towns of the Empire remained hostile to it. But Chancellor Oxenstierna had no interest in peace in Germany: his strategy was to take control of the southern coast of the Baltic, by establishing a protectorate over the Protestant States of North Germany. Nor did Cardinal Richelieu have any interest in the cessation of the war; he feared that Spain would be able to use Imperial troops liberated by the end of conflict to threaten French interests. Spain's strategy was to establish a route of free passage for her armies from Milan to the Spanish Netherlands; Richelieu's strategy was to do everything possible to hinder this plan. In his memoirs, he gives us the opinion he gave to the King on the subject at the beginning of 1629: he suggests that to defend the frontiers of the Kingdom, France should protect the small frontier states of Germany and Italy, and control the access routes to these zones, namely from the Rhine through Lorraine and Alsace, and from Italy through the Savoy:

A constant attempt to halt the progression of Spain was necessary; and, to prevent this nation from increasing its domination and extending its frontiers, France had to think only of her own fortification, and construct and open gateways to all the states of her neighbours, and be able to protect them from the oppression of Spain, when the occasion so required; for this, the first thing that needed to be done was to become powerful on the sea, which gives entry to all the states of the world; after this it was necessary to fortify Metz, and, if possible, to advance up to Strasbourg to have an entry to Germany; which needed to be done over time, with great discretion, and in a subtle and secret manner; a large citadel was needed at Versoix to gain importance in the eyes of the Swiss, to have a point of entry, and to put Geneva in a state of being one of the allies of France; we could also consider obtaining from *Maréchal* de Longueville the sovereignty of Neufchâtel, which, being in Switzerland, gives a greater foothold and more reason for France to be considered sovereign by men of little value, who respect only that which is before their eyes; and it was with these foreigners that His Majesty needed to maintain alliance most carefully, both because they separate Germany from Italy, and because, as they are ready for war, it is important to have them on our side and to deprive the enemy of them; it was necessary to consider the Marquisate of Saluce, either for an entente with *Maréchal* de Savoie .... or by making use of the poor relations between the subjects of the Marquisate and himself, and reconquering it; (…) to be even more in a position to be feared in Italy, it was necessary to maintain thirty galleys; Navarre and the Franche-Comté could still be considered as belonging to us, being contiguous to France, and easy to conquer whenever we so wished; but he did not speak of it, and it would be imprudent to think of it if, on the one hand, what is written above had not succeeded, and on the other hand, we would not be able to do so without provoking open war with Spain, which was to be avoided as far as possible.[1]

The war in Germany and Bohemia began through internal troubles, and France was not spared troubles of its own. After a revolt of the nobility supporting Queen Marie de Medici, which culminated in the battle of the Ponts-de-Cé near Angers on 7 August 1620, Louis XIII had to face a number of Protestant rebellions. An expedition of the young King to Béarn, aiming to restore certain temporal rights to the Catholic Church (here we find the same motivations as those that triggered the Thirty Years' War in Bohemia), irritated the Protestants. The Protestants met at La Rochelle on 24 December 1620 and decided to assemble their own military force. The same assembly demanded that Louis XIII retract the measures he had taken in Béarn. Each side hardened its positions, until a Huguenot force seized Privas in February 1621. The King himself took command of the army on 18 April, and besieged Saint Jean d'Angély on 16 May; the town surrendered on 23 June 1621. This was followed by the storming of Pons on 28 June, Clairac on 4 August and Nérac on 9 July. The siege of Montauban began on 17 August, but the royal troops were not able to take the town and lifted the siege on 10 November. The population of Monheurt, a small village between Agen and Marmande, was massacred by frenzied royal troops on 12 December. On 21 March 1622, the King once again took command of his army, and fought in the Battle of Riez in Lower Poitou on 16 April 1622, blockaded La Rochelle at the end of that same month, stormed Nègrepelisse on 10 June, where the entire population was massacred, and then Saint-Antonin on 21 June 1622. The King entered Béziers on 18 July. On 2 August, Praslin besieged Lunel, and Sommières was taken on 17 August. The royal troops arrived at Montpellier in September, but the siege went on until October without them being able to take the town. Lesdiguières negotiated peace with the Duc de Rohan, who surrendered on 10 October. The peace of Montpellier, signed on 18 October 1622, renewed the Edict of Nantes.

In January 1625, the Huguenots rebelled once again: Soubise seized seven vessels at La Rochelle and the Duc de Rohan raised a revolt in Languedoc, after complaining to Louis XIII of non-compliance with the clauses of the Treaty of Montpellier. Soubise landed his troops on the Île de Rhé at the beginning of September 1625; Toiras and La Rochefoucault landed on 14 September to oust them. Soubise fled to the Île d'Oléron; on 18 September, the last Protestants surrendered to Toiras. Peace was signed on 5 February 1626 with England's help. But at the instigation of the Duke of Buckingham, High Admiral of the Fleet, English diplomacy became more sympathetic to the French Protestants; Charles I feared in particular the rising power of the French fleet. On 26 July 1626, the English fleet landed an army on the Île de Rhé, which was being defended by Toiras. On 2 August, the English and the exiles laid siege to Saint-Martin de Rhé; on 15 August,

---

1   Armand du Plessis de Richelieu, *Mémoires du Cardinal de Richelieu*, Nouvelle Collection des Mémoires pour servir à l'Histoire de France (Paris: Michaud et Poujoulat, 1837), Deuxième Série, tome VII, pp.576–577.

Richelieu at La Rochelle, painting by Henri La Motte (1881), Musée de La Rochelle (Public Domain)

Gaston of Orléans besieged La Rochelle. On 8 November 1626, Toiras, with the reinforcements brought by Schomberg, forced the enemy to retreat from the island, ending the English expedition. On 12 November, Richelieu began the construction of a dyke that was to isolate La Rochelle, but the town held out until 28 October 1628. Rohan led the rebellion in the south of France; Louis XIII sent the Prince de Condé against him, who arrived at Saint-Affrique on 28 May 1628. As he was unable to take the town, he authorised widescale destruction, giving his soldiers free rein to pillage, burn, rape and kill. However, Rohan remained in charge of the Languedoc; the peace signed between France and England on 14 April 1629 allowed Louis XIII to concentrate new resources against him. On 12 May 1629, the Duc d'Estrées took Calvisson and the Royal Army took Privas on 27 May, massacring the inhabitants. All the towns in the Cévennes then surrendered to the Duc de Montmorency. Rohan sought clemency from the King, and on 27 June 1629, The Edict of Grace put an end to the Protestant uprising in Languedoc. This act allowed Richelieu to assert at the beginning of 1630 that:

> For the six years that the Cardinal has been in office, France, regaining vigour, opposed the multiple usurpations of Spain, which had largely increased since the death of the King, but with the disadvantage that most of her forces were occupied either with other wars abroad, or her own civil wars. Now that France has obliged England to make peace, and has quashed the heretic rebellion, she has all her forces available to use them in Italy to prevent Spain from invading the other states, and all the more so because Spain does not believe France to be powerful enough to halt the course of its unjust enterprises.[2]

---

2   Richelieu, *Mémoires du Cardinal de Richelieu*, Nouvelle Collection des Mémoires pour servir à l'Histoire de France (Paris: Michaud et Poujoulat, 1838), Deuxième série, VIII, p.138.

France enters the war

Before 1635, France only intervened occasionally and indirectly in the war that shook Central Europe, but when it did so it was always in the spirit of the opinion given to the King in January 1629.

In July 1620, the Catholic Grisons of the Valtelline revolted against their Protestant overlords. Spain took the opportunity to intervene through the intermediary of the Governor of Milan, occupying the valley and building fortifications. The Pope intervened in 1621, obtaining the replacement of Spanish garrisons by Papal troops, but this agreement did nothing to hinder the movement of Spanish troops through the Valtelline. The high Adda valley, between the Milan, the Tyrol and Austria, was an important Spanish communication point. On 7 February 1623, France signed an alliance with the Duchy of Savoy and the Republic of Venice. This treaty prepared for a French intervention in the Valtelline. In October 1624, François Annibal d'Estrées invaded Grison territory and ousted the Imperialists from the region by February 1625. Charles-Emmanuel of Savoy requested military aid from France to attack Genoa, a Spanish ally. Richelieu readily agreed, and Lesdiguières arrived at Turin on 1 February 1625 and at the walls of Asti, between Genoa and Milan, on 4 March. After storming Capriata, Novi and Rossiglione, Lesdiguières decided to slow his pace, preferring to lay siege to Gavi – against the advice of the Duca di Savoy. Gavi surrendered on 22 April, but it was too late to take Genoa. In the Tyrol, an Imperial army was preparing to intervene in the Valtelline, while the Spanish under the Duque de Feria prepared an army to come to Genoa's aid. The Spanish took Acqui then marched on Casale, reclaiming Gavi and Novi, while Lesdiguières beat a retreat to Piedmont. Charles-Emmanuel of Savoy, joined by Créqui, who replaced Lesdiguières as the latter had returned to the Dauphiné, entrenched his army at Verrua and the Duque de Feria was stopped on 5 August 1625 at his lines of defence. On 17 November 1625, Feria lifted the siege of Verrua and Lesdiguières took his troops back to the Dauphiné. A truce was signed on 5 February 1626 between France and Spain, which resulted in the Treaty of Monçon of 5 March 1626; the Valtelline was returned to the Vatican.

Vincenzo Gonzaga, Duca di Mantua, died in 1627. Charles Gonzaga, Duc de Nevers was the closest direct heir. His property – the Duchy of Mantua and the Marquisate of Montferrat – were both fiefdoms of the Empire, and Ferdinand II was given trusteeship at the request of Sapin and Savoy. In February 1629, the Spanish besieged Casale. As soon as La Rochelle had been taken, Louis XIII and Richelieu led an army to bring aid to Casale, crossing the Alps at Mont-Genèvre, and taking Suse on 6 March. During the night of 15/16 March, the Spanish lifted the siege of Casale. After sending an army to the Grisons on 5 June 1629, Emperor Ferdinand II ordered the French to evacuate his Italian lands. In September, he sent a second army to Mantua and a third to besiege Casale. Richelieu and the Royal Army left on 29 December 1629 for Suse, fighting off Charles-Emmanuel of Savoy, now his enemy, and took Pignerol on 21 March. On 12 May 1630, the King began his conquest of Savoy. Chambéry opened its gates on 17 May; Principe Thomas, second son of Charles-Emmanuel of Savoy, retreated to Bourg-Saint-Maurice

Cardinal Richelieu, portrait by Philippe de Champaigne (1602–1674) (Public Domain)

and was defeated by Châtillon on 6 July 1630 at the Battle of Séez. The storming of Montmélian on 19 July 1630 ended the campaign. The Duc de Montmorency, who had been given the task of taking the Marquisate of Saluces, crossed Mont Cenis on 7 July and defeated Charles-Emmanuel of Savoy on 10 July between Saint Ambroise and Avigliana. Charles-Emmanuel died of apoplexy a few days later, on 26 July. His successor, Victor Amedeo I, brother-in-law of Louis XIII, was more favourably inclined to the French, but this war had to be ended. On 17 July, the Imperialists stormed Mantua by surprise, taking Charles Gonzaga and the *Maréchal* d'Estrées prisoner. Louis XIII ordered the Duc de Montmorency to help Casale, which was being held by Toiras. Montmorency took Carignan on 6 August 1630. Victor Amedeo managed to escape, but the exhausted and diminished French did not push on to Turin and Casale. Louis XIII sent Schomberg to Piedmont, clearing the route from Suse to Turin. Schomberg's army, now reinforced by the armies of La Force and Marillac, arrived at Casale on 26 October. Opposing them were the Spanish under the Marqués de Santa-Croce and Spinola. But the battle never happened: mediation by Pope Urban VIII put an end to hostilities and led to the signing of the Treaty of Cherasco on 26 April 1631. Charles Gonzaga, Duc de Nevers, could now take possession of the Duchy of Mantua and the Marquisate of Montferrat.

At the beginning of 1632, Richelieu said to the King that:

> … to resolve the situation rapidly, it was necessary to consider that, given current state of affairs in Germany, one could only act in one of these four manners:
>
> 1° either to join with the King of Sweden to wage open war against the House of Austria;
>
> 2° or come to an agreement with the Emperor and Spain to wage war against Sweden and the Protestant princes;
>
> 3° or try to make the Catholic Electors accept neutrality in the terms proposed by the King of Sweden, if he did not wish to consent to better terms, and let him continue war in Germany without becoming involved, but only to maintain a few troops on the border to use when necessary;
>
> 4° or also, with this neutrality, take possession of Alsace, Brisach and passages of the Rhine held by the Catholic Electors, and to have there an army to use on occasions of necessity (…)'.

However, he rejected the second method, reminding the King of:

the little trust we can have in the Spanish, the danger of allowing the House of Austria to grow to the extent that it becomes a formidable force for France, and forces us to a very long war to defend ourselves against Austria or against other enemies, both external and internal, that they could enkindle in this event.[3]

But the King chose neither the first nor the second scenario, as he did not want war and wanted to avoid breaking with both the King of Sweden and the House of Austria. He therefore opted for neutrality, but events were to push him to intervene in Lorraine.

In Lorraine, Duc Charles IV had regularly welcomed enemies of Richelieu or Louis XIII since 1629 and sided in the war with Tilly against France's Swedish allies. As Charles IV had authorised the occupation of fortresses from Nancy to Strasbourg by Imperialist troops, Louis XIII, assisted by *Maréchal* d'Effiat and *Maréchal* de La Force, led the army to Lorraine in December 1631. A treaty was signed on 6 January 1632 between Louis XIII and Charles IV, but Charles IV soon resumed his active alliance with Ferdinand II, leading to other interventions by the armies of *Maréchals* d'Effiat and de La Force in 1632 and 1633. Charles IV surrendered on 20 September 1633 and the French Army entered Nancy on 25 September. The Duc de Lorraine abdicated on 19 January 1634, leaving power to his brother.

Alsace had been occupied by the Swedes, under Horn, since August 1632. The Alsatian cities, weary of pillaging, asked for help from Louis XIII. A convention negotiated on 9 October 1634 between France and Sweden, followed by a treaty signed on 22 October, authorised *Maréchal* de La Force to occupy Alsace. Under the orders of *Maréchal* de La Force, the Vicomte de Turenne fought the Imperialists in Lower Alsace from December 1634, in coordination with the army of Bernhard of Saxe-Weimar who occupied the opposite bank of the Rhine. While *Maréchals* Brézé and de La Force battled with the Imperials in Alsace, Principe Thomas di Savoy, at the head of a Spanish army, invaded the Electorate of Treves in March 1635 and took prisoner the Elector Archbishop, who was under the protection of Louis XIII. The die was cast. Richelieu, sensing that war was inevitable, reinforced his alliances with the United Provinces (8 February 1635) and Sweden (28 April 1635).

At the beginning of 1633, Richelieu once again persuaded Louis XIII to finance the war in Germany and Holland, fearing that: 'if peace is made in Germany and a truce in Holland, or one of the two, France will have to support a defensive war alone, which could spread to her own territory, with no means of avoidance…'[4] Early in 1635, he justified France's intervention by saying:

After having long fought against war, which has been the ambition of Spain for the last few years, and their bad will towards this State, which, like a mountain that hinders the flow of an impetuous torrent, has prevented their monarchy from inundating all Europe; after having spent much time protecting ourselves from their traps and continuous enterprises against this Kingdom, which we have, with

---

3   Richelieu, *Mémoires du Cardinal de Richelieu*, VIII, pp.364–365.
4   Richelieu, *Mémoires du Cardinal de Richelieu*, VIII, p.436.

God's blessing, happily remedied by indefatigable vigilance; finally, this year it is now impossible for us to withdraw further, and we are obliged to enter into open war with them, a war which we declare, but which we will not be first to begin, as it is they who attack us and force our hand by so many hostilities, so many insults, and so many preparations they began long ago to oppress us all at once, which, in order to defend ourselves, we are obliged to declare that we no longer wish to suffer the covert war that they inflict on us, and that they disguise to the world under the misleading name of peace, a peace which, all things considered, has never been the case since the Treaty of Vervins imposed the end of the rupture between themselves and Henri IV.[5]

At the beginning of 1635, Louis XIII had armies in Champagne, Picardy (under *Maréchals* Brézé and Châtillon), Lorraine (under *Maréchal* de La Force), as well as one on the Sarre under Cardinal de la Valette, who could count on aid from Bernhard of Saxe-Weimar and the Weimarians, and an army in the Valtelline under the Duc de Rohan. He also had the support of the army of the Duca di Savoy in the Alps. The army in Picardy was to cross the Meuse and join up with the army of Stadtholder Frederick Hendrick of Nassau. The French Army encountered and defeated the Spanish army of Principe Thomas di Savoy on 22 May 1635 at Avins. The combined French and Dutch armies marched on Brussels, but decimated by typhus, they could but withdraw to their bases. During this time, the Spanish and Imperial armies of the Cardinal-Infante and Piccolomini occupied the Duchy of Cleves. In September 1635 the Imperialists occupied Frankfurt and the Croats of Gallas harassed the rear of the armies of Cardinal de la Valette and Bernhard of Saxe-Weimar along the Rhine up to Metz. On 2 October, Louis XIII and the Army of Champagne retook the town of Saint-Mihiel from Charles IV, but at the end of 1635, he was firmly entrenched in the Franche-Comté while Gallas held Alsace.

During this time, Duc Henri de Rohan led a successful campaign in the Valtelline, aiming to cut Spanish and Imperial communications between North Italy and the Palatinate. Rohan entered Switzerland at the end of March 1635; although he was in a poor position, on 27 June 1635 he forced Fenarmont's Imperialists to retreat into the valley of Livigno, fought them on 3 July 1635 at the Bridge of Mazzo and seized Fort des Bains and Sainte-Marie on 17 July. At the same time, the town of Valenza was besieged by the Duca di Savoy, the Duca di Parma and *Maréchal* de Créqui. On 31 October, Rohan ousted Fenarmont from the Valtelline with a victory at Val di Fraele. The following day the armies of the Duca di Savoy, the Duca di Parma and *Maréchal* de Créqui abandoned the Siege of Valenza and timidly entered Piedmont. On 10 November at Morbegno, Rohan defeated the Spanish army of the Governor of Milan and seized his camp. However, 1635 ended to the overall advantage of Habsburg, and the war, which could have lasted only 16 years, was set to last another 14.

---

5   Richelieu, *Mémoires du Cardinal de Richelieu*, VIII, p.577.

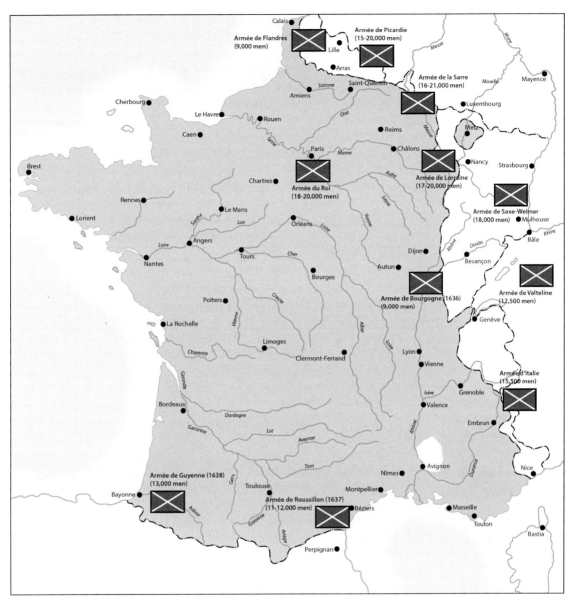

French Armies from 1635 to 1638

In 1636, Banér's Swedish armies were in Pomerania and Mecklenburg; French armies were in the Lorraine, the Valtelline and Pignerol; the armies of the Duca di Savoy were in the confines of Milan; the Spanish armies occupied Franche-Comté, the Electorates of Treves and Cologne; and the Imperial armies occupied the Lower Palatinate and Alsace. In February 1636, the Spanish invaded the Duchy of Parma, and *Maréchal* de Créqui, impatient with the hesitations of the Duca di Savoy, took the lead of an army of 6,000 French soldiers present in Casale. But he was defeated by the Marquis de Leganez, Governor of Milan, at Vespolate on 27 February. On 3 June, the Duca di Savoy relaunched the offensive and crossed the Po with Créqui in the vanguard and reached Boffalora in the Ticino on 16 June. On 22 June 1636, *Maréchal* de Créqui, supported belatedly by Victor Amedeo di Savoy, fought off the Marquis de Leganez at the Battle of Tornavento.

The Prince de Condé, Governor of Burgundy, was entrusted with an army of 20,000 infantry and 8,000 cavalry to conquer Franche-Comté, and laid siege to Dôle on 29 May 1636; but the Cardinal-Infante launched an attack on Picardy. On 2 July, Principe Thomas entered Picardy leading 30,000 infantry and 12,000 cavalry. The town of La Capelle surrendered on 9 July, and the Spanish took Le Catelet and Bray-sur-Somme before arriving at Corbie, 12 or so miles from Amiens. The country was in danger. The Army of Champagne under the Comte de Soissons was reinforced by the army of *Maréchal* de Brézé, who had returned from The Netherlands. Principe Thomas attacked, while at Bray *Maréchal* Brézé resisted; but the Comte de Soissons decided to retreat along the Oise, leaving the Imperial cavalry of Johann von Werth free to harass the rear. Corbie surrendered on 15 August while Louis XIII and Richelieu succeeded in raising a new army of 30,000 infantry and 12,000 cavalry by decreeing a levy *en masse*, thus making good use of the hesitations of the Cardinal-Infante. Faced with this sudden increase, the Cardinal-Infante took his army back to The Netherlands, fearing a counter-attack by the Dutch under Prince Frederick Hendrick of Nassau. Paris was saved – but the war had come to French territory. At the beginning of October, Louis XIII and Richelieu laid siege to Corbie, which was taken on 14 November. On 15 August, the Prince de Condé lifted the siege of Dôle, threatened by the armies of Charles IV and Gallas who had crossed the Rhine. The Imperialists crossed the Saône, entered Burgundy and laid siege to Saint Jean-de-Losne, which resisted heroically. The siege was lifted on 4 November, thanks to the aid of the Franco-Weimarian army under Cardinal de la Valette and Bernhard of Saxe-Weimar. This army was supposed to prevent the meeting of Gallas' Imperial army and the Spanish army of Principe Thomas di Savoy, who was still in Picardy.

In March 1636, Banér's Swedish army invaded Saxony and devastated the lands of the Elector of Saxony, who was 'guilty' of signing the Treaty of Prague. During a bloody battle near Wittstock on 4 and 5 October 1636, Banér defeated an imperialist and Saxon army sent to the rescue. Banér then laid siege to Leipzig in January 1637, but Imperial and Saxon forces forced him to retreat to Torgau, where he remained until June. Emperor Ferdinand II died on 15 February, and on 15 April 1637, the French fleet commanded by Cardinal de Sourdis retook the Isles of Lérins in Provence,

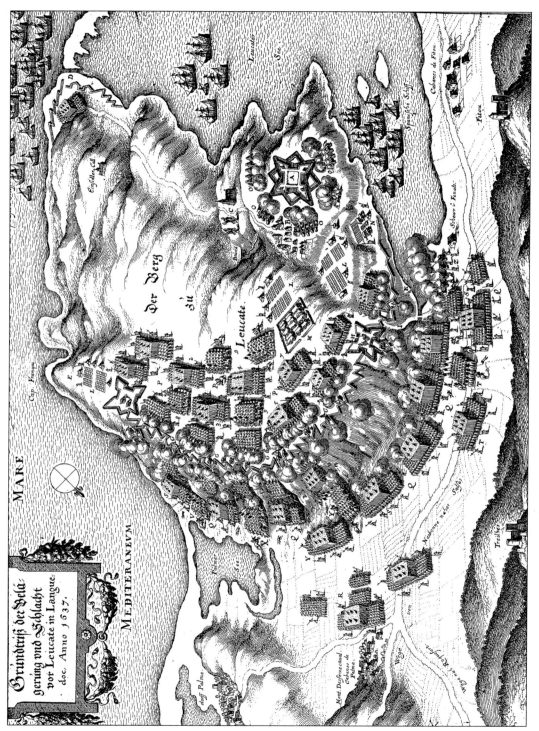

Battle of Leucate, 28 September 1637. *Theatrum Europaeum* (Public Domain)

occupied by the Spanish for the previous two years. At the beginning of June, the army of Cardinal de la Valette launched an offensive in Flanders. Cateau-Cambrésis fell on 21 June, Landrecies on 22 July and La Capelle on 15 September; the cavalry of la Valette, commanded by the Vicomte de Turenne, dealt a heavy defeat to the cavalry of Piccolomini, but a counter-offensive from Cardinal-Infante forced the French to retreat south of Maubeuge. The Spanish, fighting on two fronts, were unable to prevent the storming of Breda by the Dutch on 10 October 1637. The Army of Champagne under *Maréchal* de Châtillon, who was intending to take Luxembourg, was unable to oust the occupying Spanish and Imperialists. The army of Bernhard of Saxe-Weimar had launched an offensive in the Franche-Comté in May and dealt a defeat to the Imperial army of Charles IV, Duc de Lorraine, on 22 June at Ray sur Saône. Bernhard then returned to Alsace, but faced with the threat of an offensive by Piccolomini, left for Mulhouse in September to take up winter quarters. A second French Army under the Duc de Longueville took Lons le Saulnier on 25 June 1637 then withdrew to Burgundy. Finally, in the Valtelline a revolt from the Grison leagues erupted on 18 March 1637 and the Duc de Rohan had to flee, with his army, at the beginning of May, joining up with the army of Bernhard of Saxe-Weimar in Alsace. On 8 September Victor Amadeo of Savoy died, and with him the French alliance. At the end of August, the Spanish tried to land at Leucates, in Roussillon, but they were beaten back on 28 September by the Duc d'Halluin, Governor of Languedoc, with the support of the region's Protestants.

On 6 March 1638, France renewed its alliance with Sweden. A few weeks earlier, Bernhard of Saxe-Weimar had set out to march along the Rhine towards Austria, taking a number of forest towns. He was surprised by the Imperialists under Savelli and Johann von Werth on 28 February at Rheinfelden by Imperialists, a battle in which the Duc de Rohan was fatally injured, but he dealt them a significant defeat on 3 March with a night attack on their camp, taking Johann von Werth prisoner. Aided by Guébriant and Turenne, Bernhard of Saxe-Weimar then left for Brisgau, took Friburg on 11 August, and laid siege to Brisach, defeating the Duc de Lorraine and the Imperialists, Lamboy and Goetz, who tried to flee the town at the end of October; he finally took Brisach on 18 December after a 4 month siege. From their bases in Pomerania, the Swedes launched raids against Gallas' Imperialists and ravaged the countryside of Mecklenburg and

French officers during the siege of Saint-Omer in 1638. Stefano della Bella (Rijksmuseum, Amsterdam)

Brandenburg. In Italy, *Maréchal* de Créqui was killed on 17 March, cut in half by a cannonball while he tried to come to relieve the besieged town of Breme. Leganez took advantage of the situation to retake Breme, then Vercelli on 6 July, thus closing the Piedmont border. Later, la Valette entered the Duchy of Montferrat and defeated the Spanish on 7 October at Fellizano.

In Artois, the Army of Picardy under *Maréchals* de Châtillon and de Brézé attempted to take Saint-Omer, but had to lift the siege, threatened by the relief armies of Principe Thomas and Piccolomini; the two *Maréchals* retook Le Catelet on 14 September 1638. In the Basque Country, Cardinal de Sourdis destroyed the Spanish fleet in the Bay of Guéthary and landed reinforcements for the Prince de Condé who was commanding the Guyenne Army. But the besieged Spaniards soundly defeated the French under the command of Condé at Fontarabie on 7 September.

The Swedes under Banér began the 1639 campaign by entering Saxony and defeating the Saxons and Imperialists under Gallas at Chemnitz on 14 April. Encouraged by this success, Banér campaigned along the Elbe, arriving outside Prague in May then held his position in Bohemia. Bernhard of Saxe-Weimar had returned to Franche-Comté, taking Morteau and Pontarlier at the end of January and the Fort de Joux on 14 February. He then left for Jura and returned to Alsace in June after despoiling Franche-Comté. However, Bernhard of Saxe-Weimar, who had become an embarrassment for Richelieu, died of the plague on 8 July while preparing for an expedition to Bavaria to join Banér. During this time, Guébriant managed to convince von Erlach to retain the Weimarian army in French service.

In Italy, Principe Thomas di Savoy, who had returned to Piedmont, laid siege to Turin on 18 April 1639. Piedmont rebelled against Queen Christine, an ally of the French, while the Marquis de Leganez and Principe Thomas were in control of Turin, with the exception of the citadel and of the Po valley. The French still held Casale and Chivasso. Cardinal de la Valette died at Rivoli on 27 September 1639, and was replaced by the Comte d'Harcourt, with Turenne as his second in command and commander of the cavalry. Harcourt took Chieri on 4 November 1639, allowing him to re-establish communications with Casale, then forced Leganez and Principe Thomas to retreat to La Rotta on 20 November.

In Champagne, June 1639 saw La Meilleraye besiege Hesdin, Feuquières, Thionville. Piccolomini came to the aid of Thionville and on 7 June 1639 dealt a heavy defeat to Feuquières, but La Meilleraye took Hesdin on 29 June. In the Pyrenees, the Prince de Condé commanding the Armies of Languedoc and Guyenne seized the citadel of Salces on 9 July, which was retaken by the Spanish on 24 December. 1639, however, ended badly for the Spanish, with a fleet of 77 ships being destroyed by a Dutch squadron in the Channel on 21 October.

1640 began no better for Philip IV of Spain, as the bad feeling between Principe Thomas and Piccolomini forced him to withdraw the army from The Netherlands. Deprived of a maritime route after the disaster of Dover, and with no overland route since the loss of Brisach and the Imperial reinforcements, the Spanish situation in The Netherlands had become precarious. To crown it all, Catalonia refused to support the war effort and

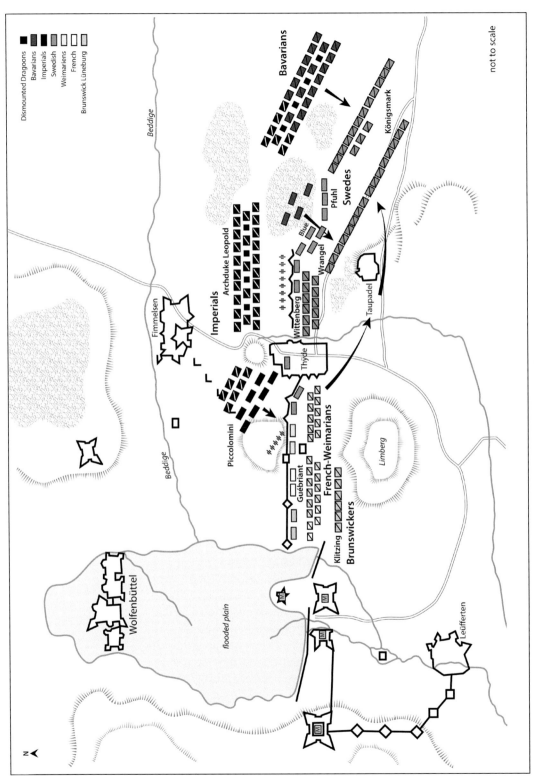

not to scale

Battle of Wolfenbüttel, 1641.

Dismounted Dragoons
Bavarians
Imperials
Swedish
Weimariens
French
Brunswick Lüneburg

Beddige

Bavarians

Königsmark

Swedes

Pfuhl

Blue

Wrangel

Archduke Leopold

Imperials

Wittenberg

Taupadel

Fimmelsen

Thyde

Piccolomini

Beddige

Guébriant

French-Weimarians

Limberg

Klitzing

Brunswickers

Wolfenbüttel

flooded plain

Leüfferten

N

rose in rebellion on 7 June 1640. This rebellion encouraged cooperation between the Catalans and Louis XIII's France and resulted in the signing of a treaty of fraternity between the two nations on 16 December 1640. This treaty led to a military alliance at the beginning of 1641. In a disaster for the Spanish navy, the Marquis de Brézé destroyed the Indies squadron in the Bay of Cadiz.

In June 1640, the French relaunched their offensive in Artois and laid siege to Arras, taking the town on 8 August. In Italy, the Spanish had taken Saluces from the French, but the Comte d'Harcourt once again beat Leganez and Principe Thomas at Casale on 29 April 1640, and then besieged Turin. Here he fought off Leganez who had come to the relief of the town, on 11 July. Leganez left for Milan, and Principe Thomas surrendered the town to the French. The Duchess Regent thus reclaimed possession of her Duchy, and Principe Thomas abandoned the Spanish alliance. To conclude this catastrophic year, Portugal, whose autonomy had been increasingly ignored and disrespected by Spain, seceded on 1 December 1640! On 1 June 1640, the newly proclaimed King of Portugal, John IV, signed a Treaty of Alliance with France, followed by a truce with The Netherlands on 12 June 1641.

Things were no better for the successor of Ferdinand II, Emperor Ferdinand III: he summoned a Diet on 26 July 1640 to try to extend the Treaty of Prague to all Princes of The Empire who had not yet signed, but the new Elector of Brandenburg, Frederick William, went back on the peace conditions and signed a separate peace with Sweden.

Banér's army, pursued by Piccolomini across Bohemia and Saxony, was now in difficulty. Banér, in command of an army reduced in size, died on 20 May 1641 at Halberstadt and was succeeded by Torstensson. On 29 June 1641, Wrangel and Guébriant, who had come to the aid of Klitzing, the General of the Brunswick forces, were victorious over the Imperialists of Archduke Leopold and Piccolomini at Wolfenbüttel in Lower Saxony. But the badly paid Swedish army mutinied and Torstensson was only able to restore the situation at the end of 1641.

In Italy, the Comte d'Harcourt ended his campaign by taking Coni on 8 September, then taking Montecalvo and Demonte. At the same time, the Kingdom of France also had troubles to face: Gaston d'Orléans had organised a new rebellion with the help of the Comte de Soissons, the Duc de Bouillon and the Duc de Lorraine. On 6 July 1641, the discontented army, reinforced by the Imperialists of Lamboy, defeated *Maréchal* de Châtillon's Army of Champagne at La Marfée near Sedan. After this defeat, Châtillon was replaced by *Maréchal* Brézé. La Meilleraye, who had seized Aire in desperation on 27 July 1641, beat a retreat from the combined armies of the Cardinal-Infante, Lamboy and the Duc de Lorraine, leaving Aire in the hands of the Spanish on 9 August 1641. Brézé's Army of Champagne then joined with the Army of Picardy under La Meilleraye; the two armies took Lens, La Bassée and Bapaume in September.

At the beginning of 1642, Guébriant's Franco-Weimarian army was in Westphalia. Lamboy was waiting near Kempen for von Hatzfeld's Bavarian reinforcements to attack in Champagne, while the Spanish attacked in Picardy. Avoiding von Hatzfeld, Guébriant crossed the Rhine to Wesel

Strategic port and fortress of Collioure, captured by the French Army in 1642. (Riksarkivet, Stockholm)

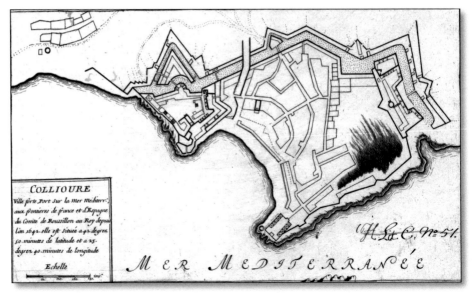

and won a significant victory over Lamboy's Imperialists at Kempen on 17 January 1642, which earned him his *Maréchal*'s baton. Then, while the Weimarians were conquering the Duchy of Jülich, Guébriant left to defend Alsace against Mercy's Bavarian Army, which was occupying the Duchy of Baden. The Swede, Torstensson, had taken his troops in hand and left for Bohemia at the beginning of 1642, seizing Glosgow on the Oder. He defeated the Saxon army on 30 May 1642 at Schweidnitz and went on to pillage Moravia. Piccolomini set off in pursuit of Torstensson who was threatening Vienna while besieging Glosgow. Torstensson then left for Silesia, liberated Glosgow and headed for Leipzig. He encountered the Imperialists of Archduke Leopold and Piccolomini on 2 November 1642, crushing them at Breitenfeld, and then went on to take Leipzig on 4 December 1642.

In The Netherlands, the Cardinal-Infante died on 9 November 1641 and Francisco de Melo took over as Governor. He retook Lens from the French on 19 April 1642 and La Bassée on 13 May, while the Comte d'Harcourt, now in Picardy, was capturing Boulogne. However, the defeat of Harcourt at Honnecourt on 26 May opened up the door to Champagne for Melo, although he preferred to head back towards Guébriant in the Rhine valley.

In the Pyrenees, La Meilleraye liberated Roussillon with the help of Turenne, took Collioure on 13 April 1642 and Perpignan on 9 September of that year, after Admiral Brézé had dispersed a Spanish fleet attempting to bring supplies to the town on 30 June. But the Catalonian army under La Mothe-Houdencourt, supported by the fleet of de Sourdis, was unable to take Tarragona and lifted the blockade on 20 August. Leganez besieged Lleida at the beginning of September while La Mothe-Houdencourt, recently promoted *Maréchal*, brought aid to Perpignan and dealt a new defeat to Leganez.

In Italy, the Duc de Longueville, supported by Thomas and Maurice of Savoy, entered Milan after storming Tortona on 26 November 1642.

1642 ended with a strong advantage to the French, Swedish and Dutch, but Richelieu, who had played a large part in French victories, died on 4 December 1642. Louis XIII replaced his prime minister with Richelieu's brilliant secretary, Cardinal Giulio Mazarin. Mazarin rapidly took affairs in hand: he sent Turenne to Piedmont, reinforced Guébriant in Alsace, La Mothe-Houdencourt in Catalonia, and the Army of Champagne, commanded by the Comte d'Espenan, while La Meilleraye led the small army of Burgundy against Franche-Comté. He then appointed Louis de Bourbon, Duc d'Enghien, then aged 21, to command the Army of Picardy.

1643 began with further major changes in the leadership of warring states. In Spain, Olivarès was removed from power on 17 January 1643. This was followed by the death of Louis XIII on 14 May 1643, leaving the Kingdom of France under the Regency of Queen Anne of Austria, ably supported by Mazarin.

In Germany, the various protagonists worked hard for peace, but peace was slow in coming. During this time, the Swedish Chancellor Oxenstierna managed to bring Prins György I[6] Ràkoczi of Transylvania into the Franco-Swedish alliance through the Treaty of Stockholm, signed on 26 April 1643.

In the Netherlands, Governor Francisco de Melo intended to sidestep the Armies of Champagne and Picardy, took Rocroi, but he was soundly defeated under the city walls on 19 May 1643 by the Duc d'Enghien. With Rocroi relieved, Enghien led the Armies of Picardy, Champagne and Burgundy to Thionville, which fell on 8 September. On 28 May 1644, Gaston d'Orléans, supported by *Maréchal* La Meilleraye and *Maréchal* Gassion, led the Army of Picardy and retook Gravelines from the Spanish. In Italy, 1644 saw the siege of Santia by Principe Thomas and *Maréchal* du Plessis-Praslin, while on the other side of the Pyrenees *Maréchal* de La Mothe-Houdencourt failed to relieve Lleida, which fell to the Spanish on 31 July 1644.

Guébriant, leading the German Army and reinforced by units from the Army of the Duc d'Enghien, crossed the Rhine in October and besieged Rottweil. The City fell on 24 November, but Guébriant died that day from a cannon injury. The same day, a Weimarian party commanded by Rantzau was surprised and defeated during the siege of Tuttlingen by the Bavarians under Mercy and Hatzfeld. The Franco-Weimarian army withdrew to Alsace, which it devastated before being restrained by Turenne, who was promoted to *Maréchal* on 3 December 1643. After wintering in Lorraine, Turenne launched an offensive in January 1644, taking back Vesoul and Luxeuil. At the beginning of May, he crossed the Rhine and took Donaueschingen before returning to Alsace at the end of June. The Bavarian, von Mercy, had taken the initiative by storming Überlingen on 11 May, then laying siege to Freiburg im Breisgau on 27 June. However, D'Enghien and Turenne were defeated by Mercy's defensive positions, notably in the bloody assault of 5 August, but they forced von Mercy to retreat to Rothenburg on 10 August. Turenne retook Philippsburg on 9 September 1644 after a 10 days siege, then Worms, Oppenheim, Mentz, and Landau before the end of September. This brilliant campaign meant that the French held practically the entire left bank of the Rhine.

---

6   Often rendered as George in English.

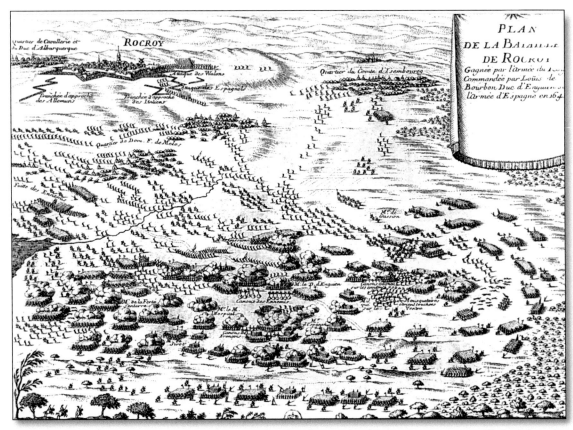

Battle of Rocroi, 19 May 1643.
(BNF, Public Domain)

In April 1643, the Swedes under Torstensson were still in Moravia. But Christian IV of Denmark had begun negotiations with Emperor Ferdinand III who sent an Imperial army commanded by Gallas, to the North as support; Oxenstierna then recalled Torstensson. Swiftly, the Swedes entered Holstein then Schleswig, and finally Jutland in January 1644, meanwhile the Swedish armies under Wrangel and Horn besieged Malmö. But with the Danes under Frederick of Denmark and the Imperialists under Gallas and Hatzfeld threatening to encircle him, Torstensson was forced to move south. The Swedes under Königsmarck, chased from Mecklenburg by Frederick of Denmark, severely defeated the Imperialists under Gallas at Magdeburg, while von Hatzfeld's army was defeated on 23 November 1644 near Wittenberg. Peace was eventually signed between Denmark and Sweden on 23 August 1645 after tortuous negotiations that had opened in February.

Prins Ràkoczi of Transylvania entered the campaign in February 1644 but was defeated on 9 April by the Imperialists under Götz. Ràkoczi lost ground throughout the rest of 1644, while Torstensson returned to Moravia in the spring of 1645, attracting the Imperialists towards him, anxious to protect Vienna. Torstensson won another bloody victory against Götz and Hatzfeld on 6 March 1645 at Jankau, in Bohemia. The Swedes then besieged Brno, and Vienna at the beginning of April; Ràkoczi's army entered Hungary and joined with the Swedes at Brünn. On the 27 July 1645, Ràkoczi opened negotiations with Emperor Ferdinand III, which resulted in a peace with the Treaty of Linz, signed on 16 December. In October, Torstensson decided not

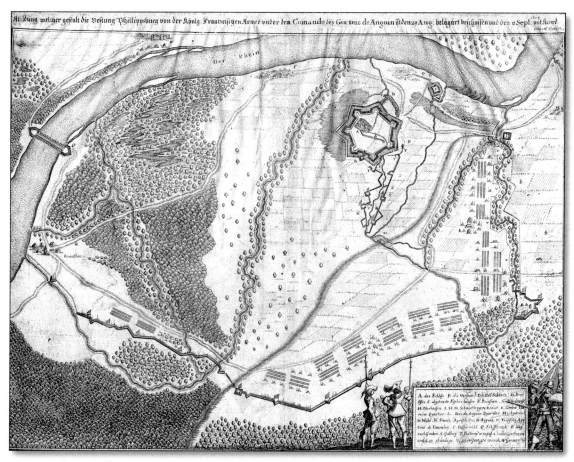

The French Army besieging Spanish-held Philippsburg, 25 August to 12 September 1644. (Riksarkivet, Stockholm)

to pursue his attack on Vienna and went back to Saxony where, because of ill health, he left command of the army to Wrangel.

At the end of March 1645, Turenne led the Franco-Weimarian army in a new offensive. He crossed the Rhine on 24 March and captured Rothenburg, but with his troops imprudently dispersed, he was defeated by Mercy on 5 May 1645 at Mergentheim (or Marienthal). Mazarin then sent the Duc d'Enghien to Turenne's aid, and on 6 August 1645 their armies won a victory over the Bavarians of Mercy and Werth at Allerheim, near Nördlingen. In October, the French returned to Philippsburg along the Rhine, escaped the combined armies of Archduke Leopold, Gallas, Hatzfeld and Johann von Werth, and retook Treves on 23 November 1645.

In July and August 1645, Gaston d'Orléans, Gassion and Rantzau took a number of towns in Artois and Flanders including Béthune, Saint-Omer and Lens, while in Catalonia the Comte d'Harcourt and Plessis-Praslin seized Rosas and Balaguer on 20 October after defeating the Spanish at Lhorens.

In April 1646, Turenne was in Mentz; Wrangel left Bohemia, took Paderborn and arrived in Hesse. The two armies threatened Bavaria, joining up belatedly on 10 August 1646; they crossed the Danube, seizing Aschaffenburg on 22 August followed by the fortress of Rain, and laid siege to Augsburg at the beginning of October. They lifted the siege under a threat from Johann von Werth. As winter arrived, they took Landsberg by surprise,

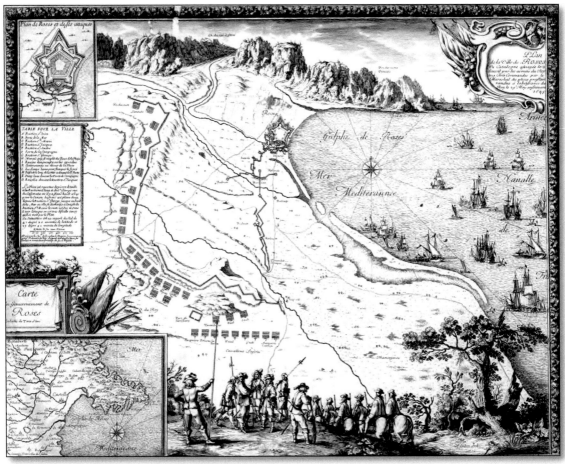

French Army besieging Rosas in Catalonia, 1 April to 29 May 1645 (Riksarkivet, Stockholm)

which served as a storehouse for arms and supplies for the Bavarians. The Imperial army withdrew to Austria, and Duke Maximilian of Bavaria, tired of war, began negotiations with Mazarin. Turenne, after suppressing a Weimarian rebellion, could manage only a few incursions into Luxembourg.

For Mazarin, there was still Spain to be dealt with. In The Netherlands, Gaston d'Orléans and the Duc d'Enghien besieged Courtrai on 15 June 1646, which surrendered on 28 June before Piccolomini, Charles IV of Lorraine and Lamboy were able to come to their aid. Bergues was taken on 29 July and Mardyck was taken back on 25 August. D'Enghien continued the conquest by taking Furnes on the 7 September, then by besieging Dunkirk on 25 September 1646. Piccolomini, Beck and the Marquis of Caracena tried without success to break the siege. D'Enghien took the Fort of Mardycke on 24 August and Dunkirk surrendered on 10 October.

To the North, the Dutch occupied the mouth of the River Escaut but, fearing an increasing closeness to France, they began negotiations with Spain – thereby ending the Franco-Dutch alliance. The Dutch negotiated a peace treaty in Münster on 30 January 1648. In The Netherlands, the Spanish also took advantage of the situation to launch a new offensive against Gassion and Rantzau: Armentières fell on 31 May 1647, followed by Commines and Landrecies, then Dixmude on 14 November. Gassion died on 23 September during the siege of Lens, and as a result Mazarin sent Turenne to the aid of Rantzau.

In Italy, Principe Thomas di Savoy and the fleet of *Amiral* Brézé besieged Ortebello on 10 May 1646, while *Maréchal* du Plessis-Praslin remained in Piedmont to face Milan's Spanish army. However, Brézé was killed, cut in half by a cannonball in a battle with the Spanish fleet on 14 May, which put an end to the intervention. Threatened by a Spanish army from Naples, Principe Thomas evacuated his army. Mazarin persevered: the armies of Plessis-Praslin and La Meilleraye landed on the Island of Elba, then seized Piombino on 16 October 1646. Spain thus lost its outlying stations, and the Duke of Modena gave his support to the French cause. *Maréchal* du Plessis-Praslin launched a new offensive and, with the help of the Duke of Modena, dealt a crushing defeat to the Marquis of Caracena on the 4 July 1647 on the banks of the Oglio River.

To complicate the Spanish situation in Italy, a revolt broke out in Sicily in the spring of 1647, followed by a similar revolt in Naples in June 1647. The Neapolitan revolt did not weaken over time, and negotiations were opened with France in order that the new Neapolitan Republic might have a chance of survival. However, at the beginning of 1648, Spain finally retook control of the City and region.

Beyond the Pyrenees, the French were in Barcelona, but their presence was irritating for the Catalans. The Comte d'Harcourt fought off Leganez who tried to break through his lines on 5 October at Lleida but Leganez then turned Harcourt's lines around, forcing Harcourt to retreat. The Spanish now held Lleida in addition to Tortosa and Tarragona. Mazarin entrusted command of the Catalonian army to the Prince de Condé (Louis II de Bourbon took the title of Prince de Condé on the death of his father at the end of 1646). The Prince entered Barcelona on 11 April 1647 and relaunched the siege of Lleida on 11 May 1647; but the besieged citizens defended themselves valiantly, and the Marqués de Aytona assembled a relief army. Condé relented, and left for Barcelona on 5 August, then for France on 7 November, having forced the Marqués de Aytona's army back beyond the Ebre.

Turenne began the year 1648 by joining Wrangel at Hanau on 23 March 1648. They headed for Munich, forcing Mélander's Bavarians back to Ingolstadt and Ratisbon as they advanced; the Bavarians, threatened by the Swedes, had resumed their alliance with the Imperialists. On 16 May, Turenne, Wrangel and Königsmarck crossed the Danube at Lautingen then dealt a heavy defeat to the Bavarian and Imperial armies of Mélander and Montecuccoli at Zusmarchausen on 17 May. They then crossed the Lech at Rain and the Iser at Freizing, only to be stopped at the Inn due to a lack of boats. Piccolomini assumed command of the Imperial army, forcing the retreat of Turenne and Wrangel up the Iser, and set up camp at Landau. While Turenne and Wrangel occupied Bavaria, Königsmarck left for Bohemia. On 26 July 1648, his troops entered the outskirts of Prague; but the old town resisted until the Treaty of Westphalia.

Artois was to be decisive. In April 1648 Mazarin entrusted the Army of Picardy to the Prince de Condé. He faced Archduke Leopold, now Viceroy of The Netherlands, who assembled a strong army around Lille. On 13 May, Condé occupied Ypres and forced Dunkirk to surrender on 27 May, while the Archduke took back Courtrai on 19 May. Archduke Leopold then opened the

French and Swedish artillery during the unsuccessful siege of the Bavarian town of Wasserburg am Inn in June 1648. (Riksarkivet, Stockholm)

siege of Le Catelet on 19 June. Condé arrived from Arras to relieve the town, and the Archduke withdrew to Landrecies on 30 June. While Condé received reinforcements from the Compte d'Erlach and his Weimarians, the Spanish retook Furnes on 2 August. Archduke Leopold confidently began to make his way to Paris on 12 August. On 14 August there was an encounter between the cavalry of the two armies; the Spanish army arrived on the plain of Lens on 18 August. The Archduke placed his army in a position that he believed to be unassailable, and awaited his enemy, who arrived on the morning of 19 August, but Condé considered the Spanish positions too strong and refused the battle. His left broke ranks to march to the right in the direction of Béthune, and Condé hoped this manoeuvre would make the Archduke leave his formidable position to attack his moving army…the Archduke fell into the trap. On 20 August, after the French cavalry had forced back both wings of the enemy cavalry, the two armies advanced towards each other. Beck, who commanded two *tercios viejos* in the centre, was injured, and his infantry routed. The Spanish defeat was total. Condé rested for eight days, then joined Rantzau at the siege of Furnes.

The Battle of Lens ended a war that had lasted 30 years. The armies of Turenne, Wrangel and Königsmark were threatening Vienna and Prague; Emperor Ferdinand's ally, Maximilian of Bavaria, fervently wanted peace; and Philip IV had lost his main army. Ferdinand had no choice other than to make peace. He approved the peace propositions from France and Sweden in Münster and Osnabrück. Since 1641, talks had been taking place between France and The Empire in Münster, and between Sweden and The Empire in Osnabrück. The definitive peace treaty, known as the Treaty of, or the Peace of, Westphalia, was signed on 24 October 1648, ending the Thirty Years' War but not the war between France and Spain, which was not to end until the Treaty of the Pyrenees was signed on 7 November 1659.

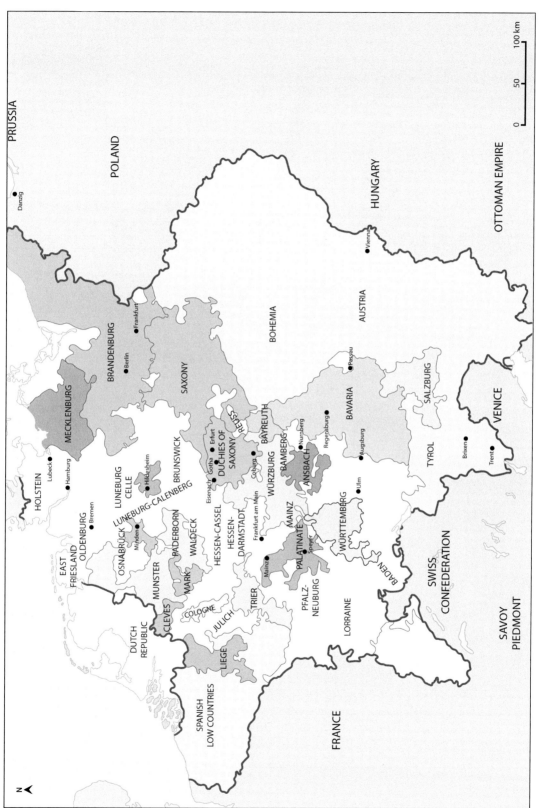

Europe in 1648

French officer of dragoons and dragoon of a regiment in service of Sweden between 1630 and 1635. Watercolor by Karl Alexander Wilke (1879-1954, photo from the author, public domain)

2

The Transformation of the French Army (1534–1616)

The various concepts underlying warfare in the early seventeenth century were the result of a slow evolution. To better understand the composition, organisation, and tactics of the French armies during the Thirty Years' War, it is necessary to go back 100 years.

The Birth of Infantry Regiments

The sixteenth century was a century of change. Europe rediscovered the military art of the ancients. And it was Machiavelli who set the ball rolling at the beginning of the century (1513–1520) with *The Art of War*. In his treatise, he proposed a way of raising an army, arranging a band and putting it into battle inspired by the Greeks and Romans. Machiavelli's *battaglione* consisted of 6,000 men, divided into ten *battaglie*, like the Roman legion and its component centuries. He divided these 6,000 men into 2,000 pikemen, 3,000 sword and buckler men and 1,000 arquebusiers.[1] Some years later, in 1559, the *Institution de la Discipline Militaire au Royaume de France* (*Institution of Military Discipline in the Kingdom of France*) by an anonymous author and dedicated to Antoine, King of Navarre, was published in France. Following in the footsteps of Machiavelli, the author proposed forming legions of 6,000 men, of whom there would be 1,000 arquebusiers, with the legionary pikemen divided into ten ensigns of 500 men, and five bands of 1,000, with each band thus comprising two ensigns.[2] Brantôme attributes this to Langey du Bellay, who is probably the author of this work, the origin of the ordinances governing the bands of the French infantry.

These treaties would perhaps have remained anecdotal if a great European sovereign, François I, had not been inspired by them. And so, on 24 July 1534,

---

1   Nicolas Machiavel, *Œuvres Complètes* (Paris: Gallimard, 1952), pp.770–771.
2   Anon., *Institution de la Discipline Militaire au Royaume de France, A Treshault & Trespuissant Prince Antoine Roy de Navarre* (Lyon: Macé Bonhomme, 1559), pp.70–71.

an edict was promulgated to raise seven legions of infantry, arquebusiers and halberdiers. Not only can this edict be considered the founding act of the French infantry, but it also inspired other great European sovereigns. Each of these seven legions was to have 6,000 men. Each legion was made up of six bands of 1,000 men commanded by a captain assisted by two lieutenants and two ensign-bearers. The edict gives the proportion of arquebusiers to pikemen, depending on the legion, to be 60 percent arquebusiers for the Brittany legion, 30 percent for the Languedoc legion and 20 percent for the other legions.[3]

At the same time, around 1535, the previous french bands, primarily those of Piedmont *and* Picardy, took on the title of old bands. Each band, headed by a captain, numbered 300 men at the end of the reign of François I and 500 under Henri I.

Charles V was quick to follow the example of Francis I, as the *prescripción/ edicto* of 1536 officially created the Spanish infantry tercios, which replaced the *coronellas*. The *tercio* was organised into 10 *banderas* of 300 men each, to a total of 3,000 men. The Habsburg Empire followed this organisation until the early seventeenth century, when Tilly continued to raise *battaglia* composed in this way. In 1560, a new *Ordonnance* reorganised the Spanish tercio into a minimum of 10 companies of pikemen and two of arquebusiers, with a strength of 250 men per company.

However, the legions were not very successful, and it was the old and new bands that formed the backbone of the French Army until the start of the Wars of Religion. Before 1560, unlike the Spanish *tercios*, the bands were only brought together when an army was being formed, with ten or twelve bands forming a battalion: these formations were only temporary.

Bands and legions were formed on the ground in massive squares – called *carré d'hommes* (square of men) or *carré de terrain* (ground square) - of pikemen and halberdiers, flanked by sleeves of arquebusiers, with squadrons (a squadron numbered 25 men) of arquebusiers formed on the front of the pikemen. Such a battalion numbered around 4,000 men.

In 1547, Henri II organised the Kingdom into three *Départements Militaires* (military departments), each administered by a *Maréchal de France*, and divided command of the French and foreign bands between five colonels and *colonel générals*.[4] A *colonel général* had a *mestre de camp général*, an colonel's ensign, a *sergente de battaile* and a *grand prévôt* to assist him. The two *colonel générals* for the French infantry were Gaspard de Châtillon, Comte de Coligny, for the infantry of *deçà les monts* (below the mountains) and François de Gouffier, Seigneur de Bonnivet, for the infantry *delà les monts* (beyond the mountains). According to Brantôme, the entire infantry owes a great deal to Gaspard de Châtillon, *Colonel Général* from 1547 to 1555, 'because it was him who regulated and policed it with the five *Ordonnances* that we have from him today, printed and so widely practised,

---

3   Decrusy & Armet Isambert, *Recueil Général des Anciennes Lois Françaises depuis l'an 420, jusqu'à la Révolution de 1789* (Paris, Belin-Leprieur, 1828), tome XII, page 390.

4   Decrusy & Armet Isambert, *Recueil Général des Anciennes lois Françaises Depuis l'an 420, jusqu'à la Révolution de 1789* (Paris: Belin-Leprieur, 1828), Tome XIII, pp.19–20

read and published among our bands.'[5] In the sixteenth and seventeenth centuries, soldiers' pay was paid during a '*montre*' (muster); a review that allowed the commissioners to check that the *roole* (or roll, i.e. the list of recruits) did not include any *passe-volants* who were fictitious recruits.

Mercenaries were one of the main sources of infantry throughout the sixteenth century. While the Swiss were still particularly popular in France, as demonstrated by the treaty of 7 June 1549, which specified that the King could raise no fewer than 6,000 of them, and no more than 16,000,[6] the German landsknechts were just as popular. In 1556, the King of France maintained seven ensigns, bands or companies and a Swiss regiment. But in 1558, there were 41,000 men in the service of France: 12,000 Swiss, 20,000 German landsknechts, and 9,000 German reiters.

In 1557, the French infantry was still made up of the old bands of Picardy and Piedmont. But on 10 August 1557, at Saint-Quentin, Duca Emmanuel-Philibert of Savoy, who commanded the army of Philip II of Spain, partially destroyed the French Army of the *Connétable de* Montmorency, including many soldiers from the old Picardie band. The Duc de Guise was recalled from Italy with his old bands from Piedmont. On 22 March 1558, King Henri II took up François I's idea and published an order creating seven new provincial legions, each with 6,000 men. Unlike the legions of Francis I, which had the same number of men, Henri II's legion had 15 ensigns of 400 men instead of six ensigns of 1,000 men. The number of legions was soon halved, and legionaries were brought in to replace the old bands in the garrison towns. Henri II's legions disappeared during the Wars of Religion: the old legionaries were usually amalgamated into the new units raised by the belligerents. Meanwhile, the Duc de Guise, with some of his old bands from Piedmont and the remnants of the old bands from Picardy, recaptured Calais from the English and took Thionville on 23 June 1558, thus provoking the Treaties of Cateau-Cambrésis. These two treaties, signed on 2 April 1559 with England and 3 April of the same year with Spain, put an end to the Italian Wars. The second was the consequence of the French defeats at Saint-Quentin in 1557 and Gravelines in 1558.

Henri II died after an accident during a tournament on 10 July 1559. He was succeeded by his son François II. With France at peace, the new bands were dismissed. All that remained were around 50 ensigns from the old Bands of Picardy and Champagne, whose *colonel général* was d'Andelot, and 36 ensigns from the old Bands of Piedmont, whose *colonel général* was the Prince de Condé. At 200 men per ensign, the French infantry therefore numbered almost 18,000 men.

Francis II died on 5 December 1560, and civil war had been tearing France apart since 15 March of that year. The old bands had split between the two sides, and less than half were with the Catholic army in Orléans when Charles IX came to the throne. All the infantry was then organised into three

---

5   Pierre de Bourdeilles, dit Brantôme, *Œuvres Complètes du Seigneur de Brantôme. Vies des Hommes Illustres et Capitaines Français* (Paris: Foucault, 1823), Tome IV, p.378

6   Decrusy & Armet Isambert, *Recueil Général des Anciennes lois Françaises Depuis l'an 420, jusqu'à la Révolution de 1789* , Tome XIII, p.85

corps commanded by three *mestres de camp*, 'in the fashion of the Spaniards', as Brantôme tells us. And under the three of them (Captains Sarlabous the elder, Richelieu and Remello) and their regiments, 'all the French infantry was organised in the style of the Spanish *tercios*'.[7] Brantôme bears witness to the birth of infantry regiments within the French Army and gives the Duc de Guise credit for them. The term regiment had already existed in Germany since 1523, but this unit was not really placed under the authority of a colonel (*obrist* or *oberst*) until around 1550: the landsknecht regiment then had ten ensigns (*fahnlein*) for a total of 3,000 to 5,000 men. Regimental organisation had also existed in Spain since 1536, in the form of *tercios* commanded by *maestro de campo*, as we have seen, whereas the legions of François I and Henri II had no permanent command of a colonel or *mestre de camp* type: there were only general colonels in charge of all the French infantry present on the battlefield.

In addition to these three regiments, the Catholic party had around 40 more bands at its disposal: garrisons on the borders and the old bands from Piedmont. For their part, the Protestant nobility raised troops in the provinces, mainly from the Gascons and Languedociens, and the Catholics soon followed suit. Four new regiments were raised by royal commission: *Charry* in Gascony, *Hémery* in Normandy, *Rieux* in Languedoc and *Sarlabous le jeune* in Poitou, Périgord and Quercy. Finally, the last ten old bands returning from Piedmont at the end of 1562 formed the *Brissac* regiment. These eight regiments were joined by new bands and legions, such as those from Picardy, Champagne, Normandy, Dauphiné and Provence.

On the eve of the Battle of Dreux, the French infantry was only part of the available resources: throughout the second half of the sixteenth century, both sides called on a large number of mercenaries: Swiss, always true to their reputation, Italians, Spaniards and German landsknechts for the Catholics, but only German landsknechts for the Protestants. The *Maréchal de Vieilleville*, referring to the Battle of Saint-Denis in 1567, expressed his concern to the King about the number of mercenaries: 'If the foreigners of both parties, who were numerous and all speaking the same language, such as 6,000 Swiss, 5,000 reiters and 4,000 landsknechts, had taken intelligence together, they would have thrown themselves on our Frenchmen in battle and would undoubtedly have defeated them all.'[8]

The Swiss were undoubtedly the most formidable troops the Royalist party had recourse to. They proved this as early as the Battle of Dreux in 1562. In 1567, Catherine de Medici asked for 6,000 Swiss to be raised. This large force, under the command of Louis Pfiffer, escorted the Court from Meaux to Le Bourget on 28 September. Pfiffer and his regiment were rewarded with the title of *Gardes Suisses du Roy*. A regiment of Guards had already been created in 1564, following an attempt by Catherine de Medici in 1563 to create ensigns of the Royal Guard from several bands of the Charry and

---

7   Brantôme, *Œuvres Complètes du Seigneur de Brantôme,* tome IV, pp.276–277.

8   François de Scepeaux, *Mémoires de la Vie de François de Scepeaux, Sire de Vielleville et Comte de Durestal,* in *Nouvelle Collection des Mémoires pour Servir à l'Histoire de France, depuis le XIIIe Siècle jusqu'à la fin du XVIIIe* (Paris: Michaud et Poujoulat, 1838), Tome 9, p.367.

Battle of Dreux, 1562, facsimile of a contemporary engraving. (Public Domain)

Richelieu Regiments. However, in the face of Protestant protests, Charles IX disbanded the regiment in 1566, sending the companies to garrison places in Picardy. The *Gardes Françaises* (French Guards) regiment was re-established in 1574, after the creation of the *Gardes Suisses* (Swiss Guards).

September 28 1567 heralded the outbreak of the second civil war and Charles IX asked Philippe Strozzi to assemble the bands scattered in Normandy, Picardy and Champagne, and the Count of Brissac, those in Piedmont. On the eve of the Battle of Saint-Denis, Charles X divided his old and new infantry bands, which must have totalled around 14,000 men excluding the Swiss, into two corps: one under Strozzi and the other under Brissac. Each of these two corps was made up of three regiments, commanded by a *mestre de camp*. It was shortly afterwards, during the Third War of Religion, following the Battle of Jarnac on 13 March 1569, that the infantry regiments known as the *Vielle Corps* (the Old Corps) were created. Ten ensigns from the old bands of the Comte de Brissac made up the regiment that later became *Piémont*. Fifteen ensigns, including six of the ensigns of the King's Guards, were brought together as the *Cosseins* regiment, which later became the *Gardes Françaises* (the French Guards). Sixteen ensigns from the old Picardie guards and bands formed the *Sarrieu* regiment, which later became *Picardie*. Finally, 26 ensigns from the old guards, new bands and old ensigns from the Lorraine garrisons made up the *Gohas* regiment, which became *Champagne*. Other regiments were created at the same time, those of *La Barthe* and *Gohas le jeune*, but they were disbanded at the end of the Wars of Religion. The last of the *Vielle Corps*, *Navarre*, was created that same year within the opposing party: the Prince de Condé having died at Jarnac, the young Henri de Navarre took over the leadership of the Protestant party. A company of 200 men was formed for his personal guard, and this company became a regiment when Henri IV took the Crown of France. It was thus the Wars of Religion that completed the transformation of the old infantry bands into infantry regiments as we know them in the seventeenth century.

On the battlefield, bands and regiments were combined into battalions of between 2,000 and 6,000 men, as was the case with the Swiss at Dreux or Saint-Denis. Around 1558, the average proportions of soldiers in a legion was one-third arquebusiers and two-thirds pikemen and halberdiers, although Montluc, before Thionville in 1588, made a different choice: 'Monsieur de Guise kept the marshal that evening; and as it was night, I took four hundred pikemen, all corselets, and four hundred arquebusiers, and went to put the four hundred corselets belly down a hundred paces from the town gate, and I went with the four hundred arquebusiers straight to the palisade.'[9] The Swiss and German ensigns were essentially made up of pikemen. At the

Morion, Musée de Brives.
(Photo: Stéphane Thion)

Battle of Saint-Denis in 1567, the Swiss battalion was flanked by French arquebusiers. And at Moncontour in 1569, Admiral Coligny's battalions of landsknechts were flanked on both sides by regiments of French arquebusiers.

The pikemen could be of 'corselets', equipped with burgonets or morions, cuirasses, pauldrons, gauntlets and tassetts, while the arquebusiers were at best protected by a morion, a jack with sleeves of mail or a *buffle* (buff coat). From 1521, and until the 1580s, the arquebus was still the main firearm used. In 1567, the musket appeared in the French infantry, a weapon that would become widespread in the 1570s.

French Artillery of the Sixteenth Century

Since the *Ordonnance* of February 1546, the artillery had depended on a *Grand Maître de l'Artillerie* (Grand Master of Artillery). His role was to arbitrate the salaries of artillery officers, appoint lieutenants and men and keep account of artillery pieces and ammunition. In 1547, Henri II appointed Charles de Cossé-Brissac *Maître* and *Captain Général* of the Artillery. With his lieutenant, Jean d'Estrées, he reorganised the artillery by limiting it to six types of guns, the six calibres of France: the *canon*, the *grande couleuvrine*, the *bâtarde*, the *moyenne*, the *faucon* and the *fauconneau*. An edict of December 1552 created 20 offices of captains of artillery and regulated their duties: each captain was required to provide 200 horses, 50 carters and 25 carts with four horse teams.

---

9   Blaise de Montluc, *Commentaires de Messire Blaise de Montluc, Mareschal de France*, in *Nouvelle collection des Mémoires pour servir à l'Histoire de France, Depuis le XIIIe Siècle jusqu'à la fin du XVIIIe* (Paris: L'Editeur du Commentaire Analytique du Code Civil, 1838), tome 7, p.191

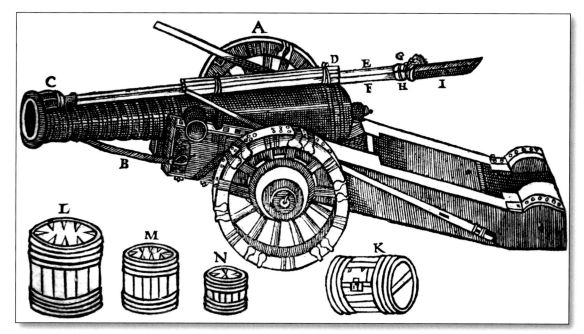

Artillery was not a decisive weapon on the battlefields of the sixteenth century. Protestant armies carried no more than five pieces with them, while Catholics carried up to fifteen. However, it proved indispensable when it came to conducting sieges and, if used properly, could have a devastating effect on morale.

Field Artillery Piece *c.* 1610. Du Praissac's manuscript 'Discours Militaires' (Photo: Stéphane Thion)

Progressive Lightening of the French cavalry

During the first half of the sixteenth century, the cavalry did not undergo any major changes compared to the regulations issued by Charles VII in 1445. On 20 January 1514, the King ordered that 'all the companies of his *Ordonnances* should be provided with a full complement of gendarmes and archers, in such numbers as they were ordered to have, equipped with coustilliers as required.'[10] The lance then provided had eight horses, i.e. one man-at-arms with four horses and two archers with two horses each. Each company, commanded by a captain assisted by a lieutenant and an ensign or guidon, always theoretically had one hundred lances, although some companies only had half that number. The *maréchal des logis* appears in the *Ordonnance* of 12 November 1549. According to this order, each man-at-arms had to wear armour, small and large armguards, breast and back plates, thigh armour and have a lance, and had, and maintained two horses, one for war service, with a pistol at the saddle bow. From that year onwards, the pistol was added to the gendarme's arms. The archer, for his part, had to wear a burgonet (a helmet

10 Decrusy & Armet Isambert, *Recueil Général des Anciennes Lois Françaises Depuis l'an 420, jusqu'à la Révolution de 1789*, Tome XII, page 2

which, unlike the morion, covers the cheeks), breastplate, forearm and thigh armour, and have a lance and a pistol.

The same *Ordonnance* also referred to *chevaux-légers* (light horse), who were more lightly armed and rode lighter horses. The first development to affect mounted troops in the first half of the sixteenth century was the development of light cavalry. The regulations of 1530 give us a better understanding of the origins of *chevaux-legers*, 'the King intends that the commissioners who will be making the next musters, tell and declare to the archers of each company that they must be ready, armed and dressed, and mounted on *chevaux-légers*[11]'. There were certainly light horse in the French Army in the past, but most of them were Albanian stradiots. Within the companies of *Ordonnance*, the term *archers* was henceforth used to designate young nobles who applied in the expectation that a position as a gendarme would become available, as the future *Connétable* de Lesdiguières did in 1588. This practice was confirmed by an *Ordonnance* of Charles IX (1574), which stipulated that 'no one could be a gendarme unless he had been an *archer* or *cheval-léger* for a continuous year, nor could he be an archer unless he was from a noble family.'

The gendarmes have the same appearance as those of the first half of the sixteenth century, as specified in an order of Charles IX dating from 1574:

> We want the man-at-arms to be armed with armet, or headgear, closed (without receiving any morion, although they had banners), good body armour, and for upper arms and forearms, tassets, thighs, with knee armour, & greaves, a good & strong lance, the estoc & an arming sword, the saddle armed in front and behind, having two good service horses, one of which will be bardable, bearing the muzzle, & the front of bards with the flanks of boiled leather. He shall also have at least one courtaut, or baggage horse, without being allowed to take any cart with him. The archer will wear an armet, or burgonet, without being allowed to have a morion with a plume; will have a good body cuirass, and armour for forearms, or armbands, tassets, & for thighs, with a good & strong lance, estoc & an arming sword, & a good service horse, in addition to the one for baggage, without him also being allowed to have any cart.[12]

But La Noüe, for his part, in *Discours Politiques et Militaires* published in 1587, deplored the heavier armour:

> As they had good reason (because of the violence of the arquebuses & pistols) to make the harnesses more massive, & better proof than before, they have however gone so far beyond measure that most have loaded themselves with anvils, instead of covering themselves with armour. And then, all the beauty of the horseman was converted into deformity, because his head clothing resembles an iron pot. On the left arm, he wears a large gauntlet, which covers him up to the elbow, & on

11 Decrusy & Armet Isambert, *Recueil Général des Anciennes Lois Françaises Depuis l'an 420, jusqu'à la Révolution de 1789,* Tome XII, page 348

12 Henri III, *Code du Roy Henri III, Roy de France et de Pologne* (Lyon: Publisher unknown, 1593), pp.1170–1171.

the right a small stump which only hides the shoulder; & usually wears no tassets, & instead of a helmet, a mandil, & without a lance. Our *gendarmes* & *chevaux-légers*, in the time of King Henri the Second, were much more beautiful to look at, wearing the sallet, brassards, tassets, helmet, lance, & baldric; & did not have all their weapons weighed down, which prevented them from wearing them for 24 hours.'[13]

At the beginning of the Wars of Religion, the *gendarmes* were still organised into companies of 25 to 100 men, and still charged *en haie*, in one or two ranks, as Castelnau tells us, referring to the Protestants at Saint-Denis (1567) : 'Nevertheless, the Prince (de Condé), who was naturally hot and ardent, in order to fight and see the enemies, resolved with the Amiral to leave Saint-Denis and put his cavalry in battle, according to the traditional French order, *en haye*, because he was not strong enough to double his ranks.'[14] For his part, La Noüe, in *Discours Militaires*, published in 1587, recommended abandoning the *en haie* formation charge in favour of forming a squadron of six or seven ranks, like the reiters, arguing that:

Armet of a Gendarme. Musée de Foix (Photograph, Stéphane Thion)

> …six or seven ranks of cavalry joined together would overthrow a single one. … In these civil wars, our gendarmerie has put to the test the strength of the reiters' squadrons; for although it has always fought courageously with them, it has not been able to break them, especially as they are so thick that there is no way of getting through. At Saint-Quentin and Gravelines, he was even more aware of what large squadrons of lances can do, from which he was easily overthrown, which is sufficient proof to induce our great men to correct the imperfections of our orders.[15]

And La Noüe then follows with the example of Montcontour in 1569, 'where the King's gendarmerie ranged itself in lancer squadrons, and also saw, when they came up against those of the Religion who were ordered *en haie*, and without any lances, that they were easily broken.'[16]

The Wars of Religion saw the development of another form of light cavalry: the mounted arquebusier and the *carabin*. The mounted arquebusier first appeared under Marshal de Brissac, who commanded Henri II's army in Piedmont. They were numerous in the armies of Henri II and Henri IV, before being replaced by dragoons under Louis XIII. Their mission was to harass,

---

13   François de La Noüe, *Discours Politiques et Militaires du Seigneur de La Noüe* (Bâle, Publisher unknown, 1587), pp.285–286.

14   Michel de Castelnau, *Mémoires de Messire Michel de Castelnau*, Collection Complète des Mémoires Relatifs à l'Histoire de France (Paris: Petitot, 1823), tome 33, p.396.

15   François de La Noüe, *Discours Politiques et Militaires du Seigneur de La Noüe*, pp.288–290.

16   François de La Noüe, *Discours Politiques et Militaires du Seigneur de La Noüe*, p.290.

Cuirassier or gendarme of the late sixteenth and beginning of the seventeenth centuries, watercolor by Karl Alexander Wilke (1879-1954, photo from the author, public domain)

capture outposts, assault and escort convoys. According to Tavannes,[17] they could fight on foot as well as on horseback. The *carabins*, who were more common under Henri IV, differed little from the mounted arquebusier in terms of equipment. Their defensive weapons were the cuirass or a buff coat, a gauntlet for the bridle hand, and a cabasset or morion, and their offensive weapon was the arquebus or *escopette*. Like the former, they were seen as scouts and flankers protecting the flanks of the *Gendarmes* and *Chevaux-Légers*. The French Army in front of Metz in April 1552 included 2,000 mounted arquebusiers and Montgommery recruited more than 3,000 in Languedoc and Dauphiné in 1569.

The main development, from the second third of the sixteenth century onwards, came with the appearance of the reiters. As early as the Battle of Dreux, the Protestants of Condé and Coligny fielded 11 *cornettes* of reiters, probably comprising 2,000 horse. In 1563, the Queen called in 6,000 German reiters. In 1567, Duc Jean Casimir reinforced the Huguenot party with 7,000 reiters and 6,000 landsknechts. In 1569, the Duc de Deux-Ponts brought 5,000 Rhinegrave reiters and 4,000 landsknechts to the Protestants, while Coligny had 3,000 and the Catholics were not to be outdone, with the Rhinegrave reiters. At the Battle of Montcontour in 1569, suspicious of his mercenaries who demanded battle or their pay, Coligny took care to surround his squadrons of reiters – he had 19 cornettes in two squadrons – with squadrons of French cavalry.

In *Discours Militaires* of 1587, La Noüe praised the fighting style of this German cavalry:

We must give them the honour of having been the first to use pistols, which I think are very dangerous when you know how to use them properly. ... Their defensive weapons are similar to those of the lancers in quality, but their offensive weapons surpass them, because the *gendarme* only uses the lance for one shot, whereas the reiter carries two pistols, from which he can fire six or seven, which cause a great deal of damage, when he uses them correctly. Everyone also carries a sword, which can have the same effect. Since the pistol can therefore distort defensive weapons, and the lance cannot, it must be concluded that the reiter has the advantage in offensive weapons, and equality in defensive ones.[18]

---

17   Guillaume de Saulx, *Mémoires de Guillaume de Saulx, Seigneur de Tavannes*, in *Collection Universelle des Mémoires Particuliers Relatifs à l'Histoire de France*, tome XLIX (London: Publisher unknown, 1789), p.325.

18   La Noüe, *Discours Politiques et Militaires du Seigneur de La Noüe*, pp.308–309.

La Noüe also admitted that the lancer was better mounted and had a psychological advantage, whereas the reiter had the advantage of fighting in a deep formation, up to 20 ranks deep. He proposed to the King of France that his army should be made up of 60 companies of gendarmes, 20 *cornettes* of *chevaux-légers*, five companies of mounted arquebusiers, making a total of 10,000 horse, and 3,000 to 4,000 reiters.[19] But the debate over the primacy of the lancer or the reiter had only just begun, since the Dutchman Walhausen, the Hungarian Basta, the Spanish Mendoza and Melzo and the Frenchman Montgomery were still debating the subject in the early seventeenth century. They all agreed that lancers had to fight in small squads and on suitable terrain to gain the upper hand.

French Wars of Religion Legacy

The French Army that took part in the Thirty Years' War was in fact the synthesis of two very different perspectives: the Catholic army and the Huguenot army of the late sixteenth century. During the first Wars of Religion, the two approaches were totally different, and this difference gave rise to an original army. To show just a few examples to illustrate this point:

On several occasions, the battles of the first Wars of Religion shared a common scenario. The Huguenots, despite being outnumbered, took the initiative: their fiery cavalry, including *gendarmes*, *chevaux-légers* and *reiters*, made magnificent and terrible charges, but were unable to break the Catholic infantry, particularly the formidable Swiss. The Huguenots, having defeated the enemy cavalry but not the infantry, who remained in control of the battlefield, were finally forced to retreat. The Battle of Dreux, between the Royalist troops of the Duc de Guise and the Protestants of Condé and Coligny, fought on 19 December 1562, and that of Saint-Denis, fought on 10 November 1567, are good example of this.

While the two sides differed in their approach to battle, their tactical choices were also very different. The Huguenot generals in particular opted for a resolutely modern approach to the organisation and positioning of troops on the battlefield. Thus, at Saint-Denis on 10 November 1567, the Prince de Condé divided his army into three corps of almost 1,000 men each, comprising 500 cavalrymen in six cornets and 400 arquebusiers. Pikemen and halberdiers were left in the town of Saint-Denis. At Moncontour, on 3 October 1569, Coligny arranged his cavalry in a particular way: he formed a 'battalion' made up of 16 cavalry cornettes – eight of *reiters* and eight of *chevaux-légers*. These were paired four by four, with two *chevaux léger cornettes* flanked on the right by two *reiter cornettes*, and on the left by a company of dismounted arquebusiers and a few mounted arquebusiers. Each squadron of four cornets was ranged behind the previous one and slightly echeloned. Nassau seems to have deployed his cavalry in the same way. During the battle, Coligny detached three regiments of French arquebusiers

---

19 La Noüe, *Discours Politiques et Militaires du Seigneur de La Noüe,* p.361.

to break up the Catholic retreating cornets, instructing them to fire at the horses, at a range of 50 paces.

At the beginning of the seventeenth century, the French infantry, influenced by Protestant practices, favoured battalions of less than a thousand men in 10 ranks. At the Battle of Ivry in 1590, Henri IV had small battalions of 500 arquebusiers formed to flank his cavalry squadrons. Following his example, around 1610, Jérémie de Billon recommended battalions of 500 men, arranged in 10 ranks of 50 men, 300 pikemen flanked by 10 ranks of 10 musketeers on each side. If necessary, two battalions could be combined to form a large battalion of 1,000 men. But this author innovated a little further by proposing to deploy the battalions in brigades of three battalions.

Sketch of a soldier by Ernest Meissonier (1815-1891), facsimile from author's collection, public domain

3

The French Army Before Entry into the War (1617–1635)

At the turn of the seventeenth century, French military commanders would take different inspirations: the lessons from their predecessors who fought in the Wars of Religion, but also the lessons from the Dutch and Spanish military theories. At the end of the Wars of Religion, Henri IV reorganised the French Army based on the Huguenot-Dutch model. This reorganisation of the army was to continue under Richelieu.

In 1600, Henri IV's army had shrunk to less than 1,500 cavalry and 7,000 infantry. During the Cleves succession crisis of 1610, the French Army had 5,000 cavalry and 25,000 infantry, plus 12,000 foreign infantry and 400 guns, both siege and campaign cannon. Sully estimated that an army of 8,000 cavalry and 50,000 infantry was needed to enter into a war and this is why he strived to fill the State's coffers. However, on the death of the King, this army was disbanded by the Regency. The army was expanded again under Louis XIII in 1620 and had more than 50,000 men by the time it was disbanded by the *Ordonnance* of 10 September 1620.

Henri IV by Jacques Onfroy de Bréville, also known as JOB (1858–1911) (Public Domain)

Between 1624 and 1635, the main developments were in administration and the organisation of services. When Lesdiguières died in 1627 the office of *Connétable* of France died with him, Richelieu thus demonstrating his desire for the centralisation of military affairs, which were passed into the hands of one of four Secretaries of State: Beauclerc took on this responsibility from 1626 to 1630, followed by Servien from 1630 to 1636. With this function now occupied by the *noblesse de robe*, the rights and duties of the soldiery could be formalised, in particular through the *Ordonnance* of 1629, called the 'Code Michaud', which aimed at increasing discipline in the French armies and controlling the condition of the troops. The objective of this section of the *Ordonnance* of January 1629, Article 220, is worthy of note:

> With regard to order and discipline of the soldiery, both cavalry and infantry, because civil war has led most of them to spread disorder and because their actions resulted in much damage which the previous military *Ordonnances* did not remedy, we consider it judicious for the good of our State, the policing of our soldiers and the relief of our people to remedy this situation by a new regulation, without modification on previous regulations and for which we determine, state, and dictate.[1]

In practice, this *Ordonnance* legislated all aspects of army life: administration of the regiment, the number of annual musters, soldiers' pay and the appointment of captains and officers, pay increase and promotions for soldiers of merit, loans to soldiers, supply of bread to a garrison, the locations of billeting throughout France, campaign hospitals, the enlisting of soldiers and checks, the duration of service (at least six months), the regulating of routes and lodgings for the troops, the order of march of regiments, the responsibilities and the policing role of captains and officers on marches, the responsibilities of the *mestres de camp* (colonels); the organisation of the regimental guard, the management of complaints from civilians; the supply of provisions to soldiers; the billeting for companies, presence of *mestres de camp* and captains in their regiment or company, presence of lieutenants, ensigns and sergeant majors in their company, the organisation of drills, the leave of and dismissal of soldiers and officers, the commissions given by the *mestres de camp*, the duties of the soldiers, and finally, military justice. These subjects are addressed in a total of 123 articles. This somewhat fastidious inventory highlights the preoccupations of Louis XIII and Richelieu regarding the army: the restoration of authority, in particular by obliging *mestres de camp* and captains to be present with their units, the recruitment of a high-quality, disciplined and less 'volatile' army by fighting against desertion and *passe-volants*; and the protection of civilians. Finally, this *Ordonnance* attempts to fight against the dishonest practices of captains and *mestres de camp*; practices highlighted by Richelieu himself in his account of an episode of the siege of La Rochelle (1628):

---

1   Decrusy & Armet Isambert, *Recueil Général des Anciennes Lois Françaises Depuis l'an 420, jusqu'à la Révolution de 1789* (Paris: Belin-Leprieur, 1828), tome XVI, p.284.

And because pay is the soul of the soldier and maintains his courage, which he seems to lose when he is not paid, and so that the soldier would always be paid on time, the Cardinal appointed one commissioner per regiment and ordered them to distribute pay directly to the soldier and not to their captains, which led to three major advantages for the army: the soldiers were actually paid, and because the captains could no longer steal their pay, they could no longer introduce *passe-volants*, and the King knew every week the number of soldiers he had in his army.[2]

As military generals had always tried to avoid Royal legislation, the King appointed *maîtres des requêtes*, who later became *intendants*, whose task was to ensure the application of the King's orders, provide reports, supervise the commissioners and war controllers and assist the Commander in Chief. The position of *intendant* was made official by an Edict of May 1635.[3]

The Dutch School

The Eighty Years' War between the Dutch and Spanish began in 1568, six years after the French Wars of Religion. At the time, the French Huguenots were already experimenting with new formations and tactics, as at Saint-Denis in 1567, where the Prince de Condé experimented with small corps of 500 cavalry and 400 arquebusiers. Based on exchanges between Huguenots and the Dutch, it is clear that the latter drew a great deal of inspiration from the advances made in France. Nevertheless, the Dutch also contributed to certain advances in the Military Arts.

Maurice, the Prince of Orange and Count of Nassau (Prins van Oranje/ Prince d'Orange and Graf von Nassau), considerably influenced the military strategy of his era. Maurice of Nassau, son of William of Nassau and Anne of Saxony, became Governor (*Stadtholder*) and Captain General of the United Provinces on the death of his father in 1584. His theories and many victories over the Spanish led him to be considered as one of the great captains of his time; he died in The Hague, on 23 April 1625. To perfect his new infantry tactics, the Prince of Orange took inspiration from Roman authors, and created lighter, and thereby more flexible formations. He was the brain behind the tactic of infantry units 10 ranks deep – which he also implemented in practice – rather than the Spanish-inspired 40 to 50 ranks that had been used up until that time. From 1594 he developed salvo fire, with the first rank of musketeers firing simultaneously, then drawing back to reload, and the next rank taking their place at the front. Each successive rank took the place of that preceding to fire. And although firepower now took precedence over hand-to-hand combat, Maurice de Nassau always maintained that it was the pikeman's duty to protect the musketeer and not the other way around. The role of the musketeers, placed in front of the pikemen, was to prepare the

---

2   Richelieu, *Mémoires du Cardinal de Richelieu*, p.513

3   Decrusy & Armet Isambert, *Recueil Général des Anciennes Lois Françaises depuis l'an 420, jusqu'à la Révolution de 1789*, Tome XVI, p.442

assault by firing at 30 *toises* (60 metres) – perhaps a quarter of the weapon's maximum range.

The works of Jean-Jacques Walhausen, Captain of the Guard of the Town of Dantzig, confirm the theories of Maurice of Nassau. His works include eight books; the first, *L'Art Militaire pour l'Infanterie*, published in 1615, addresses the use of the pike and musket, drill for an infantry company, battle arrangements for a company and a regiment, and military discipline of the infantry. The second book, *Kriegskunst zu Pferd*, published in 1616, deals with the art of war for the cavalry. The fourth book, *Archiley Kriegskunst*, published in 1617, addresses artillery. These works were written after *Les Principes de l'Art Militaire*, written in French by Jean de Billon and published in 1613–1615, although it was *written* before the death of Henri IV, probably between 1605 and 1610.

Caliverman *c.* 1608, engraving by Jacob de Gheyn (1565–1629) (Public Domain)

The French Infantry from 1617 to 1634

Around 1602, Sully reorganised the French infantry into permanent and temporary regiments that were raised only in the event of war. In March and April 1610, Henri IV raised 17 infantry regiments including five foreign regiments, bringing the army to 50,000 infantry. The *Gardes Françaises* (French Guards) now counted 20 companies of 200 men; the old regiments of *Champagne, Picardie, Piémont, Normandie and Navarre* had 20 companies of 100 men; other permanent regiments (*Bourg-l'Espinasse, Nerestang, Balagny, Sault, Deportes, Beaumont*) had 10 companies of 100 men; and the Lorraine regiments of *Vaubecourt* and *Nesmond* had 15 companies of 100 men. The *Gardes Suisses* (Swiss Guard) were established in 1616, with 20 companies of 300 men.

In 1620, permanent regiments grouped together the regiments of the Guard (*Gardes Françaises* and *Gardes Suisses),* the five regiments of the *vieux corps* (*Champagne, Picardie, Piémont, Normandie* and *Navarre)* and six regiments bearing the name of their colonel, the *petits vieux: Chappes, Rambures, Bourg-l'Espinasse, Sault, Vaubecourt* and *Beaumont*. From 1616, these permanent regiments carried the *drapeau blanc*. In times of war, a large number of temporary regiments were raised, which made up the major part of the army; these regiments generally took the name of their colonel, and a colonel could raise a number of regiments. After the pacification of 1622, the newly raised infantry regiments were disbanded. Others were raised in 1624; a regiment from Liège, *La Hocquerie*, was raised in 1629 and *Vaubecourt*, raised in 1610, was from the Lorraine.

In 1622, the number of regiments in the army reached 91 infantry regiments, and was reduced by Richelieu to 72 just before French entry into the Thirty Years' War, including 19 'maintained' regiments.

The *Gardes Françaises* – created in 1563 and France's oldest regiment – now included 30 companies of 300 men, a total of 9,000. The *Gardes Suisses* comprised 12 companies of 200 men, totalling 2,400. The *Gardes Ecossaises* (Scottish Guards) only appeared in 1635, at a strength of 13 companies of 115 men.

In theory, a permanent regiment was made up of 10 to 12 companies of 100 men, and those of the *vieux corps* had 20 or 30 companies of 100 men; *Navarre* and *Champagne* had 30 companies, most often divided into three battalions. *Normandie* appears to have had only two battalions and 20 companies. A 'temporary' regiment generally had 10 companies, as was the case of the *Bordeilles* regiment in February 1622, which had 10 companies and a total of 900 men.

In general, around 40 percent of the rank and file were pikemen and 60 percent were musketeers. On campaign, losses, illness and desertion rapidly reduced the numbers in a company to around 50 men, and only rarely more than 70 men. The two rebel regiments of the Duc de Retz, who fought in the Drôlerie des Ponts-de-Cé in August 1620, totalled only 1,500 men between them.

Henri IV had raised one foreign regiment before 1610, but this number rapidly increased to seven under the Regency, and to twelve by 1625. Foreign

A French infantry company in 1633. Jacques Callot (1592–1635), detail. (Public Domain)

regiments, notably the larger Swiss regiments, had 8 to 20 companies of 100 to 300 men: three Swiss regiments raised between 1610 and 1614 had between 2,100 and 3,000 men in companies of 300. However, in 1624, Annibal d'Estrée's three Swiss regiments (*Diesbach, Schmidt* and *Siders*) in Italy had 1,000 men each, in 5 companies of 200 men.

During the period preceding France's entry into the Thirty Years' War, the Royal Army was able to bring together all or part of its elite regiments on campaign. This was the case for the siege of Saint Jean d'Angély in 1621 with the *Gardes Françaises*, the *Gardes Suisses, Picardie, Piémont, Champagne, Navarre, Normandie, Rambures, Chappes* and *Lauzières*. In Saintonge in 1622, there were five battalions from the *Gardes Françaises*, two battalions from the *Gardes Suisses*, three battalions from *Navarre*, two battalions from *Normandie, Picardie, Piémont,* and *Champagne* – left in La Rochelle – and many other regiments, including *Nerestang. Maréchal* de Montmorency's army at Carignan in Piedmont on 6 August 1630 included the *Gardes Françaises, Champagne, Piémont, Picardie, Navarre, Normandie, Rambures, Sault, Vaubécourt* and 20 other regiments.

However, when the old regiments were together, relations were soured by quarrels over precedence, which Louis XIII settled in 1620. The Marquis de Fontenay-Mareuil gave an anecdote in his memoirs, a little before the Drôlerie des Ponts-de-Cé:

> It was on this occasion that he [the King] settled once and for all the differences that had so long divided the regiments of *Piémont, Champagne* and *Navarre,* and which on many occasions had nearly caused much ill, each of them claiming to have the right to pass before the other, and giving more importance to this advantage over the other than to fighting the enemy. The reasons they alleged were: for the regiment of *Piémont,* that it was the largest infantry regiment from beyond the mountains, as *Picardie* was the largest regiment below, and having always been on equal footing with *Picardie* when there were two colonels, and the fact that the two offices were now brought together in the person of M. d'Espernon, and all the infantry brought together in one same corps, could not lose it the place that it had kept for so long; and that although he ceded to Picardy when King Henri *le Grand* called him from Provence to serve at his side, he had no other alternative, because the Baron de Biron was at the time the *Mestre de Camp*, and the *Maréchal* de Biron, who was his brother, commanded the army and had all power, obliged him to do so; this did not prevent him from preceding all the others. *Champagne* said that he was used to marching behind *Picardie*, and that nothing had ever come between them; and *Navarre,* having been the Regiment of the Guards of King Henri *le Grand* when he was but King of Navarre, would have preceded *Picardie* if the authority of the *Maréchal* de Biron had not prevented him; this is why he should at least march behind him. But the King, without taking account of all these reasons, ordered that in the future they would alternate, and that every six months they would each have preference in turn, having drawn lots in his presence, and before the army engaged in battle.[4]

---

4   François Du Val, *Mémoires de Messire du Val, Marquis de Fontenay-Mareuil,* in *Collection Complète des Mémoires Relatifs à l'Histoire de France* (Paris: Petitot, 1826), vol. 1, pp.476–477.

In his work of military theory, *Les Principes de l'Art Militaire*, Jean de Billon recommends 2,600 men in 13 companies of 200 men in addition to the captain, the ensign, three sergeants, a drum-major, a fifer and a harbinger. But he made it clear that he preferred companies of 100 men, which he felt were easier to lead and discipline, to companies of 200 men.[5] Jean-Jacques Walhausen recommends a regiment of 3,000 men, including 1,000 to 1,200 pikemen, in 10 companies of 300 (including 100 to 120 pikemen).

Considering the size of the proposed regiments, these two theoreticians wrote their works before the beginning of the Thirty Years' War. As we have seen, in France only the *vieux corps* reached such numbers. At the end of the 1630s, the size of the regiments decreased sharply, and in his *Traité de la Guerre*, published in 1636, Duc Henri II de Rohan recommends regiments of 600 pikemen and 600 musketeers; in practice, a temporary regiment rarely exceeded 1,000 men. The regiment of *Bordeilles* in 1622 mustered 900 men, and *Chamblai* and *Lèques,* the two regiments of the Duc de Rohan that accompanied him to the Valtelline in 1633, should theoretically have had 1,000 men each, but totalled only 1,200 men between them. In 1635, the Duc de Rohan brought seven regiments into the Valtelline, with a total of 4,000 men – an average of less than 600 men per regiment.

According to the *Ordonnance* of 1629, the staff of a permanent regiment comprised: one *mestre de camp*; one sergeant major; one aide major, one provost (responsible for policing), one conduct commissioner (responsible for intendancy), one quartermaster (who arranged the quartering of troops), one chaplain and one surgeon. The officers for a company of 200 men included: one Captain, one lieutenant, one ensign (who carried the flag in the regiment colours), two sergeants, three corporals, one harbinger, two drummers and a barber-surgeon. The rest of the company included six *anspessades*, 45 appointees, 100 experienced soldiers and 37 *cadets*. As mentioned above, the battalion

On a Terrace. Oil on wood, panel by Ernest Meissonier (1815–1891) (Public Domain)

---

5   Jean de Billon, *Les Principes de l'Art Militaire* (Rouen: Berthelin, 1641), livre 2, pp.319–320.

was the combination of a number of companies, with the pikemen in the centre and the musketeers on the wings (the *manches de mousquetaires*) or in front of the first line of pikemen. The most senior of the company captains commanded the battalion. The sergeant-major took orders from the *mestre de camp* for the choice of position, battle array, alignment, and distances and intervals between the battalions.

The *Colonel Général*, who reported directly to the Crown, maintained one company – the *Colonelle* – in the *Gardes Françaises* and the five *vieux corps* (*Picardie, Piémont, Navarre, Champagne, Normandie*). This *Compagnie Colonelle* carried the *drapeau blanc* of the *Colonel Général* and was commanded by a lieutenant colonel appointed by the *Colonel Général.*

Usually, the regiments were divided into battalions of 1,000 to 1,200 men, forming as many battalions as their numbers permitted – normally one to three, and at least five in the case of the *Gardes Françaises*, as in Saintonge in 1622. However, a battalion could only be constituted of a detachment of five companies, like the *Gardes Françaises* at the Pas de Suse in March 1629, or *Champagne* on the Île de Rhé in 1627, and it was common to create detachments of 100 to 200 men from one or more companies.

In 1628, a battalion was formed from companies of the regiments of

Officers at a Entertainment.
After an engraving by
Abraham Bosse (1604–1676)
(Author's Collection)

Chappes and *Navarre* within Schomberg's army which was to reinforce the Île de Rhé (the other part of the regiment was at Fort Louis), two battalions were formed from the *Champagne* regiment, one from the regiment of *Rambures*, one from *Beaumont*, two from *Plessis-Praslin*, and two from the *La Meilleraye* regiment. The strength of these battalions could not exceed 400 men; the strength of Schomberg's army, including the cavalry, totalled 4,000 men. In 1630, Schomberg's army in the Piedmont totalled 18,000 infantry from 14 regiments and four companies from *Champagne*, which were divided into 18 battalions of 1,000 to 1,200 men.

Theoretically speaking, in combat the battalion was deployed in 10 ranks with pikes in the centre and musketeers on the wings. In his writings, Jean de Billon describes a battalion of 200 men formed in 10 ranks of 20 men abreast, with 10 files of pikemen in the centre and five files of musketeers on each side. In drills, each rank and each file was spaced at six feet. A battalion such as this occupied a space of 104 feet in width and 54 feet in depth. For an experienced battalion, the ranks and files could be spaced three feet apart or less, the battalion then occupying half as large an area. But Billon specifies that the best strength for a complete battalion is 500 men, with 10 ranks and 50 files. This battalion would then have 200 musketeers in 20 files, with 10 files on each flank, and 300 pikemen in the centre.[6] Two battalions could then form a unit of 1000 men.

On campaign, where numbers diminished rapidly, battalions were more usually drawn up in eight ranks. For battle, Billon stipulated that: 'it is necessary to be the first in the field and to draw up to await the enemy and see him arrive.'[7] Then the battalion had to move slowly, stopping 50 or 60 paces from the enemy, 'each man joining left shoulder to right shoulder, bending forwards, putting the weight on the right foot stretched behind,' then to 'move forward only five or six large paces, pikes lowered for a stronger impact.' Finally, he specified that:

> if advancing on the enemy from afar, the advance should be with small paces also, stopping every hundred paces, or less, to straighten the files, then tighten the ranks at the front, and prevent the files from closing more than one and a half feet from each other, constantly shouting that they tighten the ranks but not the files; it is necessary to consider what the enemy intends to do, and not march without that consideration.

In respect of the musketeers, he said, 'it is necessary to cause as much damage as possible to the enemy with the musketeers before engaging in hand-to-hand combat,' then he suggested a general fire from the musketeers on the flanks of the battalion 'for which the musketeers should be doubled by half files to better fire without injury.' Finally, he suggested that the detached musketeer platoons fire on the flank then 'engage hand-to-hand on the flanks of the enemy.'[8] Facing the cavalry, the pikemen advance with their pikes lowered, as the regiments of the Duc de Rohan (*La Frezelière* and *Lèques*) did in July 1635 against the German cavalry in the Val-Fresle.

On campaign, the battalions could be grouped into corps of battle (advance guard, main body, rearguard) which could include up to six battalions, as was the case for the army of *Maréchal* Schomberg on 17 October 1630 at Casale. Brigades are already mentioned in 1629, notably at the siege of Privas, during which the regiments of *Champagne* and *Piémont* formed a brigade.

In his book, Billon mentions three-battalion brigades: 'There are two facing that seem to be only one corps, and another behind these two. … Or one single battalion is placed in front and two others behind, and when it comes to hand-to-hand combat with the enemy they leave and charge the flank.'[9] There seems to have been numerous possible battalion formations, and Walhausen, like Billon, suggests a wide variety. However, on campaign, formations and manoeuvres described by the theoreticians would have rarely

6   Jean de Billon, *Les Principes de l'Art Militaire* (Rouen: Berthelin, 1641), Livre 2, p.256.
7   Jean de Billon, *Les Principes de l'Art Militaire* (Rouen: Berthelin, 1641), Livre 2, p.258.
8   Jean de Billon, *Les Principes de l'Art Militaire* (Rouen: Berthelin, 1641), Livre 2, pp.258–259.
9   Jean de Billon, *Les Principes de l'Art Militaire* (Rouen: Berthelin, 1641), Livre 2, pp.260–261.

'Disposition of an Army' around 1614, according to Sieur Du Praissac, *Les Discours Militaires Dédiez à sa Majesté* (Author's photograph, Public Domain)

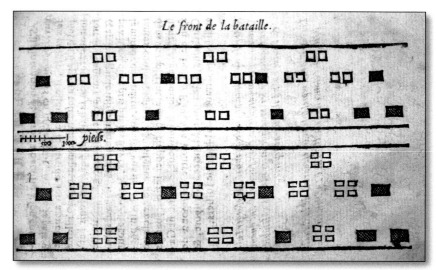

Le front de la bataille.

been applied; the experienced troops may have performed these manoeuvres but the majority of combat units and the temporary regiments most probably would not have had the time to train in such methods.

Soldiers were divided into pikemen and musketeers; Jean de Billon explains that 'some foreigners observed that, with more senior soldiers, two-thirds were pikemen and the other third musketeers. And if they were new soldiers, two-thirds were musketeers and the other third were pikemen.'[10] But he concludes that, with the war in Flanders consisting mainly of sieges, there are now more musketeers than pikemen. Among the soldiers, the *anspessades* were better paid and replaced the corporals when they were absent. The cadets were volunteers from good families. According to Billon:

> It is necessary therefore for each company to have one hundred musketeers or arquebusiers, for we are constrained to give arquebuses to the young cadets and gentlemen, who have not yet built up their strength. It seems to me that since we have found the way to carry short cannons as far as longer cannons, it would be good to make muskets in this form. ... The bandolier for the army must be of good leather, and the charges of wood, so that they do not break. In Flanders, they carry large conrainers of horn hung from a leather flask pouch, for they hold much powder. ... Swords must be short. And each soldier should have a *roupille* [a cape] for the rain, and this should be a little large.

And he adds, regarding the pikemen, 'After this, eighty or one hundred armed pikemen are required.' Their pikes should be:

> strong and of good wood; and the iron squared and of the best quality. They also need short swords, *roupilles* for those who so wish, but fitted close to the body and not large, and the best pointed burgonets. Because the straps that support the

---

10   Jean de Billon, *Les Principes de l'Art Militaire* (Rouen: Berthelin, 1641), Livre 2, p.320.

tassets break most often, it would be well to attach the tassets to the corselet with two buckles of iron.[11]

Before 1635, proportions were one pikeman to one musketeer, as we are told by the Duc de Rohan in his observations of the war in 1636: 'Nations other than the Swiss shared equally the pikes and muskets.'[12] The strength of the German regiment of Batilly, raised by capitulation, was close to this proportion: it was made up of 10 companies of 100 men, including 89 soldiers, of whom there were three corporals, three *anspessades*, 36 pikemen with corselets, and 43 musketeers. However, a company of 100 men often comprised around 60 percent musketeers and 40 percent pikemen. Thus, a company of d'Estissac regiment had 36 pikemen out of 100 men in 1622. The Scottish regiment of Hebron, raised in March 1633, in 12 companies of 100 men, had 40 pikes and 60 muskets per company. A company consisted of a captain, a lieutenant, an ensign, two sergeants, three corporals and five *anspessades*.

Helmets, morions or cabassets, and armour were given in priority to the corporals, *anspessades* and elite pikemen. The pikeman's full equipment was the pot, cuirass with tassets, a sword and a pike more than five metres in length. But as the campaign advanced, pikemen had the tendency to lighten their equipment, by replacing the corselet with a buff coat. Musketeers could wear a hat, a *boukinkan* or morion; they wore a cassock, or more rarely a buff coat, and were equipped with a sword and musket, which had fully replaced the arquebus/caliver by 1622.

The Duc de Rohan describes the equipment of the infantry just before France entered the war (1635):

Reconstruction of a *pot*, of a type worn around 1620–30 (photo showing the author)

The most ordinary arms of the Infantry at the present time for defence are the *pot*, the *cuirass* and tassets, and for the offence the sword, pike and musket, which are by and large the arms of the Greeks and Romans (…) The battle corps is made up of pikes, which is a very proper arm to resist the cavalry, with many pikes together forming a solid corps, difficult to break at the head by reason of its length, four or five rows of pikes, the blades of which protrude past the front of the soldiers and always hold the cavalry squadrons at a distance of twelve or fourteen feet.[13]

---

11   Jean de Billon, *Les Principes de l'Art Militaire* (Rouen: Berthelin, 1641), Livre 2, pp.321–322.

12   Henri II de Rohan, *Le Parfait Capitaine ; Traité de la Guerre* (Paris: Jean Houze, 1636), p.233.

13   Henri II de Rohan, *Le Parfait Capitaine ; Traité de la Guerre* (Paris: Jean Houze, 1636), pp.227–228.

The French Cavalry from 1617 to 1634

At the end of the Wars of Religion, the Catholic cavalry still followed its old organisation with its origins in the Hundred Years' War, and still charged *en haie* (in a thin, extended line) two or three ranks deep. The original *compagnies d'ordonnance* had 100 lances; a lance comprised a gendarme bearing the lance, and two archers, by this time called *chevaux-légers*. The Huguenots, inspired by German and Dutch models, rapidly adopted the pistol and reduced the weight of their armour. In 1620, there was only a part of the Gendarmerie remaining that still kept the full armour, and this became progressively lighter; the burgonet often replacing the visored helmet, and high boots in supple leather replacing greaves and sabatons. The Huguenots had also adopted a deep formation, but in contrast to the German model, they preferred the charge to the caracole. Because of this the Huguenot formation was shallower: six ranks instead of the 10 ranks of the German formations.

Henri IV reformed the cavalry in 1600, and this organisation remained until Richelieu's new reforms at the end of 1634. In 1603, the cavalry, had a total of 1,500 men, including the *Maison du Roi* (King's Household) and 19 companies of *gendarmes* and *chevaux-légers*, with 25 to 30 men in each. The *Maison du Roi* was made up of four companies of *Gardes du Corps*: a Scots Company, a Company of the King's *Chevaux-Légers,* a Company of *Gendarmes* and a troop of 100 arquebusiers and *carabins*. In 1609, cavalry numbers were brought up to 8,500 men, but contrary to what was happening in the infantry, the nobility – who were the captains of the cavalry companies – maintained their resistance to the formation of large units until 1638.

During the Regency, in 1615, bands of *carabins* were added to each company of *chevaux-légers*, armed with a carbine rather than the more cumbersome arquebus, and commanded by a lieutenant. However, in 1621, the *chevaux-légers* had practically all adopted the carbine, so the *carabins* formed a special corps commanded by a *mestre de camp des carabins*, Arnauld de Corbeville. After the pacification of 1622, cavalry companies maintained by the governors of the provinces were reduced to 15, and the King increased his Household with a company of 100 'musketeers' recruited from gentlemen volunteers.

Puysegur says, about the creation of this unit:

> After this (the storming of Montpellier in 1622), the King marched straight to Avignon and during his march he removed the carbines from the *carabins* company, and gave them muskets, and gave command of the company, which had no leader after the death of the captain, to de Montelet, the grade of lieutenant to de la Vergne and the *Cornette* to de Montalet, who bore the same name. … His Majesty asked d'Espernon for six of his Guards to put in the company; he wished – and I can even say that he forced – me to take the cassock of the musketeer … His Majesty assured me … that he had decided to put only gentlemen in this company, which he would find among his Guards, as well as a few soldiers of fortune; but that he did not wish to take any who had not served, desiring after they had served a time in the company, to remove them and disperse them in the

vieux and *petits vieux* regiments, and even give them ensigns and lieutenancies in the guards.[14]

Mousquetaires du Roi around 1630, according to JOB (1858–1911) (Public Domain)

On the 3 October 1634, Louis XIII retook charge of the unit, and thus became captain of the Company of Musketeers.

The King had his own Company of Musketeers which accompanied him everywhere; Richelieu also had his company of Guards. Gabriel Daniel reports that there was:

> emulation between these two companies that went as far as jealousy, of the sort that very often there were quarrels and combats between the King's Musketeers and the Cardinal's Guards. It was a pleasure for the King to learn that the musketeers had mistreated the Guards and the Cardinal also applauded when the musketeers were dominated. Because duels were forbidden, the duels between the Musketeers and the Cardinal's Guards were passed off as 'encounters'. The Cardinal took the occasion to make a few attempts to break the Company of Musketeers, but did not succeed.[15]

---

14 Jacques de Chastenet, *Les Mémoires de Messire Jacques de Castenet, Chevalier, Seigneur de Puysegur, Colonel du Régiment de Piedmont, & Lieutenant Général des Armées du Roy* (Amsterdam: Abraham Wolfgang, 1690), tome 1, p.35.

15 Révérend Père Gabriel Daniel, *Histoire de la Milice Française* (Paris: Jean-Baptiste Coignard, 1721), tome II, p.217.

These words seem to be inspired by the memoirs of Monsieur d'Artagnan, Captain Lieutenant of the First Company of the *Mousequetaires du Roi*:

> De Tréville had called all three from the south-west [author's note: Porthos, Athos and Aramis were all from Béarn] because they had engaged in a few battles, which gave them much reputation in the province. What is more, he was most content to choose his men thus, because there was such jealousy between the Company of Musketeers, and that of Cardinal Richelieu's Guards, that they fought each other every day. This was nothing, as it happens every day that men quarrel together, especially when there is aspersion cast on their reputation. But that which is somewhat surprising, is that the masters each boasted that they had men whose courage placed them above all others. The Cardinal constantly boasted of the bravery of his guards, and the King tried constantly to diminish this bravery because he could see that His Eminence the Cardinal sought only to elevate his Company above his own. The minister had even posted men in the provinces with the order to bring him the combatants who had excelled in fighting. Thus it was at this time when there were rigorous edicts against duels, and even when some persons of great quality were punished by death, who had fought regardless of these edicts, he offered to these persons not only exile at his side, but also, most often, his favour.[16]

In his memoirs, Richelieu describes the impression that the King's musketeers must have made in an anecdote that occurred at the siege of La Rochelle in 1627:

> As the Cardinal had, upon the order from the King, paid all the expenses of this embarkation [for the Île de Ré], all that remained was to await the wind. These troops had been so well chosen that they would have been capable to fight twice their number, and the musketeers alone, thirty-two of them that His Majesty had equipped with arms against muskets and halberds, were in such condition that they would have been able to reduce any army to pieces. But His Majesty did not content himself with this foresight and these arms; his main recourse was to God, and he ordered each man to make his peace with God, and in particular his musketeers, whom he ordered to confess and take communion before leaving.[17]

As the King had absolute confidence in his musketeers, he demanded that for the attack on the Pas de Suse on 6 March 1629, the musketeers join forces with the *enfants perdus* to force the barricades.

In 1627, the French cavalry included the *Maison du Roi* in seven companies (four *Gardes du Corps* companies, one Scottish company and three French companies, one company of *Gendarmes de la Garde*, one company of *Chevaux-Légers de la Garde* and one company of the *Mousquetaires du*

---

16   Gatien de Courtilz de Sandras, *Mémoires de M. d'Artagnan, Capitaine Lieutenant de la Première Compagnie des Mousquetaires du Roi* (Cologne : Pierre Marteau, 1701), tome I, pp.14–15.

17   Armand du Plessis de Richelieu, *Mémoires du Cardinal de Richelieu*, in *Nouvelle collection des Mémoires pour Servir à l'Histoire de France* (Paris: Michaud et Poujoulat, 1837), deuxième série, tome VII, pp.476–477.

Roi), the *Gendarmerie de France* (16 companies recruited from the lower nobility), the companies of *chevaux-légers* under the command of a *Colonel Général* of the light cavalry, the *carabins*, forming a separate corps from 1 April 1622, and the nobility of the *ban* and the *arrière-ban*, which were to serve personally, both on horseback and in arms, bringing with them a number of cavalry proportional to the size of their fiefdom. This nobility was difficult to control and was not often employed. These formations were to be abandoned when the cavalry was reorganised into regiments.

There were two types of *compagnie de gendarmerie*: the companies of the Princes of the Royal Blood, and the companies of gentlemen, these latter including those of the *Maréchals de France*, Lords and Gentlemen, after whom the company was named. Disputes were frequent over service and command, as Bussy-Rabutin relates in his memoirs:

> The Prince de Condé and the Duc d'Enghien wanted their lieutenants of *chevaux-légers* to command the lieutenants of the gendarmes of the nobility, and this was practised when one and the other commanded the army, but in their absence if a *Maréchal de France* commanded and he had a company of *gendarmes*, he claimed that the lieutenant of this company commanded the lieutenants of the *chevaux-légers d'ordonnance*.[18]

Gendarme armour *c.* 1620, Musée de l'Emperi (Photograph by the author)

The combat unit was the squadron, composed of 120 to 150 men. One or more companies (or *cornettes*) were grouped together to form a squadron. The officers of a company were: one captain, one lieutenant, one sub-lieutenant, one *guidon* (for the gendarmerie) or a *cornette* (for the *chevaux-légers*), four quartermasters, three brigadiers and three trumpeters. The eldest of the captains commanded the squadron. After the siege of La Rochelle in 1628, Richelieu brought the companies together in squadrons of at least 100 men. The companies barely reached 50 men, or even half this number, and so two to four companies had to be grouped together with the captains commanding the squadron in turn.

However, it was not until 3 October 1634 that this practice was regulated: 91 squadrons of *chevaux-légers* and seven of *carabins* (*Arnauld, Bideran, Courval, Du Pré, Harancourt, Maubuisson, Villas*), of 100 men each were created – each carrying the name of the commanding captain.

---

18   Roger de Rabutin, *Les Mémoires de Messire Roger de Rabutin Comte de Bussy, Lieutenant Général des Armées du Roi, et Mestre de Camp Général de la Cavalerie Légère*, (Amsterdam: Zacharie Chatelain, 1731), p.103.

French officer of *chevaux-légers,* watercolour by Karl Alexander Wilke (1879–1954) (Public Domain)

In *Les Principes de l'Art Militaire*, Jean de Billon specifies that the ranks of a squadron had to be of an even number, and he gives eight or 10 as an example. He also specifies that a squadron must not have more than 400 men. A squadron of 100 men should be aligned five in depth (ranks) and 20 abreast (files). The ranks and files could be spaced by six feet or three feet, as for the infantry. In the first case, a squadron occupied an area 200 feet across and 80 feet in depth, while the second arrangement occupied half this area. For 400 men, Billon suggests 10 ranks of 40 men abreast. Billon also thought that 'the most perfect number is one hundred men in each *cornette* (company), besides the officers. In this way three companies make three hundred men without the officers, and each company will be divided into five brigades .... And then, when desired, up to four *cornettes* can be joined together, which is a fairly large squadron.'[19]

In *Traité de la Guerre* published in 1636, the Duc de Rohan himself suggests regiments of 500 men, including 50 *carabins* and 50 arquebusiers.[20] But all this remained theoretical; in the Valtelline in 1635, the Duc de Rohan still spoke of the six *cornettes* present in his army. These six *cornettes* combined were a total of less than 400 men, and less than 70 cavalry per *cornette*. From July 1635, the Duc de Rohan speaks of 3 squadrons (*Canillac, Saint-André* and *Villeneuve)* and no longer of six *cornettes,* apparently in compliance with Richelieu's *Ordonnance.*

At the beginning of 1617, there were three classes of cavalry: the *gendarme,* the *chevaux léger,* and the *carabin*. The *gendarme,* already described at the beginning of this chapter, now had a lighter armour, usually known as three-quarter armour, comprising a cuirass, segmented elements protecting the shoulders, arms and the front of the thighs, tassets protecting the kidneys, and a visored helmet, which would gradually be replaced by a burgonet or a capeline. The Musée de l'Armée in Paris has many Savoyard armet helmets,

---

19   Jean de Billon, *Les Principes de l'Art Militaire* (Rouen: Berthelin, 1641), livre 2, p.324.
20   Henri II de Rohan, *Le Parfait Capitaine; Traité de la Guerre* (Paris: Jean Houze, 1636), pp.233–234.

most probably worn by gendarmes, particularly in Italy and the Savoy. Arms included a strong sword, and two cavalry pistols. The *chevaux-légers* and *carabins*, identical since the adoption of the *mousqueton* (short-barrelled musket) by the *chevaux-légers*, wore a morion, soon replaced by the capeline (the Zischägge in German, or the lobster-tailed pot in English) or the burgonet, and a cuirass or half-armour over a buff coat. They were armed with a *mousqueton* which replaced the arquebus in 1621, a strong sword and two cavalry pistols.

According to Billon, the cavalry:

> have the cuirass for protection from the arquebus, tassets, leg armour, neck piece, brassats, gauntlets, and sallet helmet, the visor of which lifts up. Besides this they have two pistols… The company of carabins shall be of sixty men… They shall have the protective cuirass and a pot or sallet helmet with no other defensive arms. And for offensive arms, a large wheel-lock arquebus of three feet or a little more, with a very large calibre, and the sword at the side, and a short pistol, as the King himself has instituted … They shall wear, if they so wish, cassocks and *gamaches* instead of boots, for greater ease in walking when necessary. Thus covered and armed, they are able to combat on foot and on horseback, and to join with the cavalry.[21]

Through this account of the *carabins,* Jean de Billon provides us with a description of the future dragoons; but it was only in 1635 that dragoon regiments were actually created.

At the beginning of the 1630s, the Duc de Rohan described the horseman's equipment in the following manner:

> As for the offensive arms of the cavalry, we have five sorts; the lance, the pistol, the sword, the carbine and the matchlock; these first two are given to the heavily armed cavalry, which should have for defensive arms cuirass, sallet helmet, brassards, tassets, leg armour and *garde-reins*, and it is not so long ago that horses wore bards; …those that carry the carbines have the pot and the cuirass; and for them to fight on horseback they should be well mounted; but those that carry matchlocks have no defensive arms; of the five sorts of offensive arms, there are no more than three in common use: the pistol, the sword and the carbine. Only the Spaniards still have a few companies of lancers that they retain more through pride than through reason; for the lance has no effect other than through the straight progress of the horse; and still there is only one rank that can use it…; the matchlock has also been as if abandoned because in the civil wars it ruined the infantry, encouraging them to steal. Nevertheless a few well disciplined troops of this type in an army are of great service; either for executions, or to win difficult passages, or to guard the cavalry quarters, or even for fighting on foot in combat like enfants perdus in front of the cavalry squadrons.[22]

---

21   Jean de Billon, *Les Principes de l'Art Militaire* (Rouen: Berthelin, 1641), livre 2, pp.324–325.
22   Henri II de Rohan, *Le Parfait Capitaine; Traité de la Guerre* (Paris: Jean Houze, 1636), pp.229–231.

A typical *chevau-léger* or *carabin* before 1630, watercolour by Karl Alexander Wilke (1879–1954) (Public Domain)

As for the breeds of horses used for riding, Pluvinel, instructor of King Louis XIII, says that:

> the ones we most commonly have come from Italy, and most of the breeds are now lost and bastardised: so much so that we no longer have any that are so good. We rarely get any from Spain, and those that do are not the best. From Turkey we get so few that we should not pay any attention to them, even though they are very excellent, and more so than those I have mentioned. Barb horse are more common to us, ordinarily good, and all fit for some purpose. Germany, Flanders and England also give us some, but as far as I am concerned, I find that those born in the Kingdom are as good as, or better than, any of those who come to us from all these foreign nations: for I have seen some very excellent ones from Gascony, Auvergne, Limousin, Poitou, Normandie, Brittany and Burgundy.[23]

French Artillery from 1617 to 1634

Sully, *Grand Maître de l'Artillerie* from 1599, assembled an arsenal of nearly 400 pieces, including around 40 that were used on campaign, at a cost of 12 million *livres*.

Sully's artillery comprised six models: a cannon firing a 33 pound ball up to 1,500 paces; the long culverin with a 16 pound ball; the bastard cannon, with a 7½ pound ball; the medium with a 2½ pound ball; the falcon with a 1½ pound ball and the falconet, with a ¾ pound ball. These pieces were mainly cast at the Paris Arsenal, and the equipment had not been renewed since.

Du Praissac, in *Discours Militaires* published in 1614, lists the following artillery pieces: the *grande couleuvrine* of 15¼ pound ball firing 10 shots per hour at 800 paces and requiring 2 *canonniers*, 24 *pionniers* and 17 horses to pull it, the *couleuvrine bâtarde* of 7¼ pound ball firing 12 shots per hour at 1,000 paces and requiring 2 *canonniers*, 12 *pionniers* and 13 horses to pull it, the *couleuvrine moyenne* of 3½ pound ball firing 13 shots per hour at 1,400

---

23 Antoine de Pluvinel, *L'Instruction du Roy en l'Exercice de Monter à Cheval*, (Paris: Michel Nivelle, 1625), pp.20–21.

paces and requiring 2 *canonniers*, 6 *pionniers* and 9 horses to pull it, the *faucon* of 1½ pound ball firing 15 shots per hour and requiring 1 *canonnier*, 4 *pionniers* and 5 horses to pull it, the *fauconneau* of ¾ pound ball firing 20 shots per hour and requiring 1 *canonniers*, 4 *pionniers* and 1 horse to pull it.[24]

Artillery personnel were as follows: for management and control, one *lieutenant général*, three general controllers, 18 provincial controllers, two *trésorier-générals*, one arsenal inspector, and 186 lieutenants and commissioners. Firearms and siege personnel were: three sap and mine captains, 67 senior gunners, 182 simple gunners and 18 firers. Personnel for the construction and repairs of equipment included: five foundrymen, three gunsmiths, 11 saltpetre makers, three tentmakers, 11 wheelwrights, five carpenters, one ropemaker, one cooper and 10 blacksmiths. The artillery train comprised: 10 *capitaines généraux*[25] and cart drivers, 29 cart captains and 27 following officers. Auxiliary staff included: one bailiff, one lieutenant and his clerks, a doctor and surgeon, chaplains, and 20 officers.

Artillery, engraving by Stefano Della Bella (1610–1664) (Public Domain)

These are roughly the same posts as those mentioned by Billon in his *Principes de l'Art Militaire*: a *Grand Maître de l'Artillerie*, one *lieutenant général de l'Artillerie*, lieutenants of artillery, commissioners, cart captains and munitions captains, marshals, master gunners, gunners, matrosses, carters, blacksmiths and carpenters.

According to Billon, the artillery lieutenant had a key role. He had to:

provide horses, carters and gunners, and make sure that everyone stayed day and night near his gun. Each gunner must also have a boy to help him. He must also have good commissioners who take care of everything, who often look at the guns to see if they are clean, the tools for loading, threshing and cleaning, and the way

---

24 Sieur Du Praissac, *Les Discours Militaires Dediez à sa Majesté*, (Paris: Guillemot & Thiboust), pp.138–141.

25 The rank/title *capitaine général* appears to have replaced the rank *mestre de camp* or *colonel* in the artillery train.

of life of everyone, to see if they observe the order and customs. He must keep all powder ammunition, balls, lead, rope, ladders, fittings, saltpetre, coal, vinegar, sulphur, all artificial fires, all rope bridges, leather or wooden bats and all other things that depend on the cannon: the mountings, forges and other necessities, and provide carts for everything that is needed, having his commissioners take care of it.[26]

Of course, he also has to know how to aim the artillery piece.

According to the Duke of Rohan, 18 men were needed to man a piece of artillery, to which must be added forge workers, wheelwrights, blacksmiths and other workers. And artillery batteries were generally guarded by an infantry company, as was the case for the *Pernes* company of the *Piémont* regiment during the siege of Marsillargues in 1622.

Rohan assigns the use of artillery mainly to sieges:

It is proper to speak of artillery after sieges, for it is mainly thanks to the artillery that towns are taken, and since it has been in use, none of these towns remain impregnable unless they are inaccessible; it has changed entirely the form and matter of fortifications.

He goes on to describe the constraints of artillery:

requires much equipment, needing one hundred artillery horses to pull a battery cannon over all types of terrain; and to be able to fire only one hundred shots; …to use a piece of battery correctly, eighteen men are needed, besides a certain number of blacksmiths, wheelwrights, marshals and other workers to repair the gun carriages, carpenters to make the bridges, scouts to repair paths; in brief, an army which transports cannon can march only slowly and heavily, and that which has none cannot be efficient.[27]

But the cannon also has its role on the battlefield, especially when an entrenched army needed to be dislodged, as illustrated by the *Maréchal* de Bassompierre during the attack of the Pas de Suse in 1629: 'We advanced also six pieces of six-pound cannon, pulled along using a hook…to force the barricades.'[28]

Command

The King of France was the Commander in Chief of all armies. Below him in the hierarchy was the *Connétable* (until 1646), followed by the *colonel générals* who commanded the infantry, cavalry and the Swiss. On campaign,

---

26   Jean de Billon, *Les Principes de l'Art Militaire* (Rouen: Berthelin, 1641), livre 1, pp.80–81.
27   Henri II de Rohan, *Le Parfait Capitaine; Traité de la Guerre* (Paris: Jean Houze, 1636), pp.315–320.
28   François de Bassompierre, *Mémoires du Maréchal de Bassompierre* (Paris: Jules Renouard, 1877), Tome IV, p.9.

each army was commanded by one or more *Maréchals*, most often highly experienced military men, although by virtue of their social position Princes of the Blood could also take command of the armies. Senior commanders – Princes and *Maréchals* – were often of a very advanced age, and relationships were soured by rivalries and conflicts of precedence. Bassompierre recounts in his memoirs that: 'M. de Montmorency, whom Schomberg had allowed through forgetfulness or otherwise to take rank before him at the King's Council, wished to do the same to me, which I did not accept. For this reason, the King refused to sit at the Council.'[29] Richelieu divided the command of his armies among many generals, but this division of responsibilities was sometimes at the expense of their efficiency. Richelieu also appointed members of the clergy, such as Sourdis or la Valette, to lead armies, with satisfactory results.

Nonetheless, the French elite had a sound training in warfare. Italian-inspired military academies had developed in France during the reign of Henri V; a number of academies were set up in the suburbs of Saint-Germain. Turenne studied in one of these academies when he was 15, before completing his training in The Netherlands with his uncle Frederick Hendrick of Nassau. Many Frenchmen, Huguenot and Catholic alike, went to study warfare in The Netherlands. Richelieu himself was interested in the school of Nassau; in 1636 he undertook the foundation of a military academy for the young nobility on the old Rue du Temple. The Duc d'Enghien, the future victor of Rocroi, studied there in 1637; this keen general interest meant that France had an ample supply of great military thinkers.

Army muster. Engraving by Jacques Callot, 1628 (Rijksmuseum, Amsterdam)

During this first period, the most remarkable 'captain' and thinker was without doubt the Duc de Rohan. Rohan published *Le Parfait Capitaine* in 1631, followed by *Traité de la Guerre* in 1636.

However, besides being a theoretician, the Duc de Rohan was above all an excellent 'captain'. The Duc d'Aumale said of him in 1886:

> He [Rohan] was not only the leader of the insurrection of the South; he was its soul; he had inspired, prepared, organised and directed it down to the smallest detail. The resistance he encountered did but stimulate his genius. In this theatre of so many bloody battles, he invented and practised a type of warfare without precedence … We can understand that a true captain such as Rohan knew how to use a mountain range, a few valleys and a curtain of rock to either show himself

---

29 François de Bassompierre, *Mémoires du Maréchal de Bassompierre* (Paris: Jules Renouard, 1877), tome IV, p.9.

Henri II de Rohan (1574–1638). Watercolour by Karl Alexander Wilke (1879–1954) (Public Domain)

or hide to take his adversaries unawares, to keep them in ignorance, to sow troubles in their combinations, and knew how to join groups of insurgents, quartered at the extremities of the Languedoc, separated by large distances, and a veritable mass of hostile populations; how he could, with a few bands of hastily disciplined peasants, hold out against the power of the Royal Household for two years.[30]

He added further that 'all his campaigns are models; if the Reformed of France could not be proud of having given their country Turenne and Duquesne, we would say that he is their first man of war. He is one of our best military writers, the best even up to the time of Napoléon.'[31]

What is striking in reading Rohan's memoirs is the care he takes in describing the geopolitical situation of the region in which he was operating. In an introduction to the chapters on his intervention in the Valtelline, he dedicates five pages to the geographical situation of the Grisons, the entire first book (around 60 pages) to the political, diplomatic and strategic situation of the region, and the whole of the third book chronicles the timeline of events in the Grisons.[32] The rest of the book details the evolution of this context. On Rohan's death in April 1638, *Maréchal* de Bassompierre said: 'This same month the Duc de Rohan died, without doubt a great loss for France; for he was a very great personage and more experienced than any other man of our times.'[33]

Like Walhausen and Billon, Rohan theorised on all aspects of warfare, but he did so as the great captain that he was. In *Traité de la Guerre* he addresses a great many military issues: the selection of soldiers and arms, military discipline, marches, encampment and entrenchment, battles, fortresses,

30   Henri d'Orléans, Duc d'Aumale, *Histoire des Princes de Condé*, (Paris: Calmann Lévy, 1886), tome 3, pp.193–198.

31   Henri d'Orléans, Duc d'Aumale, *Histoire des Princes de Condé*, (Paris: Calmann Lévy, 1886), tome 3, p.226.

32   Béat François Placide, Baron de Zurlauben, *Mémoires et Lettres de Henri Duc de Rohan* (Genève: Vincent, 1758), tome I.

33   François de Bassompierre, *Mémoires du Maréchal de Bassompierre* (Paris: Jules Renouard, 1877), Tome IV, p.255.

surprise attacks and musters, sieges, defence of town squares, artillery, baggage and pioneers, spies and guides, supplies, general duties of an army and their functions, attacks adapted to the strengths and situation of a region as well as its defences, the means to ensure a conquest, and the way to aid an ally. He also discusses the nature of the commander – the Prince or his lieutenant – who should be able to turn both the war and his reputation to his favour.

The Duc Henri de Rohan insisted on the importance of the conduct of the men, and like many others before him, he gives seven clear principles in his chapter on battle:[34]

1. Never be forced into battle against your will.
2. Choose a battlefield best suited to your army.
3. Array your army for battle in such a way as to be at an advantage.
4. Have a good general staff and an efficient chain of command (in three infantry corps and two cavalry corps).
5. Respect the distances between the different units in such a way that a disrupted unit does not disorganise the one behind it.
6. Put the best soldiers on the wings of the army and engage the battle from the strongest wing.
7. Forbid pursuit and pillage before the enemy is fully defeated.

In his chapter on arms, Rohan regrets that the Prince of Orange did not pursue his idea of reintroducing the sword and buckler into infantry equipment.[35] He praises the merits of the pike and the musket, but, taking the example of the Romans, considers that a unit of soldiers armed with sword and buckler can defeat a unit of pikemen. He therefore recommends that each battalion be accompanied by 100 or a 120 sword and buckler men to charge into the enemy's flank, specifying that an infantry regiment should have 1,440 men, made up of 600 pikemen, 600 musketeers, and 240 sword and buckler men.[36] This recommendation is in agreement with his own practices – in 1628, alongside Montpellier, he divided his advance guard of 1,500 men into six bodies:

> The first three were each of thirty armed men, chosen from volunteers, and the best men chosen from the cavalry with halberd and pistol, and eighty half-pikes, half muskets; each dozen armed men had an officer in charge, and they carried with them a few petards and ladders … The three other troops were of four hundred men each, who were to support the first; after came the Duc with his armed men, and was followed by all the rest of the battalions, of which the largest was not more than four or five hundred men.[37]

---

34 Henri II de Rohan, *Le Parfait Capitaine; Traité de la Guerre* (Paris: Jean Houze, 1636), pp.259–264.

35 Henri II de Rohan, *Le Parfait Capitaine; Traité de la Guerre* (Paris: Jean Houze, 1636), p.228.

36 Henri II de Rohan, *Le Parfait Capitaine; Traité de la Guerre* (Paris: Jean Houze, 1636), pp.233–234.

37 Henri II de Rohan, *Mémoires du Duc de Rohan, sur les Choses Advenues en France depuis la mort de Henri-le-Grand jusques à la paix faite par les réformés au mois de juin 1629, in* Nouvelle Collection des Mémoires pour servir à l'Histoire de France (Paris: Michaud et Poujoulat, 1837), Tome 5, page 573.

As explained above, the cavalry regiment was supposed to have 500 horse, with 400 gendarmes, 50 *carabins* and 50 arquebusiers.[38] In this same chapter, he considers that an army should comprise 25 percent cavalry in open country (8,000 cavalry for 24,000 infantry) and $1/6$ cavalry on rough ground.

In the following chapters he expresses his dislike of fortresses, which hindered the mobility of an army.

Richelieu's ideas were similar to those of the Duc de Rohan. He did not wish to multiply the strongholds, and therefore pushed to destroy those that were useless. Like the Duc, he favoured the offensive, saying it is better to attack without temerity, and considered that this was better suited to the French temperament, whose natural impatience was unsuited to defence. And, like the Duc, he thought that a military engagement should be prepared down to the smallest details, which postponed France's entry into this war until 1635.

French officers during the campaign in 1627. Jacques Callot, 1629–1631 (Rijksmuseum, Amsterdam)

An army could be commanded by the King, the Cardinal or by a Prince, but as a general rule it was commanded by one to three *Maréchals de France* and one to three *Maréchals de Bataille*. Until his death, the King gave the title of *lieutenant général* to his army commanders: this was the title borne by *Maréchal* de Turenne when he replaced Guébriant at the head of the Army of Alsace, and by the *Maréchal* de l'Hôpital at the Battle of Rocroi. Richelieu summarises command of an army as follows: 'In this event, command should be swiftly sent to the troops that are to obey and advance, money should be sent to pay them and also the necessary officers, say a *maréchal de camp*, an

---

38   Henri II de Rohan, *Mémoires du Duc de Rohan, sur les Choses Advenues en France depuis la mort de Henri-le-Grand jusques à la paix faite par les réformés au mois de juin 1629, in* Nouvelle Collection des Mémoires pour servir à l'Histoire de France (Paris: Michaud et Poujoulat, 1837), Tome 5, page 573.

intendant and two *maréchal de l'armée*, and the necessary money should be sent for the pay of this army.'[39] This passage takes place in the last days of the year 1628. Later in his memoirs, he describes the arrangements of Louis XIII at the beginning of 1633:

> This meant arranging with the Prince of Orange the conquests that would be made, and giving him the leadership and command of all arms. The King was required simply to send and maintain one *Maréchal de France* and two or three *maréchals de camp*, twelve thousand infantry, two thousand cavalry and everything else required by an army; that in this way the war would be easy, because all that would be required of the King would be to maintain another army in Alsace, under the command of two *Maréchals de France* and two carefully chosen *maréchals de camp*.[40]

French *Maréchal*, illustration by JOB (1858–1911) (Public Domain)

It should be noted that the Cardinal suggested this eventuality the same year because he considered that 'the difficulty to be considered in this affair was the small number of people capable of making war in France.' He already had a somewhat acerbic view of the conduct of the *Maréchals*, as he had had for the soldiers a few years earlier during the attack of the Pas de Suse in March 1629:

> It can be said in truth that all did well on this occasion; however all the order that had been desirable, and that had been decided upon, was not able to be maintained, as much through the difficulties of the terrain which was harsh and narrow, separated every hundred paces by low dry stone walls, which broke the battalions, as through the nature of the French, which has always been considered more courageous than wise, and which led each man to march as he wished, which

---

39 Armand du Plessis de Richelieu, *Mémoires du Cardinal de Richelieu*, in *Nouvelle Collection des Mémoires pour servir à l'Histoire de France*, (Paris: Michaud et Poujoulat, 1837), Deuxième Série, tome VII, p.572.

40 Armand du Plessis de Richelieu, *Mémoires du Cardinal de Richelieu*, in *Nouvelle Collection des Mémoires pour servir à l'Histoire de France*, (Paris: Michaud et Poujoulat, 1838), Deuxième Série, tome VIII, p.438.

could greatly prejudice the service of the King. In consideration of this, *Maréchals* de Créqui, de Bassompierre and Schomberg, and the *maréchals de camp* were all together at the head of the volunteers, contrary to reason which would have placed them separately in diverse locations, to give orders in all places.[41]

It was normal at the time for the *Maréchals* to advance to the middle of the battlefield with sword in hand. Witness accounts describe them at their post in the line of battle most often accompanied by a *cornette*, a company or squadron of their guards, gendarmes or *chevaux-légers*. They could thus intervene at any moment in the battle, as they would have in the golden days of chivalry.

There were many levels in the chain of command between the *Maréchals* and company captains: *maréchals de camp*, *maréchals de bataille*, *sergents de bataille*, *mestres de camp*, and colonels.

In *Histoire de la Milice Française*, Gabriel Daniel says:

> The *maréchal de camp* is one of the leading and most important officers of the troops: it is he who, together with the general, orders the encampment and lodgings of the army, and who, when the army decamps, scouts ahead to assess the lie of the land so that the troops may march in safety. After the *maréchals de camp* have determined the form and size of the camp, they leave the apportioning of the terrain to the *intendant* général and the *major général*: it is one of the functions of the *maréchal de camp* himself to post a large guard in an advantageous position, around half a league from the camp. It is they who oversee the quartering of the troops and their departure, etc. They are called *maréchal de camp* because they have the authority to order the arrangement of the camp, in the same way as the *Maréchal de France* over the entire army.[42]

Under Henri IV, and at the beginning of the reign of Louis XIII, there was a single *maréchal de camp* per army. In 1630, a *Maréchal de France* could be served by a number of *maréchals de camp*, but most often two, each responsible for one of the army corps. During the battle, the *Maréchal* or *maréchal de camp* commanded the reserve or one of the wings of the army. The office of *maréchal de bataille* appeared at the end of the reign of Louis XIII, around 1643, Gabriel Daniels explained:

> The *maréchals de bataille* were officers the main function of whom was to lead the army into battle according to a plan given to them by the general, and as we name *maréchal de camp* he who presides over the arrangement of the troops in the camps, in the same way we name *maréchal de bataille* he who, following the

---

41   Armand du Plessis de Richelieu, *Mémoires du Cardinal de Richelieu*, in *Nouvelle Collection des Mémoires pour servir à l'Histoire de France*, (Paris: Michaud et Poujoulat, 1837), Deuxième Série, tome VII, p.608.

42   Révérend Père Daniel Gabriel, *Histoire de la Milice Française*, (Paris: Jean-Baptiste Coignard, 1721), tome II, pp.27–28.

order of battle addressed to him, assigns to each officer and each corps the post that he should occupy in the arrangement of the army.[43]

The *maréchals de camp*, and later the *maréchals de bataille*, were assisted in their tasks by the *sergents de bataille*:

> In the absence of *maréchals de camp*, the *sergent de bataille* should take command, for his office is above all others; for he sits on the council, and he may enter the garrisons when the troops are garrisoned, and arrange the troops for battle, and know the number of soldiers and if they are well armed; for he must report to the King, the general and even the war secretary during wartime and sometimes even in peacetime; for such is the function of the *sergent de bataille*; before they had twenty-four ordinary guards, who went to visit by the frontiers instead of the commissioners that are sent there. Thus, they should be men chosen for their high capability and bravery.[44]

In 1630, each army corps commanded by a *Maréchal de France* sent to the aid of Casale had one or two *maréchals de camp*: *Maréchal* de Schomberg had *Maréchals de Camp* Feuquières and Frangipani as well as two aides-de-camp; *Maréchal* de Marillac had *Maréchals de Camp* Brézé and Chastelier-Barlot and two aides-de-camp; and *Maréchal* de La Force had *Maréchal de Camp* Arpajou and two aides-de-camp. In 1633, the general staff of the Army of the King, under the command of *Maréchal de* La Force, is listed as: three *Maréchals de Camp*, the Marquis de La Force, the Vicomte d'Arpajou and Hebron (Scottish); one *Sergent de Bataille* (d'Espenan); three aides-de-camp; one intendant; one quartermaster; one lieutenant of artillery and one general of army supplies. The Duc de Rohan describes the chain of command in his *Traité de la Guerre* of 1636:

> The *maréchal de camp général* receives them [the orders] from the *général* then goes to his quarters; here the commissioner for the cavalry receives the orders for the cavalry; the *sergents de bataille* for the infantry, who then sends them to the majors of the brigade; for the artillery, the quartermaster, and for supplies his own quartermaster. In brief, by speaking to these four people the *maréchal de camp général* gives orders to the entire army. All orders and commands have to be given in writing.[45]

The *mestres de camp* were originally officers: 'the function of whom was to assign, in a camp, the quarters of the bands or companies that compose a corps of troops, after taking the order from the *maréchal de camp*.'[46] However,

43 Révérend Père Daniel Gabriel, *Histoire de la Milice Française*, (Paris: Jean-Baptiste Coignard, 1721), tome II, p.73.

44 Révérend Père Daniel Gabriel, *Histoire de la Milice Française*, (Paris: Jean-Baptiste Coignard, 1721), tome II, p.75.

45 Henri II de Rohan, *Le Parfait Capitaine; Traité de la Guerre* (Paris: Jean Houze, 1636), p.344.

46 Révérend Père Daniel Gabriel, *Histoire de la Milice Française* (Paris: Jean-Baptiste Coignard, 1721), tome II, p.46.

in the time of Louis XIII the *mestre de camp* was the commander of a cavalry, dragoon, or infantry regiment. Gabriel Daniel provides us with this anecdote:

> Before, that is to say in the time of Louis XIII, it would have been improper to refer to a colonel as *mestre de camp*: for example, *Maréchal de* Bassompierre, who in his remarks on the history of Dupleix, where Monsieur Arnault is called colonel of the carabins, refers thus to this historian: 'You are an idiot. He was never *mestre de camp*, and the *carabins* are not only under the colonel of the light cavalry, but also under the mestre de camp of the *chevaux legers*.'[47] … There were no cavalry regiments in France until seventy years after the institution of the infantry regiments: for these were instituted by Henri II, and the cavalry was only regimented in this Kingdom in the year 1635 in the reign of Louis XIII. When the cavalry regiments were instituted, by the same reason the same title of *mestre de camp* was given to the commanders of these corps, the *Colonel Général* of the cavalry alone bearing the title of colonel, so that there were *mestres de camp* of the cavalry and *mestres de camp* of the infantry.[48]

Officers and foot soldiers. Illustration by JOB (1858–1911) (Public Domain)

47   Révérend Père Daniel Gabriel, *Histoire de la Milice Française* (Paris: Jean-Baptiste Coignard, 1721), tome II, pp.45–46.

48   Révérend Père Daniel Gabriel, *Histoire de la Milice Française* (Paris: Jean-Baptiste Coignard, 1721), tome II, p.48.

The office of *Colonel Général* of the infantry was discontinued by Louis XIV in 1661.

Mestres de camps had many responsibilities:

> The mestre de camp has the right to expel the captains and the junior officers of his regiment for misconduct, and to have them arrested. Justice in the regiment is performed in his own name and in the name of the King; he presents the officers for the offices of his regiment to the State Secretary of War; but they are not always approved, and sometimes others are appointed. The King always appoints the captain and the *cornette*.[49]

The title of Colonel, according to Gabriel Daniel, 'is given to the commander of a regiment of infantry or dragoons: for the dragoons are an infantry corps. It is also given to the commander of a regiment of foreign cavalry, and to the commander of a regiment of *milice bourgeoise* in a town.'[50]

Raising a company was very costly: not only did captains have to enlist men; they also had to pay for their upkeep. The money paid by the King for the levy was most often used to equip these men – they were not the owners of their arms and equipment. To remain within the budget, captains who left the service demanded a 'handover' from their successor, thereby setting the bases for venality of office. For the raising of new regiments, the King gave commissions to *mestres de camps*, who in turn gave commissions to the captains; these commissions were subject to the approval of Louis XIII. However, venality of office had the advantage of establishing ownership of the regiment, and therefore heredity of the office; the États Généraux of 1614 had condemned the principle of venality of office, as the upper echelons of society wanted military service to be the only route to enter the nobility.

The term 'officer' in the sense of military officers only entered common usage at the beginning of the seventeenth century. Walhausen speaks of 'major' officers (colonel, lieutenant-colonel, the captain of the guards of the regiment, *quartenier* of the regiment, the major and the provosts), officers (captains, lieutenants and ensigns), and 'minor' officers (sergeants, corporals and *anspessades*).[51] The Wars of Religion created many career openings, and soon the high-level ranks were no longer exclusive to the nobility, legitimising the term 'officer'. In his memoirs, D'Artagnan recounts an event that took place in 1640, telling how officers plotted against their young colonel who had much enthusiasm but little experience:

> It is not that the colonels, at this time, did not have a great authority over their captains, but when the captains were recognised for their bravery, and they had friends, if the colonel happened to wish to undertake something against them,

49 Révérend Père Daniel Gabriel, *Histoire de la Milice Française* (Paris: Jean-Baptiste Coignard, 1721), tome II, p.50.

50 Révérend Père Daniel Gabriel, *Histoire de la Milice Française* (Paris: Jean-Baptiste Coignard, 1721), tome II, p.51.

51 Jean-Jacques de Walhausen, *L'Art Militaire pour l'Infanterie* (Publisher unknown, 1615), pp.19–25.

they all plotted against him; most often he was repudiated by the Court, because the Court did not wish to remove good men from their positions to satisfy the caprice of one man.[52]

In 1633, the King's powerful army (the Army of German under *Maréchal de La Force*), also included *maréchals de camp*, the *sergent de bataille*, the quartermaster and aides-de-camp in the list of its officers.

On Campaign

Recruiting. Engraving by Jacques Callot (1592–1635) (Public Domain)

The armies of the time were never stronger than 30,000 men. The Genoese army in 1625 had 23,000 men, and in 1630 the Army of Savoy had a little over 20,000, reinforced by 6,000 Swiss troops. Armies deployed to repress Protestant rebellions rarely exceeded 10,000 men, and this is also the case with the army sent to the Valtelline in 1635. The proportion of cavalry remained low in the armies of the first third of the seventeenth century: 600 cavalry for a little under 9,000 men at the Ponts-de-Cé in 1620; 3,000 cavalry out of the 26,000 men in Piedmont in 1629; and 3,750 cavalry for 21,750 men in Schomberg's army in 1630. This is an average of 6 to 12 percent cavalry, with a peak of 17 percent in 1630. With the entry of France into the Thirty Years' War, these percentages were greatly exceeded, although there were of course exceptions, such as the small Army of the Duc de Mayenne in Montauban on the 26 July 1621, which had six companies of cavalry, four companies of *chevaux-légers* and six *carabin* companies, for only one infantry regiment and six guns. The total would have been somewhere around 4,000 men, although this was therefore an army corps rather than a full army.

At the beginning of a campaign, the preoccupations of the administration were to control troop numbers and reduce *passe-volants* ('invisible men'). The *Code Michaud* set out that muster rolls should be much more accurate than before: they should now show the first name, surname, and *nom de guerre* (nickname), age, place of birth, status and physical description of

---

52 Gatien de Courtilz de Sandras, *Mémoires de Mr d'Artagnan, Capitaine Lieutenant de la Première Compagnie des Mousquetaires du Roi*, (Cologne: Pierre Marteau, 1701), tome I, p.76.

the soldier. Misinformation was heavily punished, regardless of whether it was the *passe-volant*, the captain of the company or the commissioner of war who was found to be the perpetrator of this practice. Actual company numbers were harmed by this, and the King even conceded an allowance of a bonus to captains whose companies reached 70 men! It was on the occasion of these musters that pay was disbursed: they were termed loans. Captains, commissioners and controllers were obliged to attend these musters in person; the *mestre de camp* was only required to attend twice a year.

The *Ordonnance* of January 1629 specified the amount of pay: six *sous* per day for the soldiers, 10 for the cadets, 12 for experienced soldiers, 15 for drummers, surgeons and harbingers, 17 for *anspessades*, 20 for corporals, 30 for sergeants, 45 for *appointés*, 73 for ensigns, 100 for lieutenants, 300 for captains and 500 for the *mestres de camp*. For the regiment's staff, the daily pay was 30 *sous* for the chaplain and surgeon, 60 for the quartermaster, 100 for the *aide de major* and the conduct commissioner, 300 *sous* for the sergeant major [major] and 360 for the provost and his officers [NB between them, not each].[53] The number of musters was established at 'ten months of musters for each year, one month being 36 days' the simple soldier could therefore hope for a 'loan' of 216 sols per monthly muster.[54] Nevertheless, numbers dwindled rapidly on campaign and the Comte du Plessis, who was with Schomberg's army in 1630, recalls that:

> Regiments were strongly diminished through plague, which had lasted throughout the campaign, and had near destroyed them: but it is a fact that, despite this ravage, the regiment of the Comte de Plessis had still eight hundred men in twelve companies; and that it was far from ruined at the end of the campaign unlike the

French infantry during the campaign of 1627. Jacques Callot, 1629–1631 (Rijksmuseum, Amsterdam)

---

53   Decrusy & Armet Isambert, *Recueil Général des Anciennes Lois Françaises,* tome XVI, Article 226, p.285

54   Decrusy & Armet Isambert, *Recueil Général des Anciennes Lois Françaises,* tome XVI, Article 221, p.284

last comers, through the extraordinary care taken by the mestre de camp, who applied himself with much determination to maintain it and discipline it well.[55]

Soldiers unfit for active service, whether through injury or old age, were sometimes sent to strongholds as a part of the garrison, under the authority of the Governor: they were called the *mortes payes* – dead pay. War invalids previously benefited from *oblatus* pensions, which had been paid by the Christian *Maison de la Charité* since 1604. Beneficiaries were designated on the rolls drawn up by the *Connétable* and the *Colonel Général* of the infantry. An edict of November 1635 founded the Commanderie de Saint-Louis at Bicêtre – an establishment for the care of invalid soldiers – with the aim of replacing religious establishments; this extended the obligation of the abbeys of France set out in the Edicts of March 1624 and May 1630 to pay a pension of 100 *livres* to crippled soldiers in priories which had a high income. The *Code Michau* specifies in Article 231 that:

those captains and officers, who through age or injury have become incapable of service and reside at their expense, we shall pay or provide any other requital for the rest of their lives, for which they shall be obliged to voluntarily deliver their charge into the hands of those we deem competent; and for crippled or invalid soldiers, we shall give them a place as a lay monk, *morte paye* or other provisions sufficient for their upkeep

Then in Article 232:

hospitals shall be maintained to take care of sick or injured soldiers.[56]

The *Ordonnance* of January 1629 lays out the routes, stages and lodging of armies on campaign. The *routes* and *stations* system dated back to an *Ordonnance* by François I in 1549. The *routes* were shown in documents specifying the itinerary, and also served as 'bonds' for local authorities. Declarations of the stations were sent to the Governors and *Lieutenant Générals* of the places concerned. Article 252 of the Code Michau orders that:

All soldiers, whether in regiment, corps or companies that travel around our Kingdom should always respect these routes according to the order that they shall be given. We most expressly forbid all captains, *mestres de camp* and other commanders of these soldiers to depart from or change these routes, or to take the liberty of expanding into neighbouring villages… We desire and order that all horse and foot soldiers in numbers of six hundred or more lodging in villages, armed or unarmed, without an order signed by us or our Governors or *Lieutenant*

---

55 César, Duc de Choiseul, Comte du Plessis-Praslin, *Mémoires du Maréchal du Plessis*, in *Collection des Mémoires Relatifs à l'Histoire de France*, (Paris: Petitot et Monmerqué, 1827), tome LVII, p.159

56 Decrusy & Armet Isambert, *Recueil Général des Anciennes lois Françaises*, tome XVI, Articles 231 & 232, pp.285–286

Générals of the provinces or one of our *maréchals de camp*, shall be considered as vagabonds and thieves.[57]

The *Ordonnance* of 1629 sets out in Article 255 that:

The regiments shall be ordered to march in two or three corps, both to avoid difficulty and confusion that could be encountered in the distribution of victuals to such a large number of men, and for the commodity of the places that give them quarters and receive them, and also because it is easier to discipline a reduced number of persons.

and then in Article 260:

We desire and order that all troops, both infantry and cavalry, travel through the Kingdom in corps and in order, and … it is forbidden under pain of torture for any soldier to leave his place in line or lose his flag from view.[58]

This *Ordonnance* provides legislation for a major bane of the times: the King's soldiers took what they needed to live off the land – sometimes through indiscipline, but primarily because they were not paid regularly. In the document entitled *La Défaite des Troupes de Monsieur de Favas, La Noüe, & Bellay, au Bourg de Saint Benoît en Bas Poitou, par Messieurs les Maréchal de Praslin, Duc d'Elbeuf & Comte de La Rochefoucault*, the author relates the wrongdoing of the troops of Favas, La Noüe and Bellay: 'For their first exploit under arms, they profaned and pillaged the churches of Triaize and Saint-Denis du Perrier, without sparing the bells. Luçon saved itself from their claws with five hundred *écus* and eighteen couples of oxen, which had to be given to pull their cannon.'[59] However, the villages of Triaize and Saint-Denis du Perrier did rather well all things considered – the massacring of entire populations, the destruction of villages and the wasting of fields were all too frequent at the time.

The recruitment of soldiers was one of the captain's duties. The recruiters were assigned a region, either to complete the numbers

Shooting . Engraving by Jacques Callot (1592–1635) (Public Domain)

57   Decrusy & Armet Isambert, *Recueil Général des Anciennes lois Françaises*, Tome XVI, Article 221, p.289

58   Decrusy & Armet Isambert, *Recueil Général des Anciennes lois Françaises*, Tome XVI, Article 221, p.290.

59   Anon., *La Défaite des Troupes de Monsieur de Favas, la Noue, & Bellay, au Bourg de Saint Benoît en Bas Poitou, par Messieurs les Maréchal de Praslin, Duc d'Elbeuf & Comte de La Rochefoucault* (Lyon: Abraham Saugrain, 1621), p.4.

of their corps or to raise a new regiment. Towns were the recruiter's preferred places for raising men, especially as there were many miscreants and untrustworthy individuals, who the local authorities were keen to rid their town of. From the end of the fifteenth century, recruitment had been extended to foreigners – the Swiss in particular – and to the Germans during the Wars of Religion.

On this point, the Duc de Rohan did not agree with Richelieu. The Duc thought that:

> The French and the German armies abound with good men, and manage easily without auxiliaries; but in no manner do they choose their soldiers, they use only those who wish to go voluntarily to war; England alone of all the States of our times may choose them and take who it wishes … The other kingdoms who do not have this right must incite the men of honour and ambition to enlist, as much in the hope to be advanced to other honours, embracing the profession of warfare, as by the aim to succeed by means other than this; to refuse any office of the Kingdom, or of the King's Household, or any leadership of soldiery, to any who have not served as a soldier for a certain number of years in the bands; nor to appoint any man to the office of mestre de camp who has not been captain of the cavalry without having been officer in the cavalry … ; in brief, that none may advance in any office, who has not passed through the degrees of war; and as the hope to improve oneself is a strong incentive to encourage each man to exercise the profession of war, also the apprehension to find oneself poor and crippled after a long service is an unkindly means to retain them: this is why I would like to provide for them by establishing a fund for these people, so that they can live out the remainder of their days in comfort and with honour.[60]

Army on the march during the siege of La Rochelle. Engraving by Jacques Callot (1592–1635) (Public Domain)

---

60   Henri II de Rohan, *Le Parfait Capitaine; Traité de la Guerre* (Paris: Jean Houze, 1636), pp.221–224.

Concretely, Rohan thought that lack of promotion possibilities was at the origin of the lack of vocation of the French, while Richelieu thought that 'it is near impossible to successfully enter major wars with the French alone. Foreigners are absolutely necessary to maintain the army corps, and although the French cavalry fights well, we cannot do without the foreign cavalry for the guards and to support all the fatigues of an army.' He gives the following explanation: 'Our nation, hot and ardent in battle, is not vigilant in defence nor suited to designs nor enterprises that cannot be achieved without difficulty[61]'.

Any campaign aimed for victory by arms; the army therefore had to be both led and drawn up on the battlefield. The *Maréchal* de Bassompierre gave this order of march for the Royal Army on 15 April 1622 at the Île de Riez:

> The rendezvous for all troops shall be at ten o'clock in the evening, and the infantry shall come and array for battle to the left of our quarters, on a plain that is there, and the regiment of the guards shall have five battalions that shall be in rhombus formation, and shall lead; behind this regiment shall be the Swiss with two large battalions, then two *Normandie* battalions and finally *Navarre*, with 3 battalions; I gave their positions to their sergeant majors, then gave them the order and sent them on their way. There were seven corps in our cavalry, to whit: d'Esplans' *carabins* who were at the head on the right of my lodgings; then the company of des Roches Baritaut, followed by the *chevaux-légers* of the *Maison du Roi*; then the gendarmes; then 50 horses bearing *gendarmes* and *chevaux-légers*, which made up a squadron; behind them, the nobility of the *Reine Mère* who formed a squadron with a few volunteers; and finally the company of de Guise's *Chevaux-Légers*: and having given the order to the sergeant majors, I sent them on their way; after which we arrayed for battle, and formed three orders, to whit: the advance guard, composed of d'Espenan's *carabins*, the *chevaux-légers* of Roches Baritaut and of the guard, with the five battalions of the regiment of the guards; the main body, composed of the King's Gendarmes, and the Swiss; and the rearguard of the five battalions of *Navarre* and *Normandie* with the three last cavalry corps.[62]

The precision of such orders of battle can be seen by referring to Cardinal Richelieu's description of the Battle of the Pas de Suse in the appendix of this study.

This rhomboid/diamond arrangement appears to be standard practice as it is also in the *Mémoires* of the Duc de Rohan ; he describes the arrangement of the Army of the Duc de Montmorency at the beginning of November 1627 near Revel:

> The aforesaid Duc, his army composed of four thousand infantry and fifteen hundred highly capable cavalry, formed four battalions of his infantry, that he arranged in diamond, leaving large spaces between them for the cavalry which he put at the opposite side of the enemy army, and which he changed according

---

61   Armand du Plessis de Richelieu, *Œuvres du Cardinal de Richelieu* (Paris: Plon, 1933), p.133

62   François de Bassompierre, *Mémoires du Maréchal de Bassompierre* (Paris: Jules Renouard, 1877), tome IV, pp.26–27.

to whether he marched at the front, on the side or behind, and all with great order; and the baggage train he put in the middle of these four battalions, being resolved, in this order, either to pass or to fight.[63]

Once the army was arranged for battle, it could be required to pay compliments to a notable person, as Bassompierre reports in his memoirs in 1629:

> On Wednesday 21(March), we arranged our infantry for battle on the plain above Boussolengue. There I received Madame and Monsieur the Prince of Piedmont (who had come to see the King), halfway from Veillane; then below Saint Jory I presented the gendarmes and Chevaux-légers of the King's Guard, who marched in front and behind as they did for the King. Mr. de Luxembourg came to pay his respects, whom she kissed as she had done for me. From there I led her past the front of the infantry, who saluted her waving pikes and flags.[64]

The army was arranged in two or three lines on the battlefield as explained in Richelieu's memoirs in the description of the positions of Schomberg at the Battle of Casale on 26 October 1630:

Army on the march. Engraving by Jacques Callot (1592–1635) (Author's Collection)

After having reached the open plain, the army was arranged for battle in full view of the entrenchments and the Spanish army, and without further ado, went straight to the enemy in the best order and the greatest determination imaginable. As the army was a thousand paces from the enemy entrenchments, and as the plain was wide enough to permit the use of any order of battle, the army was halted to arrange the troops according to the order that had been decided upon for the attack, and this was as follows: seven battalions were placed in a straight line, facing the enemy, at such a distance from each other that there was space between them for the squadrons which were destined to lead the cavalry. Of the first seven battalions, there were two on the right wing from the corps of *Maréchal* La Force, who had the advance guard that day; two on the left wing from the corps of *Maréchal* de Marillac, who had the rearguard; three in the middle from the corps of *Maréchal* Schomberg, who, having command of the

---

63 Henri II de Rohan, *Mémoires du Duc de Rohan,...* (Paris: Michaud et Poujoulat, 1837), tome 5, p.566

64 François de Bassompierre, *Mémoires du Maréchal de Bassompierre* (Paris: Jules Renouard, 1877), tome IV, pp.22–23.

main body that day, consequently commanded all the army; and on the wings of the infantry two cavalry squadrons and five *carabin* companies, a little ahead of all the others. Around a hundred paces behind these first seven battalions, which made the actual vanguard of the entire army, there were seven others to defend them, and eight squadrons arranged in such a way that there was nothing directly in front of them that could prevent the enemy from seeing them, and this corps, on another straight line further back, made up the main body. Around one hundred and fifty or two hundred paces behind this second corps, there was another of six battalions and twelve squadrons, also arranged in a straight line, which were the rearguard of the main body, and fifty or sixty paces behind them, there were three reserve squadrons, and all this in such order that all were defended like a fortification. Between the main body and the rearguard was a squadron of one hundred and thirty gendarmes, commanded by *Maréchal* de La Ferté Imbault, who was to be at the place of *Maréchal* de Schomberg; a little further forward on the right was Maréchal de La Force, leading the Gendarmes and *Chevaux-Légers* of the *Maison du Roi*, and at the same distance from the enemy on the left-hand side was *Maréchal* de Marillac, leading a squadron which included his company of *Chevaux-Légers*. This was the arrangement of the whole army, in number around eighteen thousand infantry, two thousand three hundred cavalry under cornettes and four hundred and fifty noblemen of the Dauphiné, without counting the officers of the cavalry or infantry; the seven battalions that were to attack first detached their *enfants perdus*, around two hundred in number, with as many pikes as musketeers in each battalion, which advanced a few hundred paces before the rest. It was then marched straight on the enemy, up to the old entrenchments that had been made at the time of the first siege, and distanced from the new entrenchments only by the range of a musket: there it was halted to kneel and pray. After the soldiers had risen, they were given a short speech to incite them to do well; but there was not much need of this because of the good humour that the presence of the enemy gave them. The four cannon that had been brought were advanced to the rear of the first battalions, and three carts loaded with picks and shovels to force open the enemy entrenchments, and render them accessible to the cavalry. … This was the situation of the two armies when signal was given to the King's army to advance on the enemy, which may have been around four o'clock in the afternoon; so the cavalry took sword and pistol in hand, and all the officers of the infantry dismounted, and the entire army marched at the same time and at the same pace straight towards the enemy, with as much determination as gaiety; even the cannon fire from the enemy (which they did somewhat poorly) could not sow the slightest confusion among the soldiers, nor whiten a single face, although this was on passing the old entrenchments mentioned above, which was somewhat inconvenient; on the contrary, they seemed to march more resolutely and more closely, in a silence that is rare on such occasions. Until this point, the *Maréchals de France* were still marching at the head of the first battalions, although they were close enough to the enemy to be wounded by their musketry.[65]

---

65 Armand du Plessis de Richelieu, *Mémoires du Cardinal de Richelieu* in *Nouvelle Collection des Mémoires pour servir à l'Histoire de France*, (Paris: Michaud et Poujoulat, 1838), Deuxième Série, tome VIII, pp.279–280.

But that day battle would not take place; Mazarin ran between the two armies, announcing the peace negotiated by the Pope. 'After embraces and compliments were exchanged on both sides, and it had been agreed what should happen next, each man withdrew to his army, without having taken any other assurance from each other than word of honour, and the faith of the generals.'[66] This beautiful and precise description by Cardinal Richelieu gives us a perfect representation of an army in battle – in three lines, with the cavalry on the wings.

The French Army at the siege of La Rochelle. Engraving by Jacques Callot (1592–1635) (Public Domain)

Jacques Callot provides a graphic representation of the Royal Army at La Rochelle in 1628. His engraving shows three lines of infantry, nearly forming a diamond; the first is made up of two groups of two battalions, the second of three groups of two battalions and the third of two groups of two battalions. On each wing were four cavalry *cornettes*: one in the first line, two in the second line and one in the third line.

As in the previous century, each regiment could detach *enfants perdus*. Bassompierre relates in his memoirs that for the attack on Suse on 6 March 1629, 'the order was that each corps should cast before it fifty *enfants perdus*, supported by one hundred men, who would be supported by five hundred. … The King arrived at the same time with the Comte and the Cardinal: he wished his musketeers to be joined with the *enfants perdus* of the guards.'[67]

On 6 June 1630 at Bourg-Saint-Maurice, the *Gardes Françaises* detached 50 *enfants perdus* to take Séez. Two months later, on 6 August 1630, the *enfants*

---

66   Armand du Plessis de Richelieu, *Mémoires du Cardinal de Richelieu*, in *Nouvelle Collection des Mémoires pour servir à l'Histoire de France*, (Paris: Michaud et Poujoulat, 1838), Deuxième Série, tome VIII, p.281.

67   François de Bassompierre, *Mémoires du Maréchal de Bassompierre* (Paris: Jules Renouard, 1877), tome IV, p.9.

perdus of the *Picardie* and *La Meilleraye* regiments were the first to arrive at the fortifications of Carignan, and held a bridgehead there. Most often these were small groups of musketeers detached from a regiment to carry out a particular mission, or to be deployed at the front of the regiment. On the plain between Lovera and Mazzo on 3 July 1635, the Duc de Rohan arrayed his army for battle, dividing it in two corps and detaching the *enfants perdus*. At Morbegno on 10 November 1635, the *enfants perdus* who marched at the head of the battalions fought a furious battle. There is a somewhat surprising description of the composition of the units of *enfants perdus* by Richelieu, when he details his battle array at Casale on 26 October 1630: 'The seven battalions … detached their *enfants perdus*, around two hundred in number, as many pikemen as musketeers from each battalion, who advanced a few hundred paces before all the others.'[68] It should thus be noted that the *enfants perdus* could include pikemen.

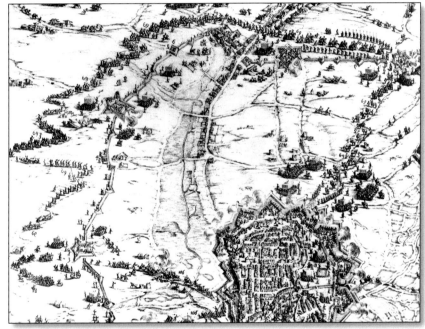

The siege of La Rochelle in 1626. Engraving by Jacques Callot (1592–1635) (Public Domain)

However, most of the time, a military campaign was a series of sieges. To be able to hope for a degree of success, these operations had to be prepared utilising a great many resources and tactics, especially cannon and mines. The *Memoires de Richelieu* provides a clear image of this, when he describes the siege of Montauban in September 1621:

> On the first of September, the battering of the town began with fifty-five cannons, which were divided into nine batteries, three for each attack. On the 4th the Duc du Maine, who had too much ardour and courage to be armed with the prudence and consideration required of a captain, decided to launch the assault after two

---

68   Armand du Plessis de Richelieu, *Mémoires du Cardinal de Richelieu*, in *Nouvelle Collection des Mémoires pour servir à l'Histoire de France*, (Paris: Michaud et Poujoulat, 1838), Deuxième Série, tome VIII, p.279.

days of battery against a *demi lune* that was before the gate of Ville-Bourbon, without having sufficiently investigated whether the breach was reasonable and the defences truly beaten, considering only that it must be so given the quantity of cannon shots that he had fired … On the sally out of the trenches, the Marquis de Thémines had hardly taken ten paces when he was killed by a musket shot; this so surprised the musketeers that followed him that it was impossible to make them advance; only the nobility, who had dismounted, gave battle and with so much courage that, although the curtains were all on fire, they managed to enter the moat, where, finding the places from which the enemy were firing, they chased them, mounted the *demi lune* and took possession of it, and also the bastion which was next to it, where they put ladders; but after a little time, because the infantry were not following to defend them, the enemy regrouped and attacked them in such large numbers that they were obliged to withdraw in great disorder and with many losses.[69]

Also in his account of the siege of Saint Jean d'Angély at the beginning of June 1621:

On the last day of May, Monsieur de Créqui immediately seized the suburb of Taillebourg, surrounded by the Boutonne River, the only bastion they had kept, before burning all the others; the Comte de Montrevel was killed here. This done, Soubise was ordered to surrender the town to the King. He answered that he was there on behalf of the assembly and that the execution of the King's commands was not in his power. The opening of the trenches began, and the batteries were installed; the King had sent for the Liégeois, who began to mine the ravelin of the Canlot tower on 13 June; the mine having been detonated on the 17th, it was not possible to prevent the nobility from launching the assault, where the Barons Desery and Lavardin were killed, and a few others injured.[70]

A siege that was poorly prepared, or conducted with few resources, was doomed to swift failure. In his *Mémoires...* the Duc de Rohan, relates his bitter experience of this at the siege of Cresseil, during the 1628 revolt:

Once all the troops had arrived, the siege was laid and the battery began with two cannon, which had not fired six rounds before the carriage of one fell to pieces, and when it had been repaired, that of the other followed suit; in this way we spent nearly all our time in remaking the carriages, and of such poor wood that, when all had been restored, it was hardly better than before: so much so that the breach was not made in one day, but it was necessary to recommence the following morning, which gave time to repair it at leisure, and stronger than it had ever been.[71]

---

69 Armand du Plessis de Richelieu, *Mémoires du Cardinal de Richelieu*, in *Nouvelle Collection des Mémoires pour servir à l'Histoire de Franc* , (Paris: Michaud et Poujoulat, 1837), Deuxième Série, tome VII, p.244.

70 Armand du Plessis de Richelieu, *Mémoires du Cardinal de Richelieu*, in *Nouvelle Collection des Mémoires pour servir à l'Histoire de France*, (Paris: Michaud et Poujoulat, 1837), Deuxième Série, tome VII, p.242.

71 Henri II de Rohan, *Mémoires du Duc de Rohan,...* (Paris: Michaud et Poujoulat, 1837), tome 5, p.583.

In his memoirs, *Maréchal* de Bassompierre relates the attack of the forts of Saint-André and Tournon on 26 May 1629, during the Protestant rebellion:

> *Pfalsbourg* opened the dance, attacked and forced entry into another house against the gate of the town, which had been fortified by the enemy. A little while after, *Picardie* attacked the 'corne' which was first won, then retaken by the enemy, and then again won by the gentlemen volunteers; at this same time, I positioned myself with the regiment of *Normandie* below the counterscarp, having arranged on the corner of this counterscarp two positions of eight musketeers each, we defended it for three hours … The same evening and at the same time, M. de Portes, with the regiments of *Champagne* and *Piémont*, attacked the Boutières area and took the forts of Saint-André and Tournon by assault, killing all who were found inside. … We held our position and at two o'clock in the morning of Monday 28th, as we had crossed the moat, we discovered a gap in the fortifications through which the enemy had access to their moat, and there was no more fire from the town. I spent some time before finding a volunteer to try this gap; having finally sent a sergeant with a roundel, he entered the town and found no one, as the enemy had abandoned it to withdraw to the Fort of Thoulon on the mountain; we entered the town, and found it already occupied by the *Pfalsbourg* regiment, who had entered it after having been told by a poor woman that the enemy had abandoned Privas; and shortly after all the regiments were sent to pillage all the districts of the town, and most had slackened in such a way that if I had not taken Swiss arms to invade Thoulon, the enemy would have been able to withdraw without hindrance. I took Thoulon with 1,200 Swiss while Privas was being pillaged, and shortly after set fire to it.[72]

This account illustrates that when a town was taken, the inhabitants had to pay the price – especially when the conqueror had few scruples. In 1628, the Duc de Rohan was witness to such behaviour by his adversary, the Duc de Montmorency, as he recounts in his memoirs:

> At the beginning of this journey, the Prince de Condé and the Duc de Montmorency began their campaign, and went to the region of Foix to attack Pamiers, a large yet weak town. By misfortune, Beaufort decided to defend it, gathering together all the forces of the region, including his own; but once the breach was made, each man was surprised to meet little resistance, and the traitors even helped to intimidate the others. Beaufort, seeing this disorder, wished to flee to Anros; they were captured, taken to Toulouse and executed. The town was pillaged, with the cruelties and liberties that can be imagined under a leader such as he.[73]

---

72   François de Bassompierre, *Mémoires du Maréchal de Bassompierre* (Paris: Jules Renouard, 1877), tome IV, pp.42–43.

73   Henri II de Rohan, *Mémoires du Duc de Rohan,...* (Paris: Michaud et Poujoulat, 1837), tome 5, p.576.

4

The French Army in the Thirty Years' War (1635–1648)

At the beginning of 1633, Richelieu urged Louis XIII to finance the war in Germany and The Netherlands, fearing that 'if peace were to be made in Germany and a truce in The Netherlands, or only one of the two, France would have to bear a defensive war alone, which would be brought to her very heart, without her being able to avoid it.'[1] The defeat of the Swedish armies at Nördlingen, on 6 September 1634, was to precipitate matters: Louis XIII embarked on a war in alliance with the Protestants against the Habsburg Empire.

On 8 February 1635, France and The Netherlands signed a treaty of alliance, stipulating that 'they would each put on the field an army of twenty-five thousand foot and five thousand horse, with the cannon and equipment necessary for such a body, and that the two armies would join in The Netherlands at a place to be agreed upon.'[2] The same treaty provided for the division of the Spanish Netherlands between France and The United Provinces. In March 1635, the Cardinal-Infante attacked the city of Trier, whose Elector had placed himself under French protection. He captured the city and took the Elector and the French garrison as prisoners. Louis XIII and Richelieu used this as the pretext to declare war on Spain.

At the beginning of 1635, Cardinal de Richelieu, remaining on the defensive with Spain, organised five armies: the first in Picardy and destined for The Netherlands, under *Maréchals* Brézé and Châtillon (3,500 cavalry and 12,500 to 16,000 infantry, according to Richelieu), the second in Lorraine, responsible for guarding Brisach, under *Maréchal* de La Force (4,000 cavalry, 1,000 dragoons and 12,000 to 15,000 infantry), the third on the Saar, under Cardinal de la Valette to oppose Galas's Imperial Army (3,500 cavalry, 1,700

1   Armand du Plessis de Richelieu, *Mémoires du Cardinal de Richelieu*, Nouvelle Collection des Mémoires pour Servir à l'Histoire de France (Paris: Michaud et Poujoulat, 1838), Deuxième Série, tome VIII, p.436.

2   Armand du Plessis de Richelieu, *Mémoires du Cardinal de Richelieu*, Nouvelle Collection des Mémoires pour Servir à l'Histoire de France (Paris: Michaud et Poujoulat, 1838), Deuxième Série, tome VIII, p.591.

dragoons and 11,000 to 16,000 men on foot), La Valette could also count on the help of Bernhard of Saxe-Weimar's Weimarians (6,000 cavalry and 12,000 infantry), the fourth in the Valtelline under the Duc de Rohan (500 cavalry and 12,000 infantry), finally, in Italy, the Franco-Savoyard army of the Duca di Savoy and the *Maréchal* de Créqui (1,500 cavalry and 14,000 infantry). A second army was being built up in Picardy in preparation to attack Flanders (1,480 cavalry, 500 dragoons and 7,000 infantry), and additionally the King kept an army of 2,000 cavalry, 1,000 dragoons and 15,000 to 25,000 infantry 'at his side'. These figures represent a total strength of 22,480 cavalry, 4,200 dragoons and 95,500 to 117,000 foot soldiers. In addition to these armies, there were garrisons totalling 30,000 men.

Before the end of 1635, Richelieu stated that he had increased the army to more than 30,000 cavalry and 150,000 infantry – theoretically more than 300 cavalry *cornettes* and 100 infantry regiments. In 1636, this total was 22,000 cavalry and 164,000 infantry, not counting the troops of Bernhard of Saxe-Weimar. The year of the storming of Corbie, the King still called on the *arrière-ban*. Paris

Louis XIII (1601–1643). Watercolour by Karl Alexander Wilke (1879–1954) (Author's photograph, Public Domain)

that year provided what was needed to raise and maintain a force of 3,000 cavalry and 12,000 infantry. In 1648, the army's manpower would reach a theoretical total of 50,000 cavalry and 273,000 infantry. In December 1648, numbers fell to the 1635 level and the accounts of the King list no more than 4,000 *Chevaux-Legers* and 40,000 infantry in service, plus a reserve of 18,000 horsemen in 100 companies and 25 infantry regiments and an additional 50,000 men from the provincial legions.

Le Tellier was now in charge at the Ministry of War, but he retained a large part of the personnel, including the brilliant Timoléon Le Roy. Military administration continued to be more and more professional under Servien (1631–1635), Sublet de Noyers (1635–1643) and Le Tellier (from 1643 to 1666). As for the pre-war period, the recruitment and upkeep of the soldiers, the numbers of which increased considerably, remained the main preoccupations of the military administration.

After the theoretical developments of the preceding period that only the Maréchals d'Estrées, de Créqui, de Montmorency and de Schomberg were able to put into practice during operations in the Valtelline, Saintonge and Piedmont, the art of warfare underwent a genuine evolution from the 1630s, thanks to experiences shared from Germany. Technological innovation complemented these new practical methods: the first flintlock rifles appeared around 1630, and the bayonet appeared around 1640, in the archaic form of a knife that was pushed into the muzzle of the musket barrel. The rifle was not commonly used by French troops until 1650, despite its light weight and ease of use.

Battles were costly in human life, and generals preferred to ruin the country rather than risk their 'capital'. The siege therefore remained the favoured type of operation during this period, and field battles were in many cases a direct or indirect consequence of this siege war. While the besieging infantry dug trenches and built protection, the cavalry foraged and brought supplies for the army. The siege then continued with the progression of trenches towards the town, followed by a war of sapping and counter-sapping, mining and counter-mining.

The French Infantry from 1635 to 1648

The French infantry was made up of so-called maintained regiments and temporary regiments, the latter were more numerous and raised for the duration of a campaign. In addition to the *Gardes Françaises, Gardes Suisses* and *Gardes Ecossaises,* at the beginning of 1635 the French Army had the six *vieux corps* - *Picardie, Champagne, Piémont, Navarre, Normandie* and *La Marine* (formerly *Cardinal-Duc*) and six *petits vieux: Nerestang* (which became *Bourbonnais* in 1673 after being *Silly* and *Castelnau*), *Rambures* (which became *Béarn* in 1762, after being *Feuquières, Leuville, Richelieu, Rohan, la Tour du Pin* and *Boisgetin*), *Auvergne, Sault* (which became *Flandres* in 1762 after being *Tessé, Tallard, Monaco, Belsunce* and *Rougé*), *Vaubecourt* (which became *Guyenne* in 1762 after being named consecutively *Mailly, Bueil Racan, La Brosse, Boufflers, Pons, Marsan, Bouzols, Talarn* and *Beaumont*).

Before entering the war, the number of regiments increased rapidly: 72 regiments in 1633, 135 regiments in 1635, 174 in 1636, 166 regiments (of which 25 were foreign) in 1641, 174 (including 25 foreign regiments) in 1642, 166 regiments in 1643 and 1644, 188 (including 36 foreign regiments) in 1645, 196 (including 46 foreign regiments) in 1646, 202 regiments in 1647 and 199 (including 51 foreign regiments) in 1648. The number of regiments returned to 170 in 1649, just after the Peace.[3]

In 1635, Richelieu reformed the infantry: regiments were to be composed of 20 companies of 53 men (a captain, a lieutenant, an ensign, two sergeants,

---

3   Lieutenant-Colonel Victor Louis Jean François Belhomme, *Histoire de l'Infanterie en France*, (Paris and Limoges: Henri Charles Lavauzelle, 1893), tomes 1 & 2.

French soldiers during an embarkation in 1627. Engraving by Jacques Callot, 1629–1631 (Rijksmuseum, Amsterdam)

three corporals, five *anspessades* and 40 soldiers); 1,060 men per regiment. The *drapeau blanc* regiments, the *vieux corps* and the *petits vieux* (*Rambures, Nerestang, Vaubecourt, La Roue, Villandry, Persan, Sault, Couvonges,* and *La Meilleraye*) were to have an establishment of 30 companies.

Establishment (theoretical) numbers established 53 men per company from 1635 to 1637, 75 men per company in 1638 and 1639, then 60 men in 1640, 56 men in 1642 and 70 men per company in 1643 and 1644. However, in practice, the number of soldiers per company or the number of companies per regiment rarely followed theory: the real numbers were something closer to 42 men per company between 1635 and 1640 (820 men per regiment) and 22 men between 1641 and 1648 (440 men per regiment). Richelieu wrote to Servien on 21 April 1635 that La Bloquerie's regiment from Liège:

> which was supposed to have 2,400 men, having only 700, it is no longer necessary, in my opinion, to count the companies at 100 men each, both because we are only giving it for that, and also because I do not believe it can have more.[4]

On 30 June 1635, Richelieu wrote to Bouthillier that:

> The six regiments that Bellefonds had led to M. de La Force, which had more than 6,000 men before leaving, now had only 3,000. It would please the King to write a letter which reads: My cousin, seeing that the troops are diminishing, and that the regiments which leave the rendezvous with 1,000 men no longer have 6 or 700 eight days later, which is what happened to those of Bellefonds, I am writing you

---

4   Armand du Plessis de Richelieu, *Lettres, Instructions Diplomatiques et Papiers d'Etat du Cardinal de Richelieu, Recueillis et Publiés par M. Avenel*, in *Collection de Documents Inédits sur l'Histoire de France*, (Paris: Imprimerie Impériale, 1861), tome IV (1630–1635), pp.714–715.

French infantry regiment of pike and shot. Illustration by JOB (1858–1911) (Public Domain)

this note to tell you that it is necessary to make levies to recruit them at the end of August.[5]

Louis XIII regularly expressed his dissatisfaction on this subject. The army of Maréchal Châtillon, in Flanders in 1641, had an average 500 men per regiment, or 20 men per company, with a differential ranging from 140 men for 20 companies to 960 men for 26 companies.

The number of foreign regiments increased sharply during the period from 1635 to 1648 – from 25 regiments in 1635 to more than 51 in 1648. Foreign regiments included Weimarian regiments (from 1636) which totalled 12,000 men in six regiments, theoretically making a strength of 2,000 men per regiment. The Swiss regiments were still a major part of the foreign regiments but saw the strength of their companies fall to 200 men in 8 to 20 companies (with an average of 10 or 12 companies). The Swiss regiment *de Roll* had 20 companies while the *Schmidt* and *Greder* regiments had only 8. The *Hebron* regiment, formed in 1633 by Sir John Hepburn, veteran of Gustav II Adolph's green brigade, was the largest of the Scottish regiments. In 1643, there were also four Scottish regiments in the French Army in addition to the *Gardes Ecossaises*: *Douglas*, *Gray*, *Lundy* and *Fullerton*.

---

5   Armand du Plessis de Richelieu, *Lettres, Instructions Diplomatiques et Papiers d'Etat du Cardinal de Richelieu, Recueillis et Publiés par M. Avenel*, in *Collection de Documents Inédits sur l'Histoire de France*, (Paris: Imprimerie Impériale, 1863), tome V (1635–1637), p.81.

The *Garde* always included the *Gardes Françaises* which theoretically counted 30 companies of 200 men. But Bassompierre relates that in April 1638, the royal troops had been denied their rations when they left their winter quarters, and:

> …forced the towns where they found themselves to provide for their upkeep, and then came with impunity to plunder the region and create much disorder … and then the soldiers, loaded with loot and plunder, and believing that they would be made to pass the summer without pay because of the subsistence they had had during the winter, preferred to spend the entire summer in peace in their houses or those of their friends, where they could live on that which they had collected, instead of going to war during the summer where they would suffer fatigue and worse, and receive no pay; with the result that, with most soldiers having abandoned their companies, these companies were so weak that when it was time to leave on campaign that there was hardly a third of the intended soldiers; he [the King] proceeded to break up Chandenier's company of the regiment of the *Gardes*, which was supposed to be of 200 men and was only of 50, and to reduce most of the other companies of the said regiment to 150 men. These examples, and the care taken to fill the companies of other regiments, reinforced them a little; nevertheless the infantry regiments were not as handsome or as complete as they had been in previous years.[6]

The Miseries of War, depicting the *Gardes Françaises.* Engraving by Jacques Callot (1592–1635) (Public Domain)

The *Gardes Suisses* had 12 companies of 200 men (2,400 men) and the newly-created *Gardes Ecossaises* had 30 companies of 150 men (4,500 men).

During the winter, infantry regiments other than those specifically reserved by the King (i.e. *Vieux* and *Petits Vieux*) were reduced to 20 companies (*cf Règlement Fait par le Roy, pour le logement & la subsistence de ses troupes pendant l'hiver prochain. Du 10 octobre 1642 à Ormeilles[7]*). Consequently, *Picardie, Piedmont, Champagne, Navarre, Normandie, La Marine, Rambures, Nerestang, Vaubecourt, La Roue, Villandry, Persan,*

6 François de Bassompierre, *Mémoires du Maréchal de Bassompierre* (Paris: Jules Renouard, 1877), tome IV, pp.251–253.

7 Archives du Service Historique de l'Armée de Terre (SHAT), 1642 A71-158.

Sault, Couvonges and La Meilleraye would still have 30 companies. In each reformed regiment, only the 20 strongest companies would be kept and the soldiers from the suppressed companies incorporated into them.

On 15 January 1643, the King wrote to Michel Le Tellier, then *Intendant* of the Army of Italy, that, because ensigns are useless in the infantry, only two ensigns will be kept per regiment, one in the *mestre de camp* company and one in that of the first captain. The ensigns of 20 company regiments will have to be dismissed immediately. In the old regiments that retained an establishment of 30 companies, the existing ensigns should be kept, but the vacancies would not be filled until there were only two ensigns per regiment. The disbanded ensigns were sent to the 12 *Compagnies Royales* which had been created a month earlier.

Although the battalion already existed before 1635, as we have seen, the origin of this tactical unit is officially accredited to Richelieu, who institutionalised it as a regimental subdivision in 1635. The size of the battalions at this time remained highly variable, shrinking as the campaign advanced, reaching 800 to 900 men for the 18 battalions of the Duc d'Enghien at Rocroi but more usually 500 to 600 men, as at Allerheim in 1645. The battalion at the time existed only as a tactical, and therefore temporary, formation the opposite of the regiment or the company, which were administrative, and permanent, formations. A regiment generally formed a battalion, particularly when it was understrength. But a full regiment could form two battalions, as suggested by Richelieu for the army of Piedmont in

Fifer and drummer. Illustration by JOB (1858–1911) (Public Domain)

September 1635: he proposed that the regiments of *Champagne, Piedmont, Navarre* and *Rambures* would each form two battalions. There is at least one example of a regiment forming three battalions: the *Vitry* Regiment, which was probably at full strength, for the attack on Sainte-Marguerite Island in 1637.[8] The regiment probably formed three small battalions of 400 or 500 men, as prescribed by Billon.

In the early 1630s, according to Rohan and Gamaliel de la Tour, the infantry battalion was drawn up in 10 ranks, with pikes in the centre and muskets on the wings. Belhomme, in *Histoire de l'Infanterie en France*, states that it was from 1633 that the battalion formed in eight ranks.[9] It was not until 1638 that the French infantry formation changed from eight to six ranks in depth. The King himself favoured six ranks for the *Gardes* regiment.[10] A depth of six ranks seems to have been formally settled on between 1638 and 1639. This is what Henri Campion states, recalling the six man files of the *Normandie* regiment during a terrible attack on the Spanish lines near Salces in 1639:

> Our battalion consisted of eight hundred good soldiers and thirty-five officers, from whom we ordered the two captains, lieutenants and ensigns of the fatigue tower[11] to stand at the rear of the unit to prevent any soldiers from running off. Two captains, two lieutenants and two ensigns were detached, to give us a little advance on our left and right, with one hundred men each. In this order we went down the mountain, and the other regiments more or less the same. ... When we were in the middle of the plain, almost within pistol range, the enemy fired all their cannons loaded grapeshot, and at the same time fired a salvo from the first rank of their musketeers. One of their cannonballs hit the middle of our battalion, and the shot, combined with the musketry, took out six files or thirty-six men.[12]

La Vallière, writing around 1644–1645, would later prescribe battalions of 700 to 800 men, 1,000 men at the most, drawn up six deep for good troops, eight deep for lesser ones.[13] The proportion of pikes and muskets were one to two, as stipulated in *Article XXIII* of the regulations of 10 October 1642: 'infantry captains will be obliged to have two-thirds of their soldiers armed with muskets and one-third with pikes.'[14]

It should be noted that, exceptionally, infantry battalions could adopt original formations, for example, cross-shaped, octagonal or in a 'hedgehog'

---

8   *Mercure François* ès Années 1635, 1636, 1637, *ou Suite de l'Histoire de Notre Temps, Sous le Règne du Très-Chrétien Roi de France et de Navarre, Louis XIII* (Paris: Olivier de Varennes, 1639), Vol.21, p.306

9   Lieutenant-Colonel Victor Louis Jean François Belhomme, *Histoire de l'Infanterie en France*, (Paris and Limoges: Henri Charles Lavauzelle, 1893), tome 1, p.356

10 Lieutenant-Colonel Victor Louis Jean François Belhomme, *Histoire de l'Infanterie en France*, (Paris and Limoges: Henri Charles Lavauzelle, 1893), tome 1, p.377

11 The French reads: *enseignes de tout pour la garde de fatigue de se tenir à la queue de la troupe.* What this tiring guard duty was, I must admit that I have been unable to discover. Maybe ensigns guarding wounded and exhausted soldiers during the battle ?

12 Henri de Campion, *Mémoires de Henri de Campion* (Paris: P. Jannet, 1867), pp.115–117

13 François de La Valière, *Pratiques et Maximes de la Guerre* (Paris: Jean-Baptiste Loyson, 1666)

14 SHAT 1642 A71-158

against cavalry. Actually, at Rocroi, the Picardie regiment adopted an octagonal formation to receive the Spanish cavalry:

> Many have commented on the battalions against the cavalry, saying that they are useless, that there is never time to form them, and that they are only suitable to see in the *Pré aux Clercs* [clerks' meadow]; but if they had sometimes found themselves in open country with infantry that had been attacked by cavalry, they would have felt quite differently. Those who were at the Battle of Rocroi, won by Monsieur le Duc d'Enghien in 1643, were able to see the great efforts and service rendered by the *Picardie* regiment, which was formed into an octagon by Sieur de Pedamons, one of its captains, who on that day distinguished himself by leading the *enfants perdus* of this corps.[15]

From *c.* 1640, only the pikemen of the *Gardes* wore the corselet, i.e. the cuirass, against the advice of previous *Ordonnances*, such as that of 14 July 1636. The pikemen got into the habit of removing and discarding these arms, or pieces of armour.

The pikes came from Biscay, and the muskets from Abbeville or Sedan. But to equip its infantry, France also sourced weapons from The Netherlands, where the work of the craftsmen was particularly appreciated: 'Unless you knew the marks of the towns, you'd think that the weapons were all made by the same craftsman,' Puysegur tells us; 'the gunpowder with which I did the test was all the best, the bandoliers were very wide, with twelve charges, and the *poulverin*, the pouches where the bullets are put, were very good.'[16] In June 1632, Puysegur went to The Netherlands to buy 6,000 stands of arms for the *Gardes Françaises*.

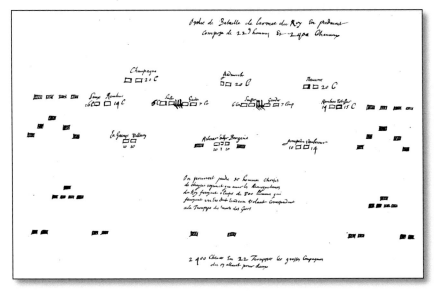

Deployment of the army of Piémont as laid down and drawn by Cardinal de Richelieu in 1635. It clearly shows the infantry battalions grouped in pairs: two battalions each from the regiments of *Champagne*, *Piémont* and *Navarre* in the front line, one battalion of *Saux*, one from *Rambures*, two battalions of the *Gardes Suisses*, two battalions of the *Gardes Françaises* (et cetera) in the second line. (Public Domain)

15   Colbert Lostelneau, *Le Mareschal de Bataille contenant le maniement des armes, les évolutions, plusieurs bataillons tant contre l'infanterie que contre la cavalerie, divers ordres de bataille* (Paris: Publisher unknown, 1647), p.244

16   Jacques de Chastenet, *Les Mémoires de Messire Jacques de Castenet, Chevalier, Seigneur de Puysegur, Colonel du Régiment de Piedmont, & Lieutenant Général des Armées du Roy* (Amsterdam: Abraham Wolfgang, 1690), tome 1, p.126.

Tactically, the French infantry was increasingly adopting the infantry brigade, whether influenced by Swedish practices or from the theories of Billon. Battalions were grouped in brigades of two to four battalions, a more flexible organisation than the large battle corps. In France, the brigade was used since at least 1629, when, at the siege of Privas, the regiments of *Champagne* and of *Piémont* formed a brigade. At this time, a brigade could include up to six battalions and 6,000 foot soldiers as in the Marillac army in 1630 in Piedmont. At the Battle of Thionville in 1639, the brigade was made up of three battalions: two from the regiment of *Navarre*, and the third from the *Beauce* regiment. In Turin on 11 July 1640, *Villandry* appears to form a brigade with *La Mothe-Houdencourt,* with *Turenne, Alincourt* and *Plessis-Praslin* as the reserve, also apparently constituting a brigade. At the Battle of Honnecourt in May 1642, *Piémont* and *Rambures* formed the Rantzau Brigade within Guiche's army. Lostelneau and La Valière, in their treatises, both refer to a group of five or six battalions called *cinquain* and *sixain*[17] but without any reference to the brigade designation.

The term brigade was used by Louis XIII to designate the two divisions formed by *Maréchals* Châtillon and Brézé from the Army of Picardie destined for The Netherlands in 1635. However, this was language used only to describe the division of this army into two parts, which the King had not wanted. Each of these two 'brigades' was made up of a large number of cavalry companies and of infantry regiments: 26 cavalry companies forming 15 squadrons and 10 to 12 infantry regiments, each forming a battalion. Each of the two 'brigades' was designated either by the name of the *Maréchal* commanding it or by the name of the old unit around which it had been formed.

In his treatise, Lostelneau also refers to *Brigade Majors* as early as 1646.[18]

The French infantry did not have to adopt the Swedish practice of musketeer detachments, as these already existed long before, either in the detachments of *enfants perdus* or through the constitution of parties of a few hundred musketeers to carry out particular missions (defence of a strategic point, attack on a barricade, protection of a wing, et cetera). The April 1638 regulations issued by the King for the *Gardes* specify the use of these units:

> If the *enfants perdus* are sent, they will be commanded by the necessary number of officers and sergeants, taken from different companies. A sergeant marches first with 12 to 15 musketeers; 30 or 40 musketeers march under a lieutenant and a sergeant; one captain with one lieutenant and two sergeants comes next with the rest of the musketeers (100 to 120 men); the battalion then moves forward.[19]

---

17 Lostelneau, Colbert (de), *Le Mareschal de Bataille Contenant le Maniement des Armes, Les Évolutions, Plusieurs Bataillons Tant Contre l'Infanterie que Contre la Cavalerie, Divers Ordres De Bataille* (Paris: Estienne Migon, 1647), pp.392–393 ; La Valière, François (de), *Pratiques et Maximes de la Guerre* (Paris: Jean-Baptiste Loyson, 1666), pp.67–68

18 Lostelneau, Colbert (de), *Le Mareschal de Bataille Contenant le Maniement des Armes, Les Évolutions, Plusieurs Bataillons Tant Contre l'Infanterie que Contre la Cavalerie, Divers Ordres De Bataille* (Paris: Estienne Migon, 1647), p.387

19 Lieutenant-Colonel Victor Louis Jean François Belhomme, *Histoire de l'Infanterie en France*, (Paris and Limoges: Henri Charles Lavauzelle, 1893), tome 1, p.377.

The Card Game. Painting by Ernest Meissonier (1815–1891) (Public Domain)

The name of these detachments of musketeers evolved towards commanded musketeers, a term possibly borrowed from the Weimarians. For instance, in his memoirs, the *Maréchal* de Gramont reports that, during the Alerheim battle (1645), 'the captain still led with the intention of reaching General Mercy, unaware that he had been killed by the first commanded musketeers on the attack of the village.'[20] There is at least one example of a regiment, the *Fusiliers du Cardinal La Valette* (1639), made up entirely of musketeers. In December 1642, Louis XIII created the *Compagnies Royales*, the 30 soldiers of which were called the *Royaux*. These companies were present at the Battle of Rocroi.

As mentioned avove, companies formed batalions of 700 to 900 men, a third of whom were pikemen who were positioned in the centre, and the other two-thirds musketeers, positioned on the wings (*les manches*). The *enfants perdus* occupied the threatened flanks. The company command was a captain, a lieutenant, an ensign or sub-lieutenant, all three armed with 9 or 10 foot half-pikes, two sergeants armed with halberds, three corporals, three *anspessades* and one drummer. The pike measured 14 feet, and the musket, which was becoming lighter, was used more and more often without a musket rest. The corporals and *anspessades* had the armament of the soldiers

---

20 Antoine de Grammont, *Mémoires du Maréchal de Grammont,* in *Nouvelle Collection des Mémoires pour servir à l'Histoire de France,* (Paris: Michaud et Poujoulat, 1839), Troisième série, VII, p.262.

they commanded. Officers and sergeants were at the front and behind the battalion, the ensigns behind the pikes and the drums on either side of the last rank.

The *Règlement* of 1633 stipulated fire by rank for the battalion when in the field and fire by file when in an entrenchment.[21] Fire by rank was simple: the first rank fired then passed behind the other rows to reload. In battle, and this was to be the case for a long time afterwards, fire at point-blank range was favoured, followed by a pike charge, as at the Battle of Lens on 20 August 1648: 'The two battalions of *Gardes* attacked a Spanish regiment and two Germans, and after a furious discharge, broke them with pikes and swords.'[22]

The offensive was also a recurrent characteristic of French behaviour during the Thirty Years' War, as it was for many periods that followed. Mercy recounts to the Baron Sirot the attack of Enghien's brigades in 1644 (*Persan, Enghien, Conti,* and *Mazarin* regiments) on his solidly entrenched infantry:

> We were entrenched in places that I believed approachable only by the birds; we had covered the entire mountain with tree trunks that we had pushed down the slope; we were fortified in different places and covered by a number of forts. These difficulties did not hinder Enghien from ousting us and neither blood nor carnage could stop his impetuosity. He fought like a lion, and the grandeur of the peril only increased his courage. In truth, there is only the French that are able to undertake such things; other nations are not capable, and it requires more than human virtue to succeed in such undertakings.[23]

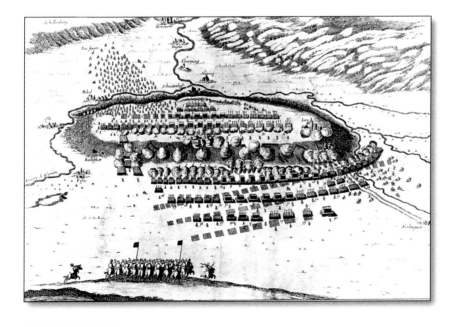

The Battle of Alerheim, or Nördlingen, in 1645. Contemporary engraving (BNF, Public Domain)

21   Lieutenant-Colonel Victor Louis Jean François Belhomme, *Histoire de l'Infanterie en France,* (Paris and Limoges: Henri Charles Lavauzelle, 1893), tome 1, p.356.

22   Anon., *Relation de la Bataille de Lens en Flandre, Gagnée par l'Armée Française, Commandée par le Prince de Condé, Recueil des Gazettes Nouvelles Ordinaires et Extraordinaires,* 129 (Paris, 1649), pp.1127–1128.

23   Claude de Letouf, *Mémoires et la Vie de Messire Claude de Letouf, Chevalier Baron de Sirot* (Paris: Claude Barbin, 1683), pp.109–110.

Maréchal de Gramont also emphasised the ardour of the French soldiers, as at Philippsburg at the end of 1644:

> The first day the trench was opened, the enemy made a sally on Persan's regiment, somewhat sluggish and with little effect, but nonetheless with a few officers and soldiers killed: which happens often in these situations, especially with the French whose ardour pushes them ever further.[24]

The French Cavalry from 1635 to 1648

In 1634, when Louis XIII and the Cardinal-Duc de Richelieu were preparing for their entry into the war, the latter made no secret of his admiration for foreign cavalry: 'I thought last night that it was better to raise foreign cavalry than French cavalry, because although the latter is more excellent for combat, it is less good for fatigue, which is what we have to deal with.'[25]

This foreign cavalry, particularly German, was equipped more lightly than the French *chevaux-légers*. The King's reply to Richelieu's memorandum is educational in this respect:

> It is very appropriate, and I believe that they should all be *carabins*, like those of Miche; because foreign cavalry is no better than ours, as soon as it has made a journey it throws away all the high and low weapons and is left only with the cuirass, which is the weapon of the *carabin*; And for M. de Bulion, it does not cost so much, and it seems to me that we should raise in Germany and Liège, because we will draw everything from the Spanish army, which will consequently become weaker.[26]

Richelieu immediately had five companies of carabins raised, but ensured that the distinction between them and the *chevaux-légers* remained:

> we have so far delayed giving the two companies of carabins that the King has allowed Coucy, because it was feared that he would claim to always keep them attached to his *chevaux-légers*, and thus stuff all the jacks of his said *chevaux-légers* in them; but finding no one who can make levies, and the said Coucy consenting to the said companies being separated as we wished, I believe it will be good to give them to him.

---

24 Antoine de Gramont, *Mémoires du Maréchal de Gramont*, in *Nouvelle Collection des Mémoires Pour Servir à l'Histoire de France* (Paris: Michaud et Poujoulat, 1839), Troisième série, tome VII, p.259.

25 Armand du Plessis de Richelieu, *Lettres, Instructions Diplomatiques et Papiers d'Etat du Cardinal de Richelieu, recueillis et publiés par Mr Avenel*, in *Collection de Documents Inédits sur l'Histoire de France*, (Paris: Imprimerie Impériale, 1861), tome IV (1630–1635), p.599.

26 Armand du Plessis de Richelieu, *Lettres, Instructions Diplomatiques et Papiers d'Etat du Cardinal de Richelieu, recueillis et publiés par Mr Avenel*, in *Collection de Documents Inédits sur l'Histoire de France*, (Paris: Imprimerie Impériale, 1861), tome IV (1630–1635), p.599.

A. An Ensign of the *Gardes Françaises* between 1620-1630
(Illustrations by Giorgio Albertini © Helion & Company)
See Colour Plate Commentaries for further information.

B. Musketeer circa 1628–35
(Illustrations by Giorgio Albertini © Helion & Company)
See Colour Plate Commentaries for further information.

C. Pikeman circa 1646–47
(Illustrations by Giorgio Albertini © Helion & Company)
See Colour Plate Commentaries for further information.

D. Musketeer circa 1646–47
(Illustrations by Giorgio Albertini © Helion & Company)
See Colour Plate Commentaries for further information.

E. Chevau-léger Officer circa 1640–43
(Illustrations by Giorgio Albertini © Helion & Company)
See Colour Plate Commentaries for further information.

F. Chevau-léger
(Illustrations by Giorgio Albertini © Helion & Company)
See Colour Plate Commentaries for further information.

G. Gendarme de la Maison du Roi
(Illustrations by Giorgio Albertini © Helion & Company)
See Colour Plate Commentaries for further information.

H. King's musketeer circa 1636
(Illustrations by Giorgio Albertini © Helion & Company)
See Colour Plate Commentaries for further information.

Flag of the
Gardes françaises (1563)
From Suzanne, Danskin,
Gerard & Lucht

Flag of the
Gardes françaises (1563)
From Callot, Gerard
& Lucht

Piémont regiment (1569)
From Suzanne, Danskin,
& Lucht

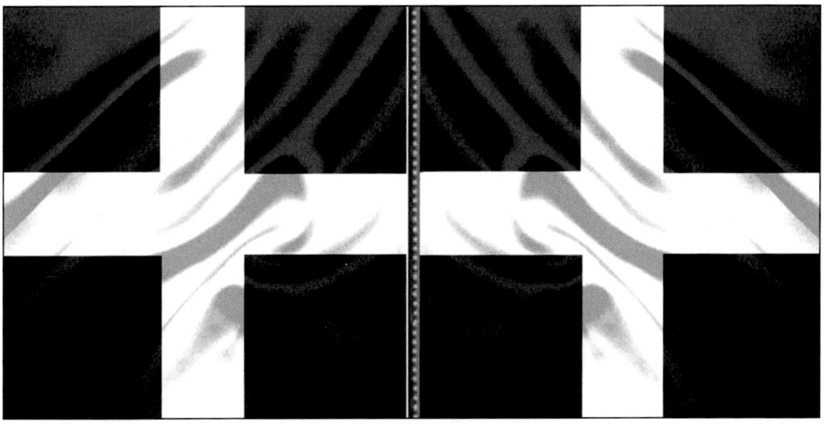

Picardie regiment (1569)
From Suzanne, Danskin,
& Lucht

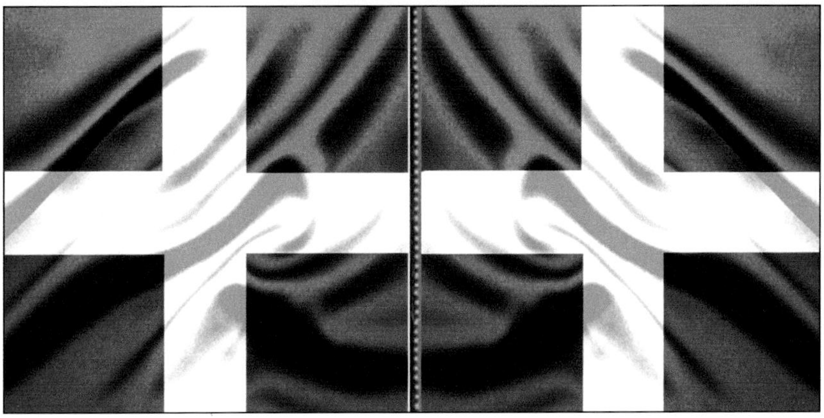

Champagne regiment (1569)
From Suzanne, Danskin,
& Lucht

Normandie regiment (1574)
From Suzanne, Danskin,
& Lucht

Balagny (1595),
Rambures (1614)
and later
Bearn regiment
From Lucht

Bourg-de-L'Espinasse (1597),
La Suze (1620),
Lauzières (1620),
Estissac (1621),
Marsillac (1629),
Leuville (1631),
Maugiron (1633),
Auvergne (1635) regiment
From Suzanne & Lucht

Créqui (1597),
Sault (1611),
And later *Flandres*
From Suzanne

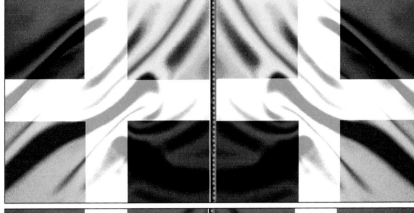

Nerestang (1599),
Chappes (1611),
Nerestang (1631),
And later *Bourbonnais*
From Lucht

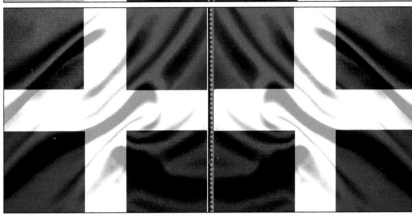

Languedoc (1622),
Montmorency (1632),
Halluyn or *Halluin* (1636)
And later *Orléans*
From Danskin

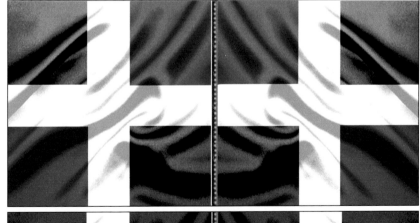

Lémont (1622),
Turenne (1625) regiment
From Danskin

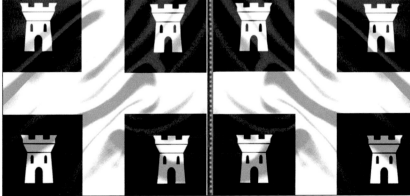

Vaubecourt (1606),
Entragues (1646),
Later *Guyenne* regiment
From Lucht

Beaumont (1610),
Chastelier-Barlot (1628),
Bellenave (1634),
Villandry (1638),
Poudenx (1642),
Navailles (1645) regiment
From Lucht

Hotel (1616),
Plessis-Praslin (1624),
Hotel (1643),
Later *Poitou*
From Lucht

Villeroy (1626),
Alincourt (1629),
Lyonnais (1635) regiment
From Danskin and Lucht

Castelbayard (1621),
Montausier (1630) regiment
From Lucht

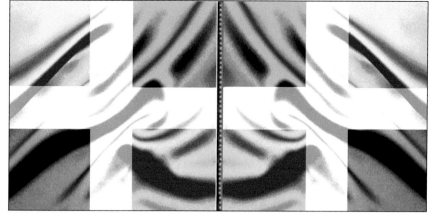

Grancey (1630) regiment
From Danskin

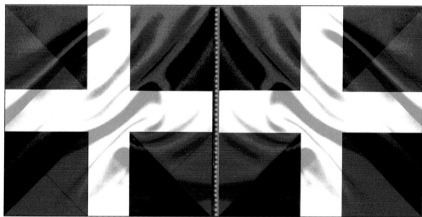

La Motte-Houdancourt (1633)
regiment
From Pierre Fourré, Club Français
de la Figurine Historique

Gardes Ecossaises (1635)
From Lucht & Fourré

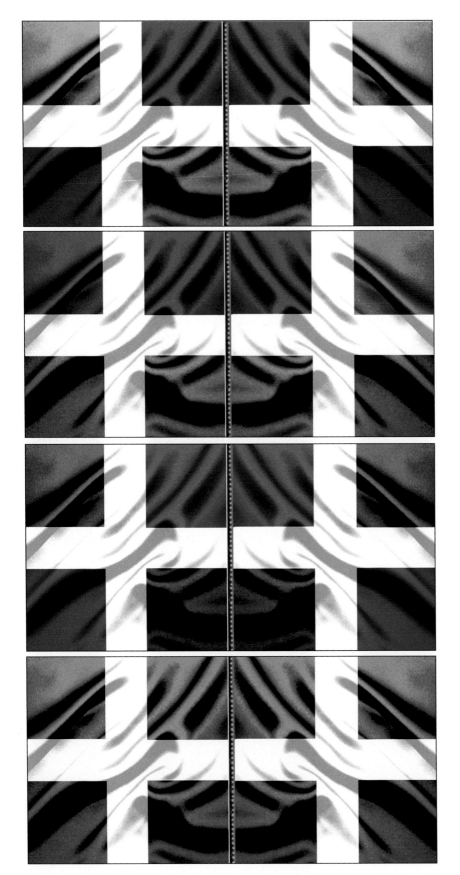

Cardinal-Duc (1635),
La Marine (1636)
From Suzanne & Lucht

Enghien (1636) regiment
From Lucht

Mazarin-italien (1642),
From Lucht

La Reine-Mère (1643),
Later *La Couronne*
From Lucht

And Louis XIII then replied to his minister: 'I think it is good, provided they are not housed with his company.'[27] Until 1636, the carabins were the real light cavalry of Louis XIII, equipped only with a cuirass and burgonet.

On 16 May 1635, Richelieu had the King sign an *Ordonnance* organising the cavalry into 12 regiments of French cavalry (created from 84 companies), 3 regiments of foreign cavalry and two *carabin* regiments (one regiment grouping together the French companies, commanded by *Arnauld de Corbeville* and one regiment grouping together the foreign companies). These 17 regiments – *Canillac, Chaulnes, Cardinal-Duc, Enghien, Le Ferron, Guiche, Matignon, La Meilleraye, Nanteuil, Sauveboeuf, Sourdis* and *Treillis* for the French cavalry, *Souvre* (Piedmontese), *Castellan* (Savoyard) and *Gassion* (German) for the foreign cavalry, plus two *carabin* regiments – were the first attempt at the creation of a regimental organisation. These regiments were made up of two or three squadrons of two companies each. In July, five new regiments were raised: *Harcourt* and *La Moussaye* (both Lotharingian), *La Meilleraye, Sirot and Espenan* (all three Hungarian), followed by three Liègois regiments in September - *Moullard, La Brocquerie* and *Leschelle.*

On 15 September 1635, non-regimented French companies of less than 25 men were dissolved. When Bernhard of Saxe-Weimar entered the service of the King of France on 26 October 1635, he was asked to maintain an army of 18,000 men, including 6,000 cavalry. In theory, the cavalry regiments had 500 men in eight companies. The 16 Weimarian regiments were *Streef, Eggenfeld, Batilly, Lee, Zillard, Muller, Schack, Tupalden, Rosen, Forbus, Watronville, Vaubecourt* (Lorraine), *Nassau* (Dutch), *Humes* (Scots), *Bouillon* (Lorraine), and *Trefski* (Polish). Before this, the Cardinal had used the *Ordonnance* of 27 May 1635 to add six dragoon regiments, made up of

Curling his Moustache. Painting of a French *chevau-léger* by Ernest Meissonier (1815–1891) (Public Domain)

---

27   Armand du Plessis de Richelieu, *Lettres, Instructions Diplomatiques et Papiers d'Etat du Cardinal de Richelieu, recueillis et publiés par Mr Avenel,* in *Collection de Documents Inédits sur l'Histoire de France,* (Paris: Imprimerie Impériale, 1861), tome IV (1630–1635), p.613.

carabin companies, for reconnoitring and raiding – these were *Cardinal, Alègre, Brûlon, Bernieules, Mahé* and *Saint-Rémy.*

However, through opposition from the captains, this first attempt at regimentation failed, and on 30 July 1636, Richelieu broke the regiments of French cavalry, returning to an organisation in *esquadrons* (squadrons, which replaced the term *escadres*). In consequence, the *Ordonnance* of 31 July 1636 reviewed the recruitment of the French cavalry by replacing the armed service of the nobility (*arrière-ban*) with a tax which allowed the recruitment of paid cavalry, even if they continued to be called *maîtres.* The regiments were replaced by three-company squadrons: the company comprised a captain, a lieutenant, a *cornette*, a quartermaster, two *brigadiers* (corporals of horse), one trumpeter and 48 troopers – a total of 55 men. The *chevaux-légers* squadron or the *dragons* were commanded by the eldest captain and therefore had 12 officers, six brigadiers, three trumpeters and 144 *maîtres.*

The gendarmerie was organised exclusively in companies. The 16 gendarmerie companies remaining in 1643 were recruited from the lower nobility; the King, Princes of the Blood and the Greater Lords were captains. The first four companies, called the *Grande Gendarmerie*, each had one captain, one lieutenant, one sub-lieutenant, one ensign, one guidon, four quartermasters, two brigadiers, two sub-brigadiers, one drummer, two trumpeters and 160 gendarmes, totalling 176 all ranks. The 12 other companies had the same officers, but the number of *maîtres* depended on the fortune of their captain.

The Cardinal did not abandon his first idea and, on 24 January 1638, ordered the creation of 36 French cavalry regiments, each composed of

La Corbie in 1636, *Gendarmes* and *Mousquetaires à Cheval.* Contemporary engraving (BNF, Public Domain)

eight companies of *chevaux-légers* and one company of *carabins* (*Alais Colonel Général, Aumont, Aubais, Beauregard, Boissac, Canillac, Cardinal-Duc, Castellan, Coislin, Crussol, Du Roure, Du Terrail, Des Roches Baritaut, Enghien, Fusiliers à Cheval du Cardinal, Gesvres, Guiche, Harambures, La Chapelle-Baloue, La Ferté-Imbaut, La Ferté-Senneterre, La Luzerne, La Meilleraye, La Valette, Lenoncourt, Lignon, Linars, Merinville, Montbrun Saint-André, Praslin Mestre de Camp, Saint-Aignan, Saint-Preuil, Saint-Simon, Treillis, Vatimont, Villeneuve*) in addition to the 25, mainly Weimarian, foreign cavalry regiments still in service. The *État de l'Armée* for 1638 and 1639 confirmed that these French *chevaux-légers* regiments included one -sometimes two – company/companies of mounted musketeers (*carabins*). These 61 cavalry regiments rapidly increased to 70 units, to which were added the non-regimented gendarme companies (*la Reine, Monsieur, Monsieur le Prince*, and the companies of other Princes and of *Maréchals*) and the *Maison du Roi* (the four companies of *Gardes du Corps, Gendarmes* and *Chevaux-Légers de la Garde*, and the *Mousquetaires du Roi*). The *Ordonnance* of 15 May 1638 states that *gendarme* companies remained *franches* (non-regimented/independent) and were to serve as the guard to the army general.

In January 1638, the *Cardinal Dragon* regiment became the regiment *Fusiliers à Cheval de son Eminence*. The unit was renamed *Fusiliers à Cheval du Roy* in the *Ordonnance* of 1 August 1643, and became a permanent cavalry regiment on 16 February 1646, the *Régiment du Roy*.

In 1646, Mazarin, who tried unsuccessfully to force the resignation of Tréville, Captain Lieutenant of the *Mousquetaires du Roi* (the King himself was the Captain), broke up the company of *Mousquetaires du Roi* under the pretext of their being an unnecessary expense. It was not until January 1657 that the King re-established this company, which then had 150 musketeers. The second company of *Mousquetaires du Roi*, the former infantry company of the Cardinal's *Gardes,* only became mounted in 1663.

Theoretical numbers (including officers) of cavalry companies varied from 100 men between 1635 and 1637, to 60 men between 1639 and 1642, 70 men in 1643–44, 50 men in 1645–1646 and 44 men in 1647–1648. However, the actual numbers were rarely more than half of this theoretical strength and there were seldom more than 40 men between 1636 and 1640, no more than 50 men in 1641, and rarely more than 40 men in the following years. Additionally, few regiments managed to muster the theoretical nine companies.

The many reorganisations complicated the situation, and sources sometimes mention squadrons, even after the aborted reorganisation of July 1636 to December 1637; in theory, these squadrons were to have 165 men. But this appellation was still used by some authors, perhaps in error, into the 1640s: in his memoirs, Turenne says that Rosen's cavalry in 1644 had eight squadrons totalling 600 men, or 75 men per squadron.[28] This figure is in reality close to the theoretical strength of the company and nearly double the

---

28   Paul Marichal, *Mémoires du Maréchal de Turenne* (Paris: Renouard, 1909), Tome I, p.23.

actual average number. However, in Turin in 1640, *Maréchal* du Plessis 'keeps only three small squadrons of 20 maîtres each,'[29] a number reminiscent of the strength of a company at the end of a campaign!

At the Battle of Rocroi, the *Cardinal-Duc* cavalry regiment, whose first captain was François Barton, Vicomte de Montbas, had:

> 400 men in all, because the remaining equipage and the large distances that we had travelled had exhausted part of my horses, which I divided into two squadrons: five companies in mine – Hocquincourt, Flavacourt, of which the captain was absent, Freigneville and Esclinvilliers; the other six with d'Estournelle, which I left with de Gassion, who gave the order to charge on the left, which was the side of the Italians and the Walloons.[30]

The Scout. Painting of a French *chevau-léger* by Ernest Meissonier (1815–1891) (Public Domain)

We can deduce from this that François Barton's regiment was formed by two squadrons divided into 11 companies of less than 40 men each.

The French squadron fought three to six ranks deep, while the depth was six to 12 ranks for the Germans, five ranks for the Dutch and three ranks for the Swedes.

In combat, many generals favoured the charge with the sword, after a preliminary firing of pistols. Gustav II Adolph's cavalry and Bernhard of Saxe-Weimar commonly attacked with the full gallop cavalry charge. Heir to the Huguenot 'millers', the French cavalry also seems to have abandoned the caracole combat relatively early on. At Leucate in 1637, for example, 'the Duc d'Halluin followed by Boissac and Sainte-Croix, attacked the cavalry with such vigour that he overthrew them and forced them to withdraw in disorder at full gallop.'[31] The cavalry of the Army of Germany, under Guébriant and then Turenne, also clearly favoured the shock of the charge to the caracole, following the example of the Saxe-Weimar regiments. Faced with steady squadrons, most of the squadrons favoured a sword attack preceded by pistol fire. Isaac de

29   César de Choiseul, Comte de, *Mémoires du Maréchal du Plessis*, in *Collection des Mémoires Relatifs à l'Histoire de France* (Paris: Petitot et Monmerqué, 1827), tome LVII, p.366.

30   François Barton, Vicomte de Montbas, in a letter dated 20 May 1643 which recounts the Battle of Rocroi in Anon., 'Un Récit Inédit de la Bataille de Rocroy', *Revue Historique du Plateau de Rocroi*, 18 (1924), p.102.

31   *Mercure François* ès Années 1635, 1636, 1637, vol.21, p.474.

la Peyrère describes such a cavalry action taking place during the Battle of Lens, on 20 August 1648:

> The Prince of Salm advanced at a trot with his first line of Walloon and Lorraine troops against Condé's first line, who advanced at a walk to receive them. The two lines met horse to horse, pistol to pistol, and remained in this position for a fairly long time, awaiting [to see] who would fire first, with neither side wavering. The enemy was more impatient and opened fire; it was as though the gates of Hell had opened! All our front line officers were killed, injured or unseated. Condé gave the signal to fire, then, with his sword held high at the head of the Gassion regiment, he crushed the squadron facing him. His other six squadrons followed him, and, on his example, charged the first enemy line so violently that it was overwhelmed.[32]

However, once the battle was underway, a charge without preliminary fire was preferred. La Peyrère describes another episode during the Battle of Lens:

> One of our squadrons, ascending by the most precipitous part of the hill, was fought off by an enemy squadron, which in return attacked Persan's battalion next to it. La Ferté-Senneterre, who had just beaten a Spanish cavalry regiment, charged this squadron with so much vigour that he forced them to flee, and pushed it into the main part of the enemy troop, where it added chaos to disorder.

Then a little further:

> Grammont was so valiant and so happy throughout the battle that his wing was not even weakened. He defeated all he charged.[33]

The cavalry could transport infantry in raids or swift-moving operations. After the Battle of Lens in 1648, a hundred cavalry from the *Chappes* regiment went ahead, with a hundred musketeers riding behind them.

It was not until the end of the summer of 1635 that the French cavalry, i.e. the *chevaux-légers* who formed the main cavalry, really lightened their equipment, as indicated in this letter, dated 11 August 1635, written by Cardinal de Richelieu and intended for Cardinal de la Valette:

> We are raising 20 regiments & 4,000 cavalry, as I have instructed you, & in addition to that we are now going to make 2,000 cavalry of the new type, of which you wrote to me, which will have only the breastplate, a burgonet which covers the cheeks, & a bar on the nose, a carbine & a pistol. I believe that this cavalry will

---

32   Isaac de La Peyrère, 'La Bataille de Lens, Donnée le 21 août 1648', in Victor Cousin, *La Société Française au XVIIᵉ siècle* (Paris: Didier et Cie, 1858), tome 1, p.407.

33   Isaac de La Peyrère, 'La Bataille de Lens, Donnée le 21 août 1648', in Victor Cousin, *La Société Française au XVIIᵉ siècle* (Paris: Didier et Cie, 1858), tome 1, p.409.

Pot helmet and cuirass.
(Museu Militar De Lisboa,
photo by the author)

be called Hungarian Cavalry, except that Monsieur Hebron wanted to give us a more appropriate name, to use his usual language. [34]

The name Hungarian Cavalry, which does not refer to the origin of the men, was used regularly.

The *chevaux-légers* protected themselves with a cuirass worn over a buff coat, or a buff coat only, leather boots, and a helmet, now usually of the *capeline* type, although the wide-brimmed hat often replaced the *capeline*. In his Mémoires, Puysegur describes these cavalry as they appeared: 'We had 6,000 horse, not including the officers and valets, all well-armed with good breastplates and helmets.'[35] However, some troopers got into the habit of discarding all of their protective equipment, and the decree of 14 July 1636 insisted that cavalry should at least have a cuirass.'[36]

The *Ordonnance* of 7 March 1639 stated that:

His Majesty very expressly orders and enjoins all *mestres de camp*, colonels, and captains of cavalry, both French and foreign, to arm their cavalrymen with breastplates in front and behind, a pot, two pistols, and a sword, without these those men who are not armed in the aforementioned manner not being able to be and deemed to have complied with the *Ordonnances*, nor with the conditions of the treaties they have made for the subsistence of their companies.'[37]

French *chevau-léger capeline*
or pot. (Public Domain)

This last *Ordonnance* is very firm on the subject – it threatens punishment for cavalry who are not armed in this way. And if the captain or officer commanding the company fails to give notice, he will be dismissed on the spot. Other *Ordonnances* would later insist on the need for such equipment, as, for example, that of 10 October 1642, stating that 'cavalry captains will be obliged to have their soldiers each armed with a cuirass, a *pot*, and two pistols, all in good condition, and that companies of gendarmes and *chevaux-légers* will be paid at the first watch on the basis of 60

34   Armand du Plessis de Richelieu, *Mémoires pour l'Histoire du Cardinal Duc de Richelieu*, recueillis par le Sieur Aubery (Cologne: Pierre Marteau, 1667), tome II, p.398.

35   Chastenet, Jacques (de), *Les Mémoires de Messire Jacques de Castenet, Chevalier, Seigneur de Puysegur, Colonel du Régiment de Piedmont, & Lieutenant Général des Armées du Roy* (Amsterdam: Abraham Wolfgang, 1690), tome 1, p.125.

36   Amblard, Vicomte de Noailles, *Episodes de la Guerre de Trente Ans, le Cardinal de la Valette, Lieutenant Général des Armées du Roi, 1635 à 1639* (Paris: Perrin, 1906), p.572.

37   *Mercure François ès Années 1639 e&1640, ou Suite de l'Histoire de Notre Temps, Sous le Règne du Très-Chrétien Roi de France et de Navarre, Louis XIII* (Paris: Olivier de Varennes), Vol.23, pp.42–43.

men each, and those of *carabins* for 50 each, all officers included.'[38] Again, the *Ordonnance* of 20 December 1643 prescribed companies of 70 men and that, 'each cavalryman be armed with a *pot*, a breastplate in front and behind and two pistols ... Each cavalry company with fewer than 30 men could not have a cornet.'[39] At the time, it was the state that provided this equipment. Sirot confirms this when he writes that in 1642, he was ordered:

that all companies would be reduced to 30 cavalrymen, and that the captain would be given 200 livres for each cavalryman, in order to recruit them to a full strength; this was immediately carried out and the money issued. The recruits were made in less than a month, and the cavalrymen being found in the numbers desired, *Maréchal* de Guiche had me issue the weapons to arm them, which I distributed to all the regiments; but there were only enough to arm 2,000 men, and there were still 1,000 unarmed.[40]

A Cavalier: Time of Louis XIII. Painting of a French chevau-léger by Ernest Meissonier (1815–1891) (Public Domain)

Another interesting source enables us to estimate the proportion of 'unarmed' cavalry in 1639: in the *Estat de l'Armée du Roy commandée par Monsieur le Maréchal de Chastillon du 27 May 1639*,[41] there are 1,333 unarmed *chevaux-légers* out of a total of 3,399.

Outside the *pot* mentioned in the *Ordonnances*, the army museum displays a *chapeau d'arme* in the shape of the wide-brimmed hat of the period, which appears to have been particularly popular in the French cavalry. Monbas wore one at Rocroi: 'The Liégeois gave me such a stroke of the sword that he made my iron hat fall'.[42] The Musée de l'Armée, in Paris, holds several examples of this type of iron hat.

---

38 SHAT 1642 A71-158.

39 SHAT 1643 A79-159.

40 Letouf, Claude (de), *Mémoires et la Vie de Messire Claude de Letouf, Chevalier Baron de Sirot* (Paris: Claude Barbin, 1683), tome II, pp.25–26.

41 Jean du Bouchet, *Preuves de l'Histoire de l'Illustre Maison de Coligny* (Paris: Jean Dupuis, 1662), p.984.

42 Anon., 'Un Récit Inédit de la bataille de Rocroy', in *Revue Historique du Plateau de Rocroi*, 19 (1924), p.114.

Among the *chevaux-légers* regiments, the *Régiment Royal*, under François Barton Vicomte de Montbas, became one of the best of the army. This regiment was the former *Cardinal-Duc*, one of the first 12 regiments organised by Cardinal de Richelieu on 16 May 1635. Montbas and his regiment were without doubt the heroes of Rocroi in 1643, as demonstrated in his letter to his wife written the day after the battle:

> We had the honour, just between you and me, of being recognised by the general, the whole French Army and all the prisoners as having won the battle ... We have such a reputation that, were it not for the displeasure of chance that our captains are experiencing, we could not be held. ... There is charm, say these Spanish officers, or rage, in seeing what our corps has done.[43]

Bravo. Painting of a French *chevau-léger* by Ernest Meissonier (1815–1891) (facsimile in the Author's Collection)

The gendarmerie still appears in some representations as heavily equipped but in reality their armour had become lighter over time. The Musée de l'Armée in Paris has armour from the end of the reign of Louis XIII, which comprises a sallet type helmet, a cuirass, tassets, and brassards, and the legs were protected only by thick leather boots. Another suit of armour from the Musée de l'Armée which belonged to a cavalryman from the *Maison du Roi* comprises an iron hat, cuirass and tassets, leg armour, a gorget, *brassats*, and gauntlets, to use the terms of Jean de Billon. An anonymous engraving of Louis XIII at the storming of Corbie in 1636 (Bibliothèque Nationale) shows a company of Gendarmes from the *Maison du Roi* wearing cuirass, tassets and brassards, but wearing superb, plumed hats rather than helmets. *L'Etat de la France* of 1648 states that 'these gendarmes have full arms – i.e. back and breast, cuisses, brassard armour, et cetera – & are paid for two horses, & are therefore obliged to have a man on duty with them.'[44]

As for clothing, only the guards, such as the *Mousquetaires de Roi* or the guards of Princes and *Maréchals*, wore any semblance of uniform, in the form of

43   Anon., 'Un Récit Inédit de la bataille de Rocroy', in *Revue Historique du Plateau de Rocroi*, 19 (1924), p.117.

44   *Estat de la France Comme Élle Etait Gouvernée en l'an 1648* (Paris : Publisher unknown, 1649), p.166.

a *casaque* (a tabard or soubreveste). The *Mousquetaires de Roi* wore a blue *casaque* with a silver cross.[45] The cavalry of the *Régiment Royal* appear to have worn a *casaque* at Rocroi, or at least its *Mestre de Camp*, François Barton Vicomte de Montbas, did. In his letter of 20 May 1643 recounting the Battle of Rocroi, Montbas says that some officers had the habit of covering their armour with a *casaque*: 'They did not think I was armoured, although I was indeed fully so, because of a small *casaque* that covered my armour with my scarf over it.'[46]

Artillery from 1635 to 1648

There were 17 types of cannon, from the basilisk firing a ball weighing 48 pounds, to the *émerillon,* which shot a ¼ pound ball (see the main types in the previous chapter). Heavy or campaign cannon were divided into brigades under the command of an artillery commissioner, seconded by the ordinary and extraordinary commissioners and 'firing officers'. The light brigades were equipped with campaign weapons that had an allocation of 25 or 30 shots in the supply train. The heavy brigades, equipped with battery cannon, were used for sieges, and the attack and defence of entrenched positions. This brigade had the ammunition, siege equipment, gunpowder, ammunition and infantry match; this was the reserve equipment and an infantry escort was given to each brigade. The Swiss had had the privilege of guarding the artillery since the time of François I, but this was less and less the case under Louis XIII.

From 1635, the French artillery closely followed the developments of its European neighbours and Swedish innovations. Thus, the French Army had either 12 or 24 pieces of artillery, depending on the source, at Avins in 1635. There were only 12 pieces of artillery at Rocroi in 1643, and *Maréchal* Guébriant's army on the Rhine had four demi-cannon, two 12-pdrs pieces, several small 6-pdr and 3-pdr cannon and a single mortar in September 1643. There were two demi-cannon and 15 falconets in Enghien's Army of Champagne and six demi-cannon and 14 falconets in Turenne's Army of Germany at Fribourg in 1644. In 1645 the French and Hessian armies at Allerheim counted 27 pieces of artillery. It appears that, from 1644, the French Army enthusiastically adopted light pieces of the falconet type, at a ratio of one or two pieces per battalion.

Earlier, the artillery adopted the exploding shell projected by a *hauwitzer,* a German term which became *obusier* in French and howitzer in English. This technique was probably first used at the siege of La Mothe in 1634.

The range of artillery was generally 1,500 paces for a ball, and 300 to 400 paces for the grapeshot or canister. French gunners were less skilled than

---

45   *Estat de la France Comme Elle Était Gouvernée en l'an 1648,* p.104.
46   Anon., 'Un Récit Inédit de la bataille de Rocroy', *Revue Historique du Plateau de Rocroi,* 19 (1924), p.115.

their Spanish, Imperial or Swedish counterparts, as noted by the Baron de Sirot at the beginning of the Battle of Rocroi:

> The town was behind them within range of cannon fire, and the two armies were only at a distance of two musket ranges from each other, and they remained thus for the entire day; but this was not without large skirmishes, and the cannon made much noise on all sides. Nevertheless, that of the enemy caused much more damage to our army than they received from us; for, besides the fact that it was better placed, it was also much better used, and their gunners were more expert and more skilful than ours.[47]

Artillery of the Thirty Years' War. Watercolour by Karl Alexander Wilke (1879–1954) (Public Domain)

This was the reason why foreign gunners were used wherever possible, especially soldiers from Liège.

As in the previous period, the artillery train required a large number of horses, for example in December 1639 760 horses were needed by *Maréchal* de Guébriant's army to transport four demi-cannon, four 6-pdrs, six 3-pdrs, one mortar, and the gunpowder, ball, fuses, grenades and all the necessary accoutrements.[48]

Command

From 1636, experience improved the efficiency of high command, in particular through the limited nomination of army commanders. But jealousies and dissensions between the *Maréchals* remained a, perhaps unavoidable, evil. *Maréchal* du Plessis-Praslin relates an anecdote from 1639:

> At the time the Comte d'Harcourt was chosen to command the Army of Italy; and as he passed through Grenoble to reach there, Cardinal Richelieu told him

47   Letouf, Claude (de), *Mémoires et la Vie de Messire Claude de Letouf, Chevalier Baron de Sirot* (Paris: Claude Barbin, 1683), tome II, pp.41–42.
48   Jean Laboureur, *Histoire du Mareschal de Guébriant* (Paris: Louis Billaine, 1676), p.166

Supplies for the French Army being unloaded on the coast during the campaign of 1627. Engraving by Jacques Callot, 1629–1631 (Rijksmuseum, Amsterdam)

that he should do nothing of importance without the counsel of the Comte de Plessis beforehand, to whom this honour gave much disquiet. He [d'Harcourt] told Cardinal Richelieu that this favour would attract much jealousy from the other *maréchals de camp* of the army, *Maréchal* de Turenne and *Maréchal* de La Mothe-Houdencourt who, having much merit, would not tolerate the Comte de Plessis appearing to have more credit than themselves in the army. To which Richelieu replied that they were too honest to be jealous and that this should not cause him difficulties.[49]

The rapid expansion of the army also allowed for the accelerated promotion of talented officers and also resulted in the creation of a military academy in 1636. In 1642 there were 12 *Maréchals*: Bassompierre, Brézé, Châtillon, La Force, Guébriant, Guiche (who became de Grammont at the end of 1644), du Hallier-L'Hôpital, Harcourt, La Meilleraye, La Mothe-Houdencourt, Schomberg and Vitry. However, at the time, the *Maréchals* still fought most often in the front line, at the head of their corps; in order to be easily recognised, French *Maréchals* always wore a white scarf, as they had done in the reign of Henri IV. This is confirmed by *Maréchal* de Gramont in his memoirs:

During the siege [the siege of Arras in 1640], which was one of the best of the entire war, the Comte de Guiche was extremely favoured by fortune; it was he who took the demi lune, so valiantly defended by the Spanish reformado officers against the attack of *Maréchal* de Châtillon, and who broke the large and formidable squadron of the Comte Bucquoy in the Battle of Bapaume, which most of our troops did not dare attack; he charged with his regiment, and broke it, but without defeating it. There were many men killed in this first charge, in which

49   César de Choiseul Comte de Plessis-Praslin, 'Mémoires du *Maréchal* du Plessis,' in *Collection des Mémoires Relatifs à l'Histoire de France* (Paris: Petitot et Monmerqué, 1827), tome LVII, p.364.

the Comte de Guiche himself was hit three times, and as they were embroiled with each other for a long period of time, he found himself enveloped and swept up into the enemy squadron when he performed a caracole to regroup and charge. It is at this point that the Comte de Guiche was saved by his presence of mind, discreetly allowing his white scarf to fall so as not to be recognised; he put himself in the first rank and charged towards his own regiment, which had reformed at the same time as the enemy; and Rouville, who was in command and recognised him, distinguished him from the enemy and then they fought so well that all were killed or taken.[50]

It was during this period that a new generation of great leaders appeared, following in the footsteps of the Duc de Rohan who died in 1638: Harcourt, Guébriant, Condé and Turenne most particularly distinguished themselves. For Condé and for Turenne, the Thirty Years' War would only be the beginning of a long and successful military career.

Louis II de Bourbon, Duc d'Enghien, who became Prince de Condé on the death of his father on the 26 December 1646, was one of the rare French generals who remained unbeaten. Even if his role in the Rocroi victory is today being questioned,[51] the fact remains that the *Grande Condé* was an excellent

Jean-Baptiste Budes de Guébriant (1602–1643). Watercolour by Karl Alexander Wilke (1879–1954) (Public Domain)

tactician, and above all a charismatic, courageous, even impetuous, general. *Maréchal* de Grammont describes these last two traits in his memoirs, with an anecdote of an event which took place near Lleida in 1646:

[The enemy] realising that most of the troops had hastily stationed themselves on the high ground, and that only five squadrons remained with *Maréchal* de Grammont on the plain, the Marquis d'Aytonne, at the head of twenty-two squadrons, charged him at a canter. *Maréchal* de Grammont, having no other choice than to fight with the few men he had, sounded the charge and marched straight towards them; for withdrawing on a flat and open plain with the enemy so close would mean certain defeat; a quarter turn to rejoin the Prince de Condé was not a safer option; and when they were one

---

50   Antoine de Gramont, 'Mémoires du *Maréchal* de Gramont', in *Nouvelle Collection des Mémoires Pour Servir à l'Histoire de France* (Paris: Michaud et Poujoulat, 1839), Troisième série, tome VII. p.250.

51   Bernard Gerrer, Patrice Petit and Juan Luis Sanchez Martin, *Rocroy 1643, Vérités et Controverses sur une Bataille de Légende* (Rocroi: Office de Tourisme..., 2007), pp.74–85.

hundred paces from each other, the Marquis d'Aytonne stopped dead; which gave extreme joy to *Maréchal* de Gramont, who also stopped, and he immediately fired four small cannon that he had just received at the Marquis d'Aytonne; which made him hesitate all the more. The Prince de Condé seeing the great danger in which the *Maréchal* de Grammont found himself, from the high ground where he was positioned, did something worthy of his stout heart and his great courage: he left his troops, alone and accompanied by a page, and went at full gallop to rejoin *Maréchal* de Grammont, embraced him warmly and told him that he wished to fight alongside him, and to share the imminent danger.[52]

But this anecdote should not allow us to forget the other great qualities of the Prince: he was an exceptional leader of men, who knew instinctively how to make the necessary decisions. None was more convinced of this than the *Maréchal* de Gramont who, speaking of 19 August 1648, the day before the Battle of Lens, says:

And it was indeed his presence of mind and this perfect knowledge he had of men which put him always above the others in the most perilous and the greatest occasions; for everything he had to do came to him in an instant. Such men are a rare genius of warfare, a species of which there are only one in a hundred thousand.[53]

Condé's strategy was relatively conventional: depending on the layout of the battlefield, a frontal attack of the main infantry body at the centre, as at Fribourg or Allerheim, or a charge of a stronger wing of cavalry as at Rocroi. Usually, Condé himself led the main effort. But what set this him apart was above all his energy and self-confidence, which could however lead to stubbornness.

Henri de la Tour d'Auvergne, Comte de Turenne, became one

Louis II de Bourbon, Duc d'Enghien (1621–1686). Watercolour by Karl Alexander Wilke (1879–1954) (Author's photograph, Public Domain)

---

52 Antoine de Gramont, 'Mémoires du *Maréchal* de Gramont', in *Nouvelle Collection des Mémoires Pour Servir à l'Histoire de France* (Paris: Michaud et Poujoulat, 1839), Troisième série, tome VII, p.274,

53 Antoine de Gramont, 'Mémoires du *Maréchal* de Gramont', in *Nouvelle Collection des Mémoires Pour Servir à l'Histoire de France* (Paris: Michaud et Poujoulat, 1839), Troisième série, tome VII, p.280.

of the greatest generals of his time through his qualities of leadership and strategy. He knew perfectly how to apply the principles of war: well-trained and well-maintained troops; a detailed analysis of the conditions and the environment; caution before action but decisiveness once the decision had been made. And as a grand general should, he also knew how to recognise his errors, especially that of Mergentheim in 1645.

Napoléon himself praises the qualities and demonstrate the weaknesses of both generals. In *Précis des Guerres du Maréchal de Turenne*, Napoléon reproaches Condé for his impetuosity at Fribourg:

> The Prince de Condé violated one of the principles of mountain warfare: never attack troops occupying good positions in the mountains, but flush them out by occupying camps on their flanks or their rear.[54]

Napoléon also condemns Condé's choices at Nördlingen in 1645:

> The Prince de Condé was wrong to attack Mercy in his camp, with an army nearly completely composed of cavalry and having so little artillery; the attack on the village of Alerheim was a grand affair.'

But further on he concedes that:

> Condé deserved victory by this obstinacy, this rare intrepidity that distinguished him for, even if this trait did not serve him well in the attack of Alerheim, it is this that advised him, after having lost the centre and the right, to recommence the battle with the left, the only troop left to him; for it is he who directed all movements of this wing, and it is he to whom glory should be given.[55]

On the other hand, he approved of Turenne's manoeuvre after Friburg:

> The conduct of Turenne, after the departure of the Prince de Condé, was skilful; it is true that he was much aided by the terrain. The armies of Bavaria and Lorraine were separated by the Rhine and mountains; their junction was difficult.[56]'

Then, evoking the campaign of 1645, he says:

> Turenne, with his army, was cornered below Philippsburg by a very large army; he found no bridge over the Rhine, but made use of the terrain between the river and the town to establish his camp. This should be a lesson for engineers, not only for the construction of strongholds, but also for the construction of bridgeheads.[57]

---

54   Napoléon Bonaparte, *Précis des Guerres du Maréchal de Turenne* (Paris: Hachette, 1872), p.119.
55   Napoléon Bonaparte, *Précis des Guerres du Maréchal de Turenne* (Paris: Hachette, 1872), pp.124–126.
56   Napoléon Bonaparte, *Précis des Guerres du Maréchal de Turenne* (Paris: Hachette, 1872), pp.119.
57   Napoléon Bonaparte, *Précis des Guerres du Maréchal de Turenne* (Paris: Hachette, 1872), pp.127.

Napoléon becomes even more admiring when he talks about the campaign of 1646:

> Turenne's march along the left bank of the Rhine is worthy of him. His march along the Danube and the Lech to take war to Bavaria, thus making use of the ruses of the Archduke was full of audacity and wisdom … The manoeuvres to remove the Archduke from his camp between Memmingen and Landsberg were full of audacity, wisdom and genius, producing excellent results. The military should study them.[58]

That same year, Turenne and Wrangel put a screen of 2,000 cavalry in front of the Army of the Archduke to mask their march to Landsberg. Concluding with the campaign of 1648, Napoléon could not speak more highly of Turenne:

> Turenne is the first French general to have planted the national colours on the banks of the Inn. In this campaign, and in that of 1646, he traversed Germany in all directions, with a mobility and hardiness that foreshadows the way in which war has been conducted since. This stems from his skilfulness, and the sound principles of warfare of this school.[59]

Henri de la Tour d'Auvergne, *dit* Turenne (1611–1675). Watercolour by Karl Alexander Wilke (1879–1954) (Public Domain)

The Swedish Influence

Gustav II Adolph did not revolutionise the art of war, but he was able to perfectly synthesise the teachings of his time. Indeed, many of his reforms were rooted in the teachings of the earlier Wars of Religion. He used small infantry formations, taking inspiration from the small Huguenot and Dutch battalions, and organising brigades of three battalions as suggested by Billon and Walhausen. He also adopted Condé's, Coligny's and Henri IV's innovation of mixing formations of commanded musketeers with cavalry squadrons. Finally, for his cavalry, he favoured

---

58   Napoléon Bonaparte, *Précis des Guerres du Maréchal de Turenne* (Paris: Hachette, 1872), pp.129.
59   Napoléon Bonaparte, *Précis des Guerres du Maréchal de Turenne* (Paris: Hachette, 1872), pp.134.

Bernhard de Saxe-Weimar (1604–1639). Watercolour by Karl Alexander Wilke (1879–1954) (Author's photograph, Public Domain)

the shock over the caracole, as the Huguenots had done earlier. However, from 1635 onwards, the French Army benefited from the re-importation of these innovations. The Swedish example would speed up the reduction in armour, particularly in the cavalry. Thus, the integration of the regiments of Bernhard of Saxe-Weimar, Rantzau and Gassion into the French Army in 1636 would have some influence on this development, to the point where armies commanded by Protestant generals would behave differently in the field than armies commanded by Catholics.

Beyond that, Gustav II Adolph was also able to improve on these lessons thanks to a number of personal contributions. The two main ones were salvo fire and the small 3-pdr battalion guns.

Firstly, when he reorganised the Swedish army at the beginning of the seventeenth century, not only did he set up a modern organisation based on conscription and the creation of regional regiments, but he was also the originator of many tactical and technical developments. In 1634, the Swedes had 12 regional infantry regiments and five cavalry regiments, recruited on the basis of compulsory conscription for a three-year period. The Swedish infantry regiment had eight companies and a theoretical strength of 1,160 men. The regiment was the administrative and command unit but, on campaign, the companies were organised into two squadrons (battalions) of four companies or more totalling 568 men (504 soldiers and 64 officers and NCOs). Although in theory these battalions had four companies, an average of six companies was actually needed to make up a unit of this size. On campaign, squadrons were regrouped into permanent brigades, commanded by a brigadier; a brigade such as this had two squadrons until Breitenfeld, but three at Lützen. The Swedish infantry used *feu de chaussée* – salvo fire – by squad, section or company; the average range of fire was 200 feet (65 metres). Gustav II Adolph also promoted the lightening of the musket for the Swedish infantry, which lead to the abandonment of the rest.

Gustav II Adolph used the Swedish cavalry for impact: it charged at a trot from 50 or 60 metres from the enemy formation, then, when within a dozen metres, increased speed to contact at a gallop; the first ranks fired their pistols at very close range (less than five metres). A regiment was made up of eight companies, for a theoretical strength of 1,000. On campaign, the

Musket drill. Illustration by Jacques Callot, 1635 (Rijksmuseum, Amsterdam)

tactical formation was the cavalry squadron, which grouped together two or three companies arrayed three rows deep. At the beginning of the action, the Swedish cavalry was strengthened by platoons of 50 to 200 musketeers who were interspersed between the squadrons.

But Gustav II Adolph pushed mixed-arm tactics beyond what had been done before, by integrating the artillery into this approach. In the Swedish army, the field artillery, the infantry and the cavalry provided each other with mutual support and defence. His army adopted a small iron cannon, four feet long and weighing only 625 pounds including the carriage, which fired a 3 pound ball. This cannon, which was loaded rapidly like a musket, followed the brigade and was pulled using ropes attached to the trail. Gustav II Adolph focused on simplifying his artillery and retained only three calibres: the 24-pdrs, 12-pdrs and 3-pdrs guns operated by two men. The artillery was organised in a regimental structure made up of a number of companies: one company grouping together the regimental 3-pdrs guns (in theory two per regiment); three companies including the 24-pdr and 12-pdr heavy artillery, one company of sappers and one company of workers. In 1630, this artillery "regiment" had around 1,200 men; Wallenstein's artillery never numbered more than 80 guns, and Tilly's never more than 30 guns, but Gustav II Adolph's artillery regularly exceeded 100 cannon, distributed mainly between the infantry brigades. In the mid–1640s, France emulated the Swedes and adopted these small battalion guns.

On Campaign

From 1635, a French Army on campaign was barely larger than at the beginning of the century – rarely exceeding 30,000 men – but the cavalry rapidly accounted for a larger proportion. Rarely exceeding 20 percent until 1638 – except for the army of Condé in 1636 which had a total of 20,000 infantry and 8,000 cavalry – the cavalry frequently represented 20 to 30 percent between 1639 and 1643, in some cases it reached 45 to 50 percent in 1644 and 1645, then returning to around 28 percent in 1646. Army numbers diminished rapidly as the campaign progressed, with losses, illness and desertions all taking their toll, but also because garrisons had to be left in

French infantry, with pikemen in armour and musketeers still using musket rests. Illustration by Jacques Callot, 1633 (Rijksmuseum, Amsterdam)

towns. This represented a few hundred men each time, as occurred during Turenne's campaign of 1644, where 200 to 300 men were left in Worms and nearly 400 men in Mentz, while the Bavarians had nearly 700 men in Philippsburg. Sieges immobilised many thousands of men; Turenne left a corps of 2,000 in Philippsburg in 1644. At the beginning of the 1644 campaign, Turenne's army had 6,000 infantry and 3,000 or 4,000 cavalry; there remained a little under 1,500 infantry and less than 4,000 horses at the beginning of 1645 before the arrival of the 6,000 strong Hessian reinforcements. Regimental numbers dwindled rapidly, as in 1644, when Turenne ordered the regiments of *Montausier* and *Melun* to form a battalion before the first Battle of Fribourg.[60]

As for the previous period, *Ordonnances* show the difficulties encountered in recruiting soldiers. Compliance with the specifications and instructions of the 1629 *Ordonnance*, extensively covered in previous chapters, became much more difficult with the war. Volunteers stayed only the minimum three months, and desertions remained a blight on the armies beyond the Rhine and the mountains, especially as the number of musters decreased from eight musters of 45 days in 1634, to six musters of 45 days in 1636 – another reason for the increase in devastations and other miseries of the war. Consequently, *Ordonnances* used to order that captains who didn't bring their company up to the right number had to be dismissed. Each year, an *Ordonnance* published in October or November specified the provisions for winter quarters. That of October 1642 ordered that, 'the complete companies of the infantry regiments will be paid at the first watch on the basis of 56 men each, and that the infantry captains will be obliged to have two-thirds of their soldiers armed with muskets and one-third with pikes.'[61]

Later *Ordonnances* would provide a bonus for captains with a company of 60 men and even more for those with a company of 70 men. The main preoccupation of many captains at the time (happily not all!) was then to obtain the bonus for reaching a target number of recruits, no matter where or how these soldiers had been recruited, and regardless of their aptitude. Until they attained this bonus the recruits would be taken care of, but then the captain would lose interest, leading to the abovementioned conduct. And yet, although these French soldiers had a poor reputation, it was they who were to be the architects of the many victories of this war. Thus lived and died the soldier of Rocroi and Lens.

---

60   Paul Marichal (ed.), *Mémoires du Maréchal de Turenne* (Paris: Renouard, 1909), tome I, p.10.
61   SHAT 1642 A71-158.

One of the ways to increase the number of soldiers was to increase the recruitment of foreign mercenaries – German, Swiss, Italian, Scottish, Irish, Swedish, Hungarian and Croatian.

On campaign, the troops had of course to be fed, and the musters rarely provided for this. At the beginning of the campaign all went well, as for the army of Turenne at the beginning of the campaign of 1644:

> Alsace being too much ruined, in the month of January he entered the mountains of Lorraine, where he put the Army into quarters: he enlarged them afterwards, by the taking of two small places, called Luxeul and Vesoul in Franche-Comté, where he left three or four regiments. At the same time some money was received from the Court, with which, and the help of the quarters, the army, that is to say the cavalry, was put in a good condition; but as for the infantry, it was a very hard matter to complete them again during the winter.[62]

We see the same situation at the beginning of the 1645 campaign, with the troops ready to march:

> M. de Turenne thought fit not to go to Court during the winter, that he might be in a condition to take the field the sooner; and the Cardinal having approved of it, he stayed at Spires: from thence he sent to desire M. de La Ferté, Governor of Lorraine, to pay the troops with all expedition their winter quarters. M. de La Ferté did it most punctually in all the places of his Government, and ordered three months pay to be given them. Thus the cavalry, amounting to five thousand,

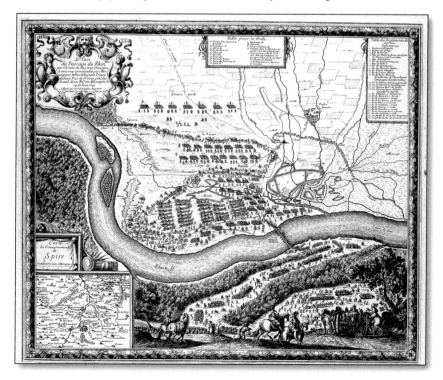

Spire, Rhine crossing, 1645. Engraving by de Beaulieu (Service Historique de la Défense, Public Domain)

---

62 Paul Marichal (ed.), *Mémoires du Maréchal de Turenne* (Paris: Renouard, 1909), tome I, p.4.

and the infantry to five or six thousand, with twelve or sixteen pieces of cannon, about the end of the month of March were ready to recross the Rhine, upon a bridge of boats that was made at Spire.[63]

However, after a few weeks, they had to forage for food and naturally, these resources were fairly nonexistent in a ravaged area, as for Turenne's army at the end of 1644:

M. de Turenne finding that there was no danger of the Bavarian Army's passing the Rhine, and that all his cavalry was perishing for want of forage, kept only three or four regiments of cavalry, without baggage, which he put into the towns, and furnished them with straw, but very little oats, and sent away all the rest of his cavalry into the hills of Lorraine, having written to the Court that directions might be given to provide them with winter quarters in that country, and in the Bishoprics of Metz, Toul, and Verdun, keeping all the infantry with him in Germany, and leaving a body of two thousand men at Philippsburg, until he should know that the Bavarian Army had broken up, which was not till the month of December.[64]

In winter, not only did food and animal fodder have to be provided, but also provision of new, and repair of old, equipment; Turenne did so in February 1648, which required:

…ten days for repairing the artillery, sent into Switzerland for horses, in the month of February returned to Mentz, where he recrossed the Rhine, and marched into Franconia to join the Swedes, although he was eight days during this march, scarce finding in this way straw for the horses. As for the infantry, because the winter was very severe, he ordered cloaks to be made for them. When he got on the other side of the Rhine, he found his strength consisted of four thousand infantry, four thousand cavalry, and twenty pieces of cannon, with twelve or fifteen captured towns in very good condition.[65]

This need for supplies could put the army in a delicate situation, as Turenne learnt to his expense when he lost a part of his army at Mergentheim at the beginning of May 1645:

To speak the truth, M. de Turenne's too easy compliance that the cavalry might not suffer for want of forage, his great desire that they might quickly put themselves in a good condition, several of the officers promising to buy horses in their quarters for their dismounted men, and likewise the distance from the enemy, who were

63   Paul Marichal (ed.), *Mémoires du Maréchal de Turenne* (Paris: Renouard, 1909), tome I, p.40.
64   Paul Marichal (ed.), *Mémoires du Maréchal de Turenne* (Paris: Renouard, 1909), tome I, p.37
65   Paul Marichal (ed.), *Mémoires du Maréchal de Turenne* (Paris: Renouard, 1909), tome I, pp.118–119

near ten leagues from thence, the parties reporting that they were separated, made him unadvisedly resolve to send them into little close places.[66]

The soldiers continued to live off the land and to extort money from the towns, when they did not simply destroy them totally. Turenne's Weimarians even mutinied in 1647, as he recounted in his memoirs:

M. de Turenne had orders to march into Flanders; he had plainly foreseen that the German cavalry would with difficulty be persuaded to follow him, because there was five or six months pay due to them. This he had represented to the Court, which not being in a condition to give any considerable sum, promised only one month's pay, and even this, because of the difficulty the merchants made of accepting the bills of exchange, was not ready at the time the army was to march. In order to remedy this evil, M. de Turenne sent the cavalry into good quarters, divided the whole country among them, treated them in the best manner he could, and marched with the French infantry to take Hoeft and Stanheim, and other small places, which secured his conquests along the Rhine. ... None of the German horse passed but the *Régiment de Turenne*: the old *Régiment de Rosen* having presently sent to the other German regiments, they all joined it in two hours. The next day, the chief officers of the army came to M. de Turenne and demanded all the pay that was due. He gave them to understand that it was impossible for them to have any money before the opening of the campaign; but if they would march, he promised them to get full assurance from the Court for their complete payment. They returned with this answer. ... When M. Rosen and M. Tracy came to the cavalry, those of the officers who had been the most intimate with M. Rosen remonstrated to him that the affair was come to that pass that there was no accommodation to be hoped; and that if he did not resolve to put himself at their head, they would choose another, and so he would remain amongst the French without being in any consideration. M. Rosen determined to stay with them, alleging that the troops kept him by force.[67]

The Franco-Swedish Army in 1648. *Theatrum Europeaum* (Public Domain)

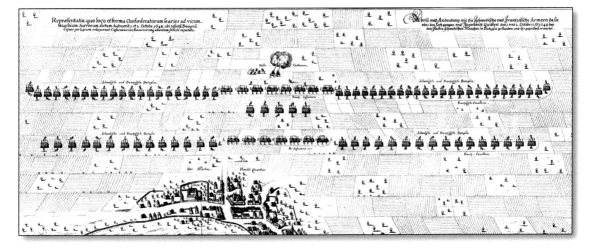

---

66   Paul Marichal (ed.), *Mémoires du Maréchal de Turenne* (Paris: Renouard, 1909), tome I, pp.43–44

67   Paul Marichal (ed.), *Mémoires du Maréchal de Turenne* (Paris: Renouard, 1909), tome I, pp.103–107.

In the end, Turenne charged the mutinied regiments with his cavalry.

A marching army was divided into three bodies: the advance guard, the main body, and the rearguard. In principle, marching troops maintained 40 paces between the squadrons and 25 paces between the battalions.

In battle, the deployment of a large army on the battlefield and its first contact were critical phases. The units took their positions according to the arrangements made by the *maréchal de bataille*. The distance between units depended on the context: the number and the size of battalions and squadrons, the size of the battlefield, et cetera.

In late September 1635, Cardinal de Richelieu proposed different distances between units as well as between ranks and files in his order of battle of the King's army in Piedmont:

> Between 2 lines there are to be 3 feet, between 2 ranks 6 feet when marching, and 3 in battle.
> Between 2 battalions fighting together, 100 feet in battle, and to fight, 50.
> Between pikemen and musketeers, when marching behind, 50 feet.
> Between the vanguard and the battle, 300 feet.
> And between the battle and the rear, 600.
> The battalions of the battle are to the left and right of the straight line of the vanguard by 100 feet.
> Between each line of horse, 3 feet.
> Between each rank, 12 feet.
> Between each cavalry cornet of the same squadron, 50 feet.
> Between one squadron and another, 150 feet.[68]

A decade later, La Valière suggested that the vanguard and the battle should be 100 paces apart, while 200 paces should separate the battle from the rearguard.

> To maintain a fair distance, the army is placed in three lines, the first of which is called the vanguard, the second the battle, which are roughly equal in strength, and the third the rearguard, when it is roughly equal in strength to the others, or the reserve corps, when it is much weaker. The infantry is placed in the middle, and the cavalry on the wings; … The *Carabins*, Musketeers, General's Guards and Croats were placed on the slightly more advanced wings of the army.
>
> One hundred paces is given between the vanguard and the battle, and two hundred between the battle and the rearguard.
>
> The squadrons and battalions of the battle must face each other at the intervals left between those of the vanguard, so that the troops of the battle can pass between those of the vanguard to go to the enemy, and so that those of the vanguard, being broken, can pass into the interval of those of the battle without falling on them. This gap is the width of the front of the squadron or battalion, which supports eight or ten paces more on each side.

---

68   Armand du Plessis de Richelieu, *Lettres, Instructions Diplomatiques et Papiers d'Etat du Cardinal de Richelieu*, pp.265–266.

A squadron of one hundred and twenty horse, which is forty abreast and three deep, will have a two hundred feet frontage, which is five feet for each rider, and a battalion of one thousand men will be six deep and one hundred and sixty-five abreast, and will have a pace of three feet for each soldier. However, by closing up to fight, they reduce the front by a third.

The battalions and squadrons of the rearguard are usually placed opposite the intervals of the troops in the battle. There are various ways of arranging these three corps, each of which has been given specific names, such as the cross, the chequerboard, the *cinquain*, the *sixain*, and several others that have no names. But the most common is the cross, and this is the tightest order, because the troops of the rearguard are opposite those of the vanguard.[69]

Because the depth of a battalion was reduced from eight men to six men between 1635 and the time of La Valière, the front of a battalion had widened and the distance between two units had increased accordingly. The same applies to the cavalry.

The Battle of Rocroi, 1643. Engraving by Alexandre Boudan (1600–1671) (Public Domain)

La Valière was *maréchal de bataille* on the day of Rocroi. The distances he laid down on that day were 170 paces between battalions, a figure close to the 165 paces suggested in his treatise. Nevertheless, he ordered 300 paces between the first two lines of infantry and 400 paces between the second line and Sirot's reserve, figures closer to those suggested by Richelieu in 1635:

The right wing of the main body: *Picardie*, on the right wing. *La Marine*, after, shall double on its left, on the same line, at 170 paces. *Persan*, after, and shall double as above. The first battalion of *Molondin* shall march after and shall double

---

69   François de La Valière, François, *Pratiques et Maximes de la Guerre* (Paris: Jean-Baptiste Loyson, 1666), pp.63–68

as above. The second battalion of *Molondin* shall march after and shall double as above. *Vervins* and *La Prée* shall march after, and shall remain behind *Picardie* and *La Marine*, at 300 paces in the second line. *Vidame* shall march at the rear of *Vervins* and shall double on the left at 170 paces. The first battalion of *Watteville* shall march after *Vidame* and shall double on the left at 170 paces. The *Gardes Ecossais* shall array for battle to the left of *Watteville*.

The left wing: *Piémont* shall march on the left wing. *Rambures* shall follow after and shall double on the right at 170 paces on the same front. *Bourdonné* and *Biscaras* shall march after and shall double as above. *Bussy* and *Guiche* shall remain in battle array at 300 paces behind the interval of *Piémont* and *Rambures*, in the second line. *Brézé* and *Langeron* shall double on the right of *Bussy* and *Guiche*, at 170 paces. Roll shall march after *Brézé* and shall double on the right at 170 paces.

Reserve: *Harcourt*, *Aubeterre* and *Gesvres* shall march at the head of the reserve corps and shall remain in the line of battle at 400 paces below the interval of *Vidame* and the first battalion of *Watteville*. Second battalion of *Watteville* shall march after, and shall double on their left at 300 paces to support the first battalion. The *Royaux* shall march after and shall double on the left at a same distance.[70]

French pikeman *c.* 1645–46, from Lostelnau's *Le Mareschal de Bataille* (Paris: 1647) (Public Domain)

To complete the picture, the cavalry of the Duc d'Enghien was arranged thus: on the right wing under Gassion, 15 squadrons in two lines, 10 in the first line and five in the second line, with musketeer 'sleeves' (commanded musketeers) in the intervals; on the left wing, 13 squadrons in two lines, eight in the first line and five in the second line, commanded by La Ferté-Senneterre, and also with 'sleeves' of musketeer in the intervals.

During the course of a battle, the distances between the lines, which allow the units to support each other, are important. As in this example from the Third Battle of Fribourg in 1644:

M. de Mercy ... faced about upon M. de Rosen with the whole body of his troops; but some of the enemy's squadrons advancing before their infantry, M. de Rosen beat them back, and following them in order, three or four battalions

---

70   Henri d'Orléans, Duc d'Aumale, *Histoire des Princes de Condé pendant les XVIe et XVIIe Siècles* (Paris: Calmann Lévy, 1886), tome. 4, pp.489–490.

fired upon him, which stopped his detachment, however, without putting them into confusion; seeing himself very near the enemy's main body, and their front very much larger than his own, he began to retire. Two or three squadrons of the second line sustained those of the first, that were very little moved by so great a fire, and after having lost four or five standards, they retired very slowly in good order.[71]

The *maréchal de bataille*, an office that had appeared shortly before the Battle of Rocroi, was in charge of the line of battle and the combat formation of the army during the battle. He was aided in this task by *sergents de bataille*. He had not only to lay down distances, but also kept a scrupulous eye on the alignments, while reminding the deployed units of their orders. This is illustrated by Prince de Condé instructions at Lens, on 20 August 1648:

> In the evening, we halted the line of battle, and we gave three most important recommendations to all the troops: the first, to watch each other as they marched, so that the cavalry and the infantry would remain on the same line, and so that they could keep their distances and intervals; the second, to charge only at a walking pace; the third, to allow the enemy to fire first.[72]

Then the generals encouraged their troops, as the *Maréchal* de Gramont did at the Battle of Lens in epic style:

> *Maréchal* de Gramont left the Prince de Condé and returned to his wing; and passing to the head of the troops, he told them that battle had just been decided; he asked them to remember their valour and what they owed the King, and also to observe well the orders they had been given; he said that this action was of such importance given the current state of affairs, that it was either victory or death, and that he was going to show them the example by entering first into the enemy squadron that was opposite his own. This short and moving speech was infinitely pleasing to the soldiers; all the infantry shouted for joy and threw their hats in the air; the cavalry took their swords in hand and all the trumpets sounded fanfares of an inexpressible joy. The Prince de

French Cavalry *c.* 1635. Engraving by Jacques Callot (1592–1635) (Public Domain)

---

71 Paul Marichal (ed.), *Mémoires du Maréchal de Turenne* (Paris: Renouard, 1909), tome I, pp.23–24.

72 Antoine de Gramont, *Mémoires du Maréchal de Gramont*, in *Nouvelle Collection des Mémoires Pour Servir à l'Histoire de France* (Paris: Michaud et Poujoulat, 1839), Troisième série, tome VII, p.279.

Condé and *Maréchal* de Gramont embraced warmly, and each thought of their own business.[73]

The battle itself progressed in a succession of charges and counter charges, the battalions and squadrons supporting each other. La Peyrère, in his account of the Battle of Lens, describes such an engagement:

It was around eight o'clock in the morning when the army began to march in excellent array to the sound of trumpets, drums and cannons. The Prince called a halt from time to time to redress the lines and to maintain distances and, the cannon of the Comte de Cossé was so well and so diligently used that it fired while marching, which is a significant feat; they had the advantage that, by firing from the plain onto the hillock of the enemy position, all shots reached either the squadrons, or the battalions, and created great confusion for them to array themselves for battle. Their cannon, which fired from the top of the hill to the foot, did not have the same effect as ours, although the numbers were unequal, with the Archduke having 38 and the Prince 18.

The enemy was impatient to fight; they looked brave and marched resolutely towards us. However they were attempting two things at the same time, marching and arraying for combat, which is a hindrance when marching to a decisive battle …

The two armies were at 30 paces from each other when three shots were fired from the left wing of the enemy into our right wing. Condé, who feared the precipitation of his soldiers, halted them and forbade the musketeers from opening fire before the enemy had fired; fire should not begin until at point-blank range. This halt had three good effects; it tempered the ardour of our troops, readjusted the battle array and confirmed the soldier in his resolution to withstand the enemy discharge.

The Prince of Salm advanced at a trot with his first line of Walloon and Lorraine cavalry against Condé's first line, who advanced at a walk to receive them. The two lines met horse to horse, pistol to pistol, and remained in this position for a fairly long time, awaiting who would fire first, with neither side wavering.

The enemy was more impatient and opened fire; it was as though the gates of Hell had opened! All our front line officers were killed, injured or unseated. Condé gave the signal to fire, then, leading the Gassion regiment with his sword held high, he crushed the squadron facing him. His six other squadrons followed him, and, on his example, charged the first enemy line so violently that it was overwhelmed.[74]

The Duc d'Enghien attempted to hold the fire of his regiments until the last moment, well under 30 paces. It would appear from various accounts that 50

73   Antoine de Gramont, *Mémoires du Maréchal de Gramont*, in *Nouvelle Collection des Mémoires Pour Servir à l'Histoire de France*, (Paris: Michaud et Poujoulat, 1839), Troisième série, tome VII, p.279.

74   Isaac de la Peyrère, 'La Bataille de Lens, donnée le 21 août 1648', in Cousin, Victor, *La Société Française au XVIIᵉ Siècle*, (Paris: Didier et Cie, 1858), tome 1, p.407.

paces was the "safe" distance for two enemy armies. An army wishing to put itself out of range withdrew to more than 40 paces, as Mercy's Bavarians did in 1644:

> The Bavarians lost a great many men, and retired about forty or fifty paces from our infantry, having all their cavalry, and a body of infantry of the second line, to sustain them. The two armies continued thus facing one another, the Bavarians not daring to come to a close engagement again with those regiments that were ready to receive them with their pikes, and the French not daring to enter further onto the plain, having no cavalry to sustain them.

And a little later that day:

> The night did not put an end to the fight, but the troops on both sides remained for seven hours continually firing at the distance of forty paces until it was day.[75]

Musketeer *c.* 1645–46 from Lostelnau's *Le Mareschal de Bataille* (Paris: 1647) (Public Domain)

Infantry fire could be terrible at close range. In his memoirs, de Grammont relates this episode from the battle of Nördlingen (or Alerheim) on 3 August 1645:

> All I could do was to put myself at the head of the two infantry regiments of *Fabert* and *Wal*. They did not move from their positions in the slightest, and muzzle to muzzle they fired such a furious discharge into the enemy cavalry, that they were forced open, and I made use of this to enter in with what remained of his men.[76]

Henri de Bessé gives a graphic account of the effects of continuous infantry fire in his account of the Battle of Friburg:

> The two parties fired with such fury that the noise and the smoke confused everything, and they could only make each other out by the light of cannon and musket fire. All the woods around echoed with a terrible booming which further added to the horror of the battle.

---

75   Paul Marichal (ed.), *Mémoires du Maréchal de Turenne* (Paris: Renouard, 1909), tome I, p.14.

76   Antoine de Gramont, *Mémoires du Maréchal de Gramont*, in *Nouvelle Collection des Mémoires Pour Servir à l'Histoire de France* (Paris: Michaud et Poujoulat, 1839), Troisième série, tome VII, p.262.

The soldiers were so fierce and unrelenting, both those trying to force the entrenchments, and those trying to defend them, that, if night had not fallen, both sides would have seen the greatest carnage ever seen in our times.[77]

Sometimes the battlefield was not as clear and flat as at Rocroi or Lens, and the generals had to adapt to the situation, as was the case of the Duc d'Enghien at Nördlingen (or Alerheim) in 1645:

About twelve o'clock the army advanced into the great plain, and about four o'clock the two armies came into distance of one another. It took up a good deal of time to extend and put ourselves in a posture of fighting. That village, which was before the enemy's army, justly made it doubtful, whether it were better to attack it, or march towards the two wings with the horse only: but as it is not very safe to attack wings, without at the same time charging the foot posted in the centre, it was not judged proper, whatever difficulty there might be in attacking the village, to charge with the horse, without the infantry marching in the same front ; and as the village was above four hundred paces more advanced than the place where the enemy's army was, it was thought best to halt with the two wings, while the infantry should attack and make themselves masters of the nearest houses of that village, or at least of some of them. For that end, our cannon were brought up, that we might not be annoyed by those of the enemy, without annoying them with ours: but as cannon that are planted have a great advantage over those that march, because the horses must always be put to the carriages in order to advance, whereby a great deal of time is lost, those of the enemy did a great deal more damage than ours. In this disposition the infantry of the King's army marched straight to the village; the right wing being opposite to the enemy's left wing in the plain, and the left wing to the enemy's right, which was upon that hill, from which there was an insensible descent to the village.[78]

When the terrain did not permit the assembling of large cavalry wings, the cavalry's role was to defend the infantry. On many occasions we find the following arrangements, as exemplified in the Battle of Friburg:

Then M. the Prince thought fit that M. de Turenne should march with his infantry, the *Maréchal* de Gramont was to have charged the enemy in the flank, or to have sustained with the horse, if the attack had succeeded. We marched straight to the fall of trees which was in the middle of the hill, and opposite to the left of the Prince's army. The cavalry regiments of M. de Turenne and Tracy, sustained the Prince's infantry, who were repulsed after a very obstinate fight, where this cavalry performed wonders, in bearing the fire without moving.[79]

---

77   Henri de Bessé, *Relation des Campagnes de Rocroi et de Fribourg* (Paris, Delangle, 1826), p.116.
78   Paul Marichal (ed.), *Mémoires du Maréchal de Turenne* (Paris: Renouard, 1909), tome I, pp.62–63.
79   Paul Marichal (ed.), *Mémoires du Maréchal de Turenne* (Paris: Renouard, 1909), tome I, p.20.

In open country, the cavalry was used on the wings, and was a decisive element in defeating the enemy. In his account of the Battle of Rocroi, Henri de Bessé relates the effect of a cavalry charge:

> But nothing is as dangerous as making wide movements in front of a powerful enemy when about to come to hand-to-hand combat. These squadrons, already weakened, were broken at the first charge, and all the troops of Albuquerque were knocked down on top of each other. Enghien, seeing them take flight, ordered Gassion to pursue them and turned instantly against the infantry.[80]

Between charges, the cavalry rallied and reformed behind the infantry, as recounted by this officer of the Prince de Condé present at the Battle of Lens in 1648:

> Our cavalry suffered greatly for the enemy had always three squadrons against one, but when they were broken, they always came to rally behind *Picardie*; (many officers) after having charged twenty times and breaking the corps that they fought, came here to refresh themselves, and Streif came here to die.[81]

However, when circumstances required, the cavalry could also simply skirmish, as during the Battle of Friburg on 5 August 1644:

> The French *gendarmerie* performed excellently; La Boulaye, who was in command, took it to the edge of this entrenchment of trees, and, in spite of the enemy fire, he skirmished for a very long time with pistols.[82]

Or again in this description a little after Friburg:

> The enemy's cavalry dare not pursue them briskly, for fear going too far from their foot; or else, because being as yet stunned with the battles of the preceding days, their main design was to retire without fighting. Rosen's foremost squadrons being sustained by those of the second line, and the whole body of the enemy's cavalry and infantry continuing to march against them, and being between forty and fifty paces from one another, they retired five or six hundred paces, mixed with the enemy, who made more use of the fire of their infantry than of their cavalry.[83]

As in the earlier period, during the Thirty Years' War the French armies used skirmishers, or *enfants perdus*. They were generally detached from their regiment and could be commanded by a captain, such as Pédamont, commanding the *enfants perdus* of regiment of *Picardie* at Rocroi. However, the generals of the Army of Germany, such as Turenne and Grammont, used

---

80   Henri de Bessé, *Relation des Campagnes de Rocroi et de Fribourg* (Paris: Delangle, 1826), p.32.
81   Archives du Château de Chantilly, Manuscrit MS933, 'Relation de la Bataille de Lens, le 20 août 1648, par un officier de Condé.'
82   Henri de Bessé, *Relation des Campagnes de Rocroi et de Fribourg* (Paris: Delangle, 1826), p.116.
83   Paul Marichal (ed.), *Mémoires du Maréchal de Turenne* (Paris: Renouard, 1909), tome I, p.24.

Drummers. Engraving by Jacques Callot, 1635 (Rijksmuseum, Amsterdam)

the term commanded musketeers, which could equally well designate a musketeer unit, or musketeers detached from a regiment.

When battles did not go to their advantage, the *Maréchals* had to take steps to maintain the cohesion of their troops. In his memoirs, Sirot describes this episode from the Battle of Rocroi:

> The *Maréchal de Bataille*, the Chevalier de La Vallière, gave the order to retreat to the discouraged troops from the left wing, whom I had rallied, for the battle was lost. These were *Picardie*, *Piémont*, *La Marine*, the Swiss of *Monlondin*, and *Persan*. They had suffered greatly and obeyed willingly; but upon seeing that they abandoned me, I went to them and told them to hold fast.
>
> As they withdrew in spite of my remonstrances, I blamed them for their lack of heart and I had a serious dispute with the Chevalier de La Vallière, to whom I said that it was not for him to command my troops. Prayers and threats had such an effect on the spirits of the officers that I hardened them; but as I led the charge, La Vallière halted them a second time and I was followed only by what remained of my reserve, *Harcourt*, *Bretagne*, the *Royaux*, and for the cavalry, my own regiment, which had suffered greatly. I charged the Spanish troops, but I was not able to crush them because our men were too weak in numbers. I therefore ran to the five withdrawing regiments which were at more than 100 paces from me, and I shouted:
>
> "Are you cowards, men of little honour and little heart, to withdraw without seeing the enemy? I shall proclaim it throughout France; I shall complain to the King and the Duc d'Enghien. Stay and we shall win the battle! Do not abandon me for a man who shall lose you your reputation forever; rally my troops, I promise to give you victory!"
>
> Officers and soldiers replied: "To the Baron de Sirot!" I led them to join my troops that were waiting for me.[84]

Siege warfare remained the main form of action during the various campaigns that took place between 1635 and 1648 even if many generals, such as Rohan and Turenne, tried to avoid it. The siege of Lleida, led by the Prince de Condé in 1647 and recounted by the Duc de Gramont, illustrates this type of warfare:

---

84 Claude de Letouf, *Mémoires et la Vie de Messire Claude de Letouf, Chevalier Baron de Sirot* (Paris: Claude Barbin, 1683), tome II, pp.44–45.

The beginnings of the siege gave hope for a happy success; for we found all the old circumvallation of the Comte d'Harcourt, which the negligence of the Spaniards had left nearly whole and in defensive condition: this won us much time, and meant the troops were not fatigued through work. What is more, the town had been well reconnoitred, and appeared neither easy, nor difficult to take.

The Spanish army, always slow in its operation, was not yet ready to begin their campaign, which gave us all the time necessary to bring into the camp the cannon, victuals and munitions required to realise the siege at our leisure. Besides this, the Chevalier de La Vallière, who had led our attacks in the grand sieges of Flanders, had been Governor of the town, and gave mathematical assurance that the town was worth nothing at all; which further strengthened our hopes, because with knowledge of the fortifications, and because he had commanded in the town, he had a perfect knowledge of the enemy' strengths and weaknesses. …

There were three thousand native Spanish in the town, and the Governor was the Portuguese, Don Antonio Brit, a man of honour and valour, and with perfect manners, sending every morning ices and lemonade to the Prince de Condé for his refreshment; he was proud and intrepid in his manner of defending his town, of which we were not able to take an inch without the sword, and without being constantly fought off.

Army besieging a stronghold. Engraving by Jacques Callot (1592–1635) (Public Domain)

We made two attacks, one on the side of the Prince de Condé, and the other on the side of *Maréchal* de Grammont: these attacks pushed fairly energetically to the foot of the battlements that Brit had made halfway up. But when we wished to attach the mine to explode it, we found the rock so hard that we were not able to do so; and despite all our efforts, the nights passed by without any headway being made: which distressed the generals, the officers and the soldiers. Also the fire was terrible, continuous, and casualties very heavy. The Governor made two significant sallies, both on the trench of the Prince de Condé. At the first, the Swiss who were guarding it were so severely attacked that they abandoned it entirely, and were never able to rally; in such a way that it was necessary for the Prince de Condé and the *Maréchal* de Gramont to come to the camp to regain it and to retake all the positions that had been abandoned, which was done at extreme peril; for because the enemy had retaken possession a sufficiently long time ago to repair and improve them, it was necessary to regain the lost positions in full daylight and without cover, under the tremendous fire of the whole town, and put back the guard where they had been in the first place: this made the pill even more difficult to swallow.

The other sally was also to attack the Prince. The regiment that had the guard did not abandon him completely, for he was supported by *Persan*, who was in *Maréchal* de Gramont's trench. However, the enemy killed a great number of officers and soldiers, and generally all the miners, whose work they ruined totally: after which the Governor was not remiss in sending his two little mutes to the Prince de Condé, laden with ice and cinnamon water for refreshment after the fatigues of the day.

To this poor success was added the desertion of the troops, in number more than four thousand, who surrendered to the enemy: which so weakened the army that the trench Guards, ordinarily of twelve hundred men, were no more than three hundred, and nearly all the circumvallation abandoned.[85]

The siege of Ypres in 1648, once again narrated by *Maréchal* de Gramont, was more positive from his side. He gives a thorough description of the system of trenches, moats, counterscarps, and the way to reduce enemy defences:

The same evening, we opened the trench in two places in close proximity to each other: the front that we attacked was large, the moat very wide, deep and full of water, and a most handsome counterscarp, with excellent palisades. The *Gardes Françaises* defended against both attacks and pushed up to a hundred paces from the corner of the counterscarp. The ninth day after the trench was opened, the Poles, leading the attack of *Maréchal* de Gramont, swam across the moat of the *demi lune*; and after hacking through the palisades of the moat, they entered within; and having killed all those who were inside, they constructed a superb position on the point. This was done in daylight, and was one of the most hardy [actions] ever seen: the mine was attached to the *demi lune* on the side of the attack of the Prince de Condé; after which the enemy beat a retreat, with the advantage of being very poorly defended. The man they sent to surrender was a Walloon lieutenant colonel, one of the most ridiculous personages ever seen.[86]

A fort could be composed of bastions, fortifications with two corners and two sides; curtains, battlements separating the bastions; scarps, slopes inside the moats and ditches; and counterscarps, which were the outer slopes of these moats and ditches. A *demi lune* was an advance bastion outside the fort. The attackers used fascines – bundles of branches – to fill moats and ditches, and dug saps, or approach trenches, while the besieged attempted to prevent them by digging countermines, or mine tunnels.

---

85   Antoine de Gramont, Antoine, *Mémoires du Maréchal de Gramont*, in *Nouvelle Collection des Mémoires Pour Servir à l'Histoire de France* (Paris: Michaud et Poujoulat, 1839), Troisième série, tome VII, p.272.

86   Antoine de Gramont, Antoine, *Mémoires du Maréchal de Gramont*, in *Nouvelle Collection des Mémoires Pour Servir à l'Histoire de France* (Paris: Michaud et Poujoulat, 1839), Troisième série, tome VII, pp.276–277.

5

Uniforms and Colours

The infantry was dressed in a short coat, most often with button sleeves, but which could be left unbuttoned. Ribbons or laces could be used for decoration. Officers often wore a cloak over this jacket, and were recognisable on the battlefield by their white scarf. Breeches were tied just below the knee by a ribbon, and could be decorated by a series of buttons on the seam. Stockings covered the legs, and shoes completed the outfit, although on campaign, the infantry preferred to wear boots if they had the possibility of doing so, as Captain Lieutenant d'Artagnan relates in his memoirs: the major of an infantry regiment sent 'a captain that he had with him to the regiment to inform the lieutenant colonel of the inspection that the King wished to perform … Those wearing boots removed them on hearing this, and put on shoes, as was proper for an inspection of infantry.'[1] The uniform of the drummers was usually more decorated. Cavalry and certain infantry officers were protected by a leather coat – the buff coat.

Swords were generally worn on the left from a belt or a baldric. Musketeers were also equipped with a bandolier, which held 12 powder charges. Officers were equipped with a halberd or partisan.

Game Lost. Painting by Ernest Meissonier (1815–1891) (Facsimile in the Author's Collection)

---

1 Gatien de Courtilz de Sandras, *Mémoires de Mr d'Artagnan, Capitaine Lieutenant de la Première Compagnie des Mousquetaires du Roi* (Cologne: Pierre Marteau, 1701), tome I, p.73.

In the first half of the seventeenth century, units generally did not yet wear uniforms, as they would from around 1660; only a few guard units did so, such as the four companies of the King's *Gardes du Corps* and the *Mousquetaires du Roi*. The latter wore a blue cassock with white edging and a white cross embroidered in the middle. Cardinal de Richelieu's Guards wore a red cassock with a white cross. According to Henri Campion, in 1635 'the *Maréchal* [de La Force] was reinforced by fifteen hundred well mounted and highly gilded gentlemen from Normandy and two thousand dragoons, all dressed in helmets in the colours of Cardinal de Richelieu.'[2]

The *Gardes Françaises* (French Guards) also seem not to have had any semblance of a uniform. The young d'Artagnan, who was in the *Gardes Françaises* at the time, bears witness to this when he writes that of all the assassins sent by his enemy Rosnay to kill him, 'not one of them recognised me as being from the regiment (of the *Gardes Françaises*). As they were from the first battalion, and I was only from the second, we had not yet found each other. ... When they had seen me it had only been in a different outfit to that of the regiment.'[3] According to a letter from Louis XIII to the Provost of Merchants, dated 27 October 1627, the Guards' clothing consisted of a coat, long stockings, breeches, of minimal bure dyed wool.

It is however highly probable that many regiments had a certain 'uniformity' at the beginning of a campaign. Equipment and clothing were mainly provided by the government or the *mestre de camp* of the regiment, and this would become more and more the case under Richelieu's administration. It is therefore likely that clothing was made out of the same cloth and was of the same cut throughout a unit. For instance, in the winter 1627, Richelieu ordered the large towns of the Kingdom to provide clothing. Paris dressed the regiment of *Gardes* by sending 2,500 coats, breeches, stockings and shoes. Each town bought a batch of cloth,

Bad Mood. Painting by Ernest Meissonier (1815–1891) (Public Domain)

---

2   Henri de Campion, *Mémoires de Henri de Campion* (Paris: P. Jannet, 1867), p.53.
3   Gatien de Courtilz de Sandras, *Mémoires de Mr d'Artagnan, Capitaine Lieutenant de la Première Compagnie des Mousquetaires du Roi* (Cologne: Pierre Marteau, 1701), tome I, p.112.

so each regiment was uniformed in the same colour, albeit not the same throughout the Army.[4]

On 27 October 1641, Mazarin wrote to Le Tellier, then *intendant* of the army of Piedmont, that he was 'ordered to have clothes made for all of the infantry in the army.'[5] He received 5,400 suits of clothes a month later. On 29 July 1642, Le Tellier wrote to Des Noyers stating that he had 4,434 suits of clothes distributed to the majors of each infantry regiment for distribution to the soldiers of each unit who had wintered in Piedmont.[6] In 1644, when he took command of the army in Germany, Vicomte de Turenne 'had 5,000 cavalry remounted at his expense and 4,000 infantry clothed.'[7] On 24 July 1646, the Parlement of Brittany ordered the communities to provide each soldier with a new suit of good clothing, complete with two shirts, a hat, a pair of shoes and a sword. Finally, on 10 October 1647, the King ordered the City of Paris to provide 1,600 complete suits. Dull colours, especially grey and brown, appear to have been dominant. Of course, as the campaign advanced, wear on the equipment and plunder increasingly added to the variation of this general appearance.

While there was a semblance of uniformity within a regiment, this was not the case for the army as a whole. To distinguish themselves, officers generally wore a white scarf. But as that was not enough, some commanders could order a *camisade* to distinguish their troops in the middle of the melee, as this account from Puysegur in 1622 relates:

> the King wanted a camisade to be given, and told me that I had to put my shirt out of my breeches. I replied to him, Sire, the two enemy battalions behind the lost ditch also have their shirt out of their breeches, which is why we will not distinguish one from the other. If your Majesty wishes, we will put our shirts on over our doublet and breeches, which the King thought was a good idea and so ordered. With the attack resolved in this way, orders were given to the troops. *Monsieur* de Bassompierre, who commanded the attack by the *Gardes*, had me put on the shirt over my coat and led me to the head of the works. All the officers and soldiers put on their shirts in the same way as me. I was ordered to march at the head of the *enfants perdus*, who were commanded by two sergeants of the *Gardes*.[8]

Each regiment had its own colours. Those of the guards and the *vieux corps* are best known as they did not change when a new colonel was appointed.

4   Lieutenant-Colonel Victor Louis Jean François Belhomme, *Histoire de l'Infanterie en France*, (Paris and Limoges: Henri Charles Lavauzelle, 1893), tome 1, pp.341–342.

5   Narcisse Léonard Caron, *Michel Le Tellier, Son Administration Comme Intendant d'Armée en Piémont 1640–1643* (Paris: Pedone-Lauriel, 1880), p.120.

6   Caron, Narcisse L., *Michel Le Tellier, Son Administration Comme Intendant d'Armée en Piémont 1640–1643* (Paris: Pedone-Lauriel, 1880), p.CXLI.

7   James II Ramsay, *Histoire du Vicomte de Turenne, Maréchal-Général des Armées du Roi* (La Haye: Jean Neaulme, 1736), Tome 1, p.115.

8   Jacques de Chastenet, *Les Mémoires de Messire Jacques de Castenet, Chevalier, Seigneur de Puysegur, Colonel du Régiment de Piedmont, & Lieutenant Général des Armées du Roy* (Amsterdam: Abraham Wolfgang, 1690), tome 1, p.30.

The Standard-Bearer. Painting by Ernest Meissonier (1815–1891) (Public Domain)

This was also the case for the regiments which bore the name of a province; it is much more difficult to find the colours of the temporary regiments. The colours of the *vieux corps* were a single colour with a white cross throughout: green for Champagne, black for Piedmont, red for Picardie, brown for Navarre and yellow for Normandie.

From at least January 1643, French infantry regiments had carried only two colours: the regimental colour and the white colour of the *Compagnie Colonelle*. This practice is attested to in the King's letter to Le Tellier, Intendant of the Army of Piedmont, dated 15 January 1643:

> Monsieur Le Tellier, I will tell you that having recognised that ensigns are very useless in infantry companies, even that in the new regiments several captains do not have any, or that they put people there who depend on them to draw their *appointments* [salaries], I have resolved to keep only two ensigns in each infantry regiment, one in the colonel's company, in regiments with a white colour, the other in the *mestre de camp* company; and in the other regiments, one in the company of the *mestre de camp* and the other in that of the first captain.[9]

Removing the ensigns from the companies meant that they no longer carried a colour. It is difficult to know how long the practice of keeping only one or two colours had existed. Belhomme noted that in October 1634, the French Army crossed the Rhine to join Bernard of Saxe-Weimar's army: the old regiments took only one colour each and left the others at Manheim with the army *intendant*.[10] This transformation necessarily took place after that date. According to Belhomme, each company had its own colour in the hue and pattern of the regiment. The colours did not change for regiments with a province name, whereas they did for those bearing the name of their *mestre de camp*, when the latter changed. And he adds that not all the company

9   Caron, Narcisse L., *Michel Le Tellier, Son Administration Comme Intendant d'Armée en Piémont 1640–1643* (Paris: Pedone-Lauriel, 1880), p.268.
10   Lieutenant-Colonel Victor Louis Jean François Belhomme, *Histoire de l'Infanterie en France*, (Paris and Limoges: Henri Charles Lavauzelle, 1893), tome 1, p.360.

colours were flown when the strength of the companies fell below 100 men. The company colours were deposited at the ensign's lodgings. When the ensigns were abolished, the colours were deposited in the captain's lodging.[11]

One exception was the *Gardes Françaises*. Because its 30 companies were spread across several armies, each company was allowed to keep a different colour.

In addition to the company colour, permanent regiments were given the white colour. In 1632, the army had five white colour regiments: *Picardie, Piedmont, Champagne, Navarre* and *Normandie*. The *Ordonnance* of 15 September 1635 gave the white colour and the *compagnie colonelle* to the regiments *Nerestang, Rambures, Maugiron* (ex-*Estissac* and which became *Auvergne*), *Sault, Vaubecourt, Vaudemont Lorrain, Bellenave* (ex-*Chastelier-Barlot*), Scottish *Hepburn*, which also had the white colour of the *Colonel Général* of the Scots, *Plessis-Praslin* and *Alincourt* (ex-*Villeroy* which became *Lyonnais*) regiments. There were 17 white colours, including 2 for the Swiss and Scottish regiments.[12] On 26 September 1635, the *Cardinal-Duc* regiment was raised, changing its name to the regiment of *La Marine* in December. It carried a white colour. Other regiments subsequently obtained the white colour over time, e.g. *Perche, Turenne, Rebé* and *Nettancourt* on 8 December 1635, and *Menillet* (which became *Bourdonné*), *Montausier* and *La Frezelière* in May 1636.[13]

Pikemen and infantry ensign. Stefano della Bella (Rijksmuseum, Amsterdam)

Regarding mounted troops, each cavalry company displayed its own standard, even when grouped together in regiments.

The colours carried by the infantry regiments were large, and usually square in shape. Those of the *Gardes Suisses* measured 3 x 3 metres, while the colours of other regiments measured 2.80 metres or a little less. They were carried on a pole which measured up to 3.60 metres in length.[14] The cavalry standards were of a more modest size around 62cm square, and were edged with gold or silver fringe.

11   Lieutenant-Colonel Victor Louis Jean François Belhomme, *Histoire de l'Infanterie en France*, (Paris and Limoges: Henri Charles Lavauzelle, 1893), tome 2, p.35.
12   Lieutenant-Colonel Victor Louis Jean François Belhomme, *Histoire de l'Infanterie en France*, (Paris and Limoges: Henri Charles Lavauzelle, 1893), tome 1, p.364.
13   Lieutenant-Colonel Victor Louis Jean François Belhomme, *Histoire de l'Infanterie en France*, (Paris and Limoges: Henri Charles Lavauzelle, 1893), tome 1, pp.365 & 368.
14   Neil Danskin, *The French Army in the Thirty Years' War,* (The Pike & Shot Society), p. 68.

6

Operations of the French Army from 1620–1648: main actions and Orders of Battle

The French Army fought extensively during the first half of the seventeenth century, both to repress internal revolts and to combat its secular enemy, Spain. For example looking at the service record of the *Gardes Françaises*, and the four oldest of the *vieux corps*: *Piémont*, *Picardie*, *Champagne* and *Navarre*. These five regiments were present during the internal campaigns against the Huguenots: in 1620 at the Battle of Les Ponts-de-Cé in Normandy; in 1621 at the sieges of Saint Jean d'Angély and Montauban; and in 1622 in Nègrepelisse and the siege of Montpellier. The *Gardes Françaises*, *Champagne* and *Piémont* were at the siege of La Rochelle in 1627, then the *Gardes Françaises*, *Navarre* and *Piémont* were with the King's army in Piedmont at the beginning of 1629. The charge of the *Gardes Françaises* at the Pas de Suse gave a magnificent and memorable example of France's offensive spirit, the famous *furia francese*. The *Gardes Françaises, Champagne* and *Piémont* were present in the spring of 1629 in the repression of a Huguenot revolt in the Languedoc. On this occasion, the brigade of *Champagne* and *Piémont* launched an assault on the Fort Saint-André. The regiments of the *Gardes Françaises*, *Picardie* and *Champagne* were also in the army that went to conquer the Savoy in 1630, and all five regiments were in the King's army in Piedmont in1630.

After a few years' rest, the *Gardes Françaises*, *Picardie*, and *Navarre* were a part of the Army of La Sarre in 1635, and then in 1636, the *Gardes Françaises, Piémont,* and *Champagne* were in the Army of Champagne. Note that during the French campaigns of the Thirty Years' War, the *Gardes Françaises* and the *vieux corps* rarely formed a brigade together; the King had to divide his experienced troops among a number of armies: Champagne, Germany, Lorraine, Franche-Comté, Italy and the Pyrenees. The regiments of *Picardie* and *Navarre* were destroyed at Thionville in 1639, while the *Gardes Françaises, Piémont* and *Champagne* contributed to the storming of Hesdin in the same year. The *Gardes Françaises*, *Picardie*, *Piémont* and *Navarre* were present at the siege of Thionville in 1643 while at Rocroi the same year, the Army of the Duc d'Enghien included the *Picardie* and *Piémont* regiments. It was *Picardie* that massacred the 1,000 Spanish musketeers in a dawn ambush. *Piémont* was attacked by the entire cavalry of Alsace, it held out, although it suffered heavy losses. However, during the battle both *Picardie* and *Piémont* had to be rallied with the rest of the French infantry, which was done with difficulty. In April 1646, *Champagne* was decimated at the siege of Lleida. At Lens, in 1648, the *Gardes Françaises* and the *Gardes Suisses* crushed three enemy battalions, one Spanish and two German, but then, drunk on success, they allowed themselves to be surrounded by the Spanish *Tercio Viejos*. *Picardie*, the only *vieux corps* present at Lens alongside the guard regiments, was one of the regiments that rushed to the aid of the *Gardes Françaises*, breaking the *tercios*.

The service of these regiments did not, of course, stop there – *Picardie*, for example, retook Saumur from the rebels in April 1650 – but this is where our story ends, interrupting a list of military actions that would only end with the French Revolution.

The composition of the main French armies during the 1620 to 1648 period.

At the *Drôlerie des Ponts-de-Cé,* on 7 August 1620, the French Army had 8,000 infantry and 600 cavalry, commanded by the Prince de Condé; the *Maréchal* de Praslin was *Lieutenant Général* and the *Maréchals de Camp* were Tresnel, Créquy, Nerestang and Bassompierre.

Present were: companies of *chevaux-légers* and *carabins*. The *Gardes Françaises, Piémont, Picardie, Champagne* (two battalions), *Navarre*. The *Gardes Françaises* were at the centre, *Picardie* on their right and the two battalions of *Champagne* on their left. Each infantry regiment deployed *enfants perdus*.

The French Army at the Siege of Saint Jean d'Angély, June 1621

The cavalry was made up of seven *cornettes*: the *Chevaux-Légers* of the *Maison du Roi*, the *Gendarmerie*,[1] the *Chevaux-Légers de la Reine, Guise, Châteaubriant,* and the *Carabins d'Esplans.*

The infantry comprised the *Gardes Françaises,* the *Gardes Suisses,* the *Picardie, Piémont, Champagne, Navarre, Normandie, Rambures, Chappes* and *Lauzières* regiments.

Siege of Montauban, August-November 1621

Three corps were formed to assault the town at different points.

The first was formed of the *Gardes Françaises* and *Gardes Suisses* reinforced by *Piémont, Normandie, Chappes* and *Estissac.*

The second comprised *Picardie, Champagne, Navarre, Villeroy* and *Vaillac.*

The third grouped together *Languedoc, Rambures, Saint-Étienne* and *Lauzières.*

---

1 The records that I have consulted do not specify *which* Gendarmerie this was.

In October 1621, the Duc de Montmorency reinforced the Royal Army in Montauban with 500 cavalry and five Languedoc regiments of *Rieux*, *Réaux*, *Moussoulens*, *Fabrègues* and *La Roquette*, totalling 6,000 men (1,200 men per regiment).

The Army of the Duc d'Elbeuf that fought against the Marquis de La Force, February 1622

Five companies of *chevaux-légers*.

The infantry regiments of *Piémont*, nine companies of which had been left to garrison Duras, *Riberac* and *Grignaux*. This small army was joined by the regiments of *Bordeilles, Curson, Loson, Ramburges* and the cavalry[2].

The Army of Louis XIII in 1622, from Saintonge to the Siege of Montpellier (April-October)

The *Maison du Roi* (the *Cent-Suisses*, the *Cent Gentilshommes à Bec-de-Corbin*, the *Gardes de la Porte*, the *Gardes de la Manche*, the *Gardes de la Prévôté* and the four companies of mounted *Gardes du Corps*, one French and three Scottish, of 336 Guards each), the *Gendarmes* and *Chevaux-Légers* of the *Maison du Roi*.

Some companies of gendarmes, including the *Gendarmes de Condé*, *Chevaux-Légers*, including those of *la Reine, Chateaubriand, Condé, Guise, Praslin, Vitry*, and the *Carabins d'Esplans*.

The infantry included the *Gardes Françaises* (five battalions), the *Gardes Suisses* (two large battalions), *Navarre* (three battalions), *Normandie* (two battalions), *Picardie, Piémont, Champagne* (left at La Rochelle), and a number of other regiments including *Nerestang, Berry, Estissac, Saint-Chamond, Fontenay-Mareuil*, et cetera,

Seven culverins.

---

2   The records do not give any details as to which cavalry this was.

In July 1622, *Maréchal* de Praslin went to take Bédarieux with *Picardie*, *Navarre* and nine cannon. On 2 August, he laid siege to Lunel and the Duc de Montmorency took Massillargues with *Normandie*, five regiments from the Languedoc – *Rieux*, *Réaux*, *Moussoulens*, *Fabrègues* and *La Roquette*, a culverin and six other cannon.

At the siege of Montpellier in September 1622, two attacks were made: the attack on the left, with the *Gardes Françaises*, *Gardes Suisses*, *Navarre*, *Piémont*, *Picardie*, *Estissac* and *Saint-Chamond;* and the attack on the right with *Normandie*, *Nerestang* and the five regiments from the Languedoc - *Rieux*, *Réaux*, *Moussoulens*, *Fabrègues* and *La Roquette*.

For the siege of Montpellier on 7 October, six infantry regiments of the Dauphiné arrived as reinforcements: *Tournon*, *Sault*, *Trémond*, *Calard*, *Labaume* and *Montchamp*.

On 20 October, the King entered Montpellier and *Picardie*, *Navarre* and *Normandie* were left there when he departed. *Champagne* was still at La Rochelle.

The newly raised infantry regiments were disbanded.

The Army of Annibal d'Estrées, Marquis de Coeuvres, in Italy, 1624

Included 10 companies of the *Normandie* regiment, *Vaubecourt* (a regiment from the Lorraine), six companies of the *d'Estrées* regiment and the three Swiss regiments of *Diesbach*, *Schmidt* and *Siders* of 1,000 men each.

The Army of Genoa, commanded by *Connétable* Lesdiguières, 4 March 1625

23,000 men, including:

The *Gendarmes* and *Chevaux-Légers Dauphinois*.

The infantry regiments *Sault*, *Chappes*, *Trémond*, *Bonnes*, *Blacon*, *Sancy*, *Tallard*, *Beaufort*, *La Grange*, and *Uxelles*.

The artillery had only two small cannon.

The Two Armies of the King at the Siege of La Rochelle, 1627

The first Army, commanded by Bassompierre, had *Monsieur's Gendarmes*, and six companies of *chevaux legers* and three companies of *Gardes Suisses*, the Fort Louis detachment of *Champagne*, *Navarre*, *Vaubecourt*, *Beaumont*, *Plessis-Praslin*, *Riberac*, *Chastelier-Barlot*.

The second army, that of the King, with the Duc d'Angoulême and *Maréchal* Schomberg. The *Gendarmes* of the *Maison du Roi*, and several companies of gendarmes, including the *Gendarmes* of the *Reine Mère* and the *Chevaux-Légers de la Garde*, the *Gardes Françaises*, *Gardes Suisses*, *Piémont*, *Rambures*, *Chappes*, *Estissac*, *La Meilleraye*,

Piedmont Campaign, February 1629 to liberate Casale and for the attack of the Pass de Suse on 6 March 1629: Richelieu reinforced the permanent corps and raised six new regiments in Dauphiné, Lyonnais and Provence. Three

French infantry and camp followers during the campaign in 1627. Jacques Callot, 1629–1631 (Rijksmuseum, Amsterdam)

armies were to invade the Piedmont: the King's Army, the Army of Provence (on the right) commanded by the Duc de Guise and *Maréchal* d'Estrées, and the Army of Lyons (on the left), which was to be commanded by Schomberg. But only the King's army, at the centre, would be assembled in time.

This Army had 3,000 cavalry and 23,000 infantry.

The cavalry comprised that of the King's Household, 12 companies of *chevaux legers*, including *Toiras, Canillac, Boissat, Cournon, Maugiron, Meigneux* and *Arnaud de Corbeville's carabins*. The *Gardes Françaises, Gardes Suisses, Navarre, Piémont, Sault, Estissac, Vaubecourt, La Grange* and *Riberac*, the *Chasseurs des Alpes*.

The Army of Lyons, drawn up at the beginning of April.

Comprised eight regiments (it was planned that it would have 10,000 men), the regiments of *Picardie, Normandie, Phalsbourg, Lestrange, Pérault, Montréal, Logères* and *Annibal*.

On 28 April 1629, the King left the army of *au delà les monts* to suppress a new uprising of Rohan in the Cévennes with,

The *Gardes du Corps, Gendarmes, Chevaux-Légers, Mousequetaires*, and six companies of *Gardes Françaises*.

He joined with the **Army of Languedoc**, commanded by the Duc de Guise and the Duc de Montmorency which included *Picardie* and four regiments from Languedoc.

The Prince de Condé and the Duc d'Epernon were at the head of the **Army of Guyenne** which was watching over Montauban.

The Army of Provence, commanded by *Maréchal* d'Estrées: it included 6,000 infantry (including the *Montréal* and *Lestrange* regiments) and 400 horses before the arrival of the reinforcement of 1,500 voluntary *chevaux-légers*. **On 19 May 1629, Richelieu and Bassompierre** arrived to reinforce the armies of the Languedoc and Provence with the *Gardes Françaises, Gardes Suisses, Champagne, Piémont, Rambures, Languedoc, Vaillac* and *Annonay*.

The rest of the infantry of the **Army of *Au delà les monts*** left behind in Suse under the command of de Créqui included: *Navarre, Estissac, Sault, Pompadour, La Bergerie, Vaubecourt* and one company of *Gardes Suisses*.

At the end of May 1629, the Army of *Au Delà les Monts*

(totalling 10,000 men)

The Army, commanded by Créqui, had remained in Suse against Charles-Emmanuel of Savoy. It was to be reinforced by the Languedoc Army. On 29 December 1629, Richelieu left for Suse with the Duc de Montmorency, the Cardinal de la Valette, *Maréchals* d'Estrées, Schomberg and Bassompierre and 10 companies of *Gardes Françaises* of 300 men each. Richelieu sent Bassompierre to raise 6,000 men in Switzerland. In addition to the six detached regiments at Casale, and two regiments guarding the Pas de Suse, Richelieu had 21,000 men from:

Cavalry regiment companies including *Gendarmes* and *Chevaux-Légers* of the *Maison du Roi, Créqui* and *Bassompierre Guards, Bussy Lauriéres, Boissac* and *Arnault* companies.

Infantry regiments *Gardes Françaises, Gardes Suisses, Navarre, Sault, Estissac* and *Mousquetaires du Roi*.

Richelieu's *Lieutenant Générals* were *Maréchals* Charles de Créqui, Jacques de Caumont, La Force and Henri de Schomberg. The *Maréchals de Camp* were Etienne d'Auriac, Jean de Toiras and the Marquis de Feuquières.

French soldiers carrying additional pikes and muskets during embarkation in 1627. Jacques Callot, 1629–1631. (Rijksmuseum, Amsterdam)

Conquest of Savoy, 1630

The army of Savoy with which Richelieu joined on 2 May 1630, had:

Eight companies of *Gardes Françaises*, and was commanded by the *Maréchals* de Créqui, de Bassompierre and de Châtillon. The *Maréchals de Bataille* were de Vignolles and du Hallier and the *intendants* were de Chastellet, Servien and d'Hemery (or d'Emery).

The army had 8,000 infantry and 2,000 cavalry before being joined by the 6,000 Swiss of Bassompierre. It included the

Gardes Suisses, Picardie, Champagne, Normandie, Rambures, Chastelier-Barlot, La Meilleraye, Plessis Besançon, Juigné, Autremont, Maillard, Montausier, Pizieux, Jauson, Verdun, Langeron, Chouain, the garrisons of the Dauphiné, and 18 *cornettes* of cavalry. At the Battle of Séez on 6 July 1630, *Gardes Françaises, Picardie, La Meilleraye, Plessis Besançon, Juigné,* 1,500 Swiss and *cornettes* of cavalry were present under Châtillon.

On Saint Ambrosius' Day, 10 July 1630: the infantry was on the right and the cavalry on the left; the rearguard of the army, which was to be engaged, was composed of 4,000 infantry: four companies of *Gardes Françaises, Picardie, Normandie, Rambures*, and 320 horse: 80 *Gendarmes* and 80 *Chevaux-légers* of the *Maison du Roi*, the *gendarme* companies of *Monsieur* and the *Comte de Noailles. Picardie* was on the right and the *Gardes Françaises* on the left, with *Normandie* and *Rambures* in the second line. On the left of the *Gardes* were four cavalry companies, each forming a squadron of 80 cavalry, including the *Gendarmes* of the King and Noailles.

The Army of the King in Piedmont under the Duc de Montmorency, commanded by *Maréchal* de La Force, Battle of Carignan, 6 August 1630

Maréchals de Bataille: Feuquières and Villeroy

The cavalry was composed of: half of the King's *Gendarmes*, the King's *chevaux-légers*, six *gendarme* companies: *Monsieur, Montmorency, Alaincourt, Ventadour, Créqui, Noailles.* 34 *chevaux-légers* companies: *Monsieur, Mestre de Camp, Condé, Montmorency, Monceaux, Hocquincourt, Roches, Saint-Trivier, Montgon, Marcillac, La Borde, Lignières, Busay, Laurière, Arbourse, la Roque-Massebaut, Canillac, Morconnay, Créqui, Dizimieux, Gerboulle, Roche-Baritaut, Lesche, Montastruc, la Flocellière, Cluis, Aubais, Bandol, Saint-Julien, Beauregard, du Hallier, Luserna* and *Philippes.* 12 *carabin* companies: *Arnault, de Corbeville, Maubuisson, Autichamp, Saint-Angolin, Bellot, Saint-Fargeau, Conflans, Cendre, Cavois, Biderau, Saint-Martin*, and *Evreux.*

The infantry had 29 regiments: the *Gardes Françaises, Champagne, Piémont, Picardie, Navarre, Normandie, Phalsbourg, La Meilleraye, Rambures, La Rochefoucault, Sault, Plessis-Praslin, La Bergerie, Vaillac, la Tour, Longjumeau, Bussy, Blacons, Goudrin, Vaubecourt, Languedoc, Annibal, Perrault, Jeanson, Saint-Forgeux, Mirepoix, Naves*, the Swiss of *Ariac* and the Liégeois of *La Hocquerie.*

The army of Toiras in Casale had three infantry regiments: *Ribérac, Pompadour, La Grange*, and six companies of *chevaux legers*: *Toiras, Canillac, Brissac, Courvoux, Maugiron, Migneux.*

The Army of *Maréchal* de Schomberg in Piedmont, 1630, from 17 August 1630

Comprised, for the cavalry: a detachment of the *Maison du Roi*: *Gendarmes* and *Chevaux-Légers*, the Duc de Bellegarde's *Gendarmes* and seven companies of *chevaux-légers*: *Bligny, La Palice, Schomberg, Chambray, Mollinet, La Chapelle-Baloue* and *Faucon*

For the infantry: six companies of the *Gardes Françaises*, eight companies of the *Gardes Suisses* and 20 regiments: *Aiguebonne, Saint-Paul, Plessis Joigny, Grancey, Lecques, Longueval, Maugiron, Conches, du Pallais, Chabrilles, Urfé, Sautour, Turenne, Croisille, Montréal, Thoré, Vercoiran, Soyécourt, Crussol* and *Danti*. Most of these regiments were new levies.

The army of *Maréchal* de Marillac, sent as reinforcements for Schomberg in Piedmont, October 1630

Cavalry: three companies of *gendarmes* – de Chaulnes, Effiat, Tavannes, 450 nobles of the *ban* and *arrière-ban* of Dauphiné, 22 companies of *chevaux-légers*: *Effiat, Bonneval, Linars, La Ferté-Senneterre, du Terrail, du Mascheix, Feugly, Chaulnes, Sesseval, Lignières, Allamont, Beaucourt, Boufflers, Verneuil, Thouars, Marillac, Marinville, Boury, Lignon, du Jeu, Quinçay, Commarin.*

Infantry: four companies from *Champagne* and 14 regiments: *Chappes, Bonnivet, Brazey, Houdancourt, Espagny, Hocquincourt, Piles, Beaulieu, Persac, Peslières, Tonneins, Nicey, Magland, Fiémarcon.*

On 17 October, the cavalry companies were grouped together in squadrons of 100 to 150 men and the regiments were divided into battalions of 1,000 men (three brigades of six battalions of 1,000 men).

The Army of Schomberg and Marillac

(18,000 infantry and 3,750 horses)

was divided into three brigades (the advance guard commanded by Schomberg, the main body by Marillac and the rearguard commanded by La Force) of six battalions and six squadrons. One of the three brigades was reinforced by the battalions of the *Gardes Françaises* and the *Gardes Suisses,* and also by the 450 nobles of the Dauphiné.

The army had four cannon.

At Casale on 26 October 1630: the three brigades were placed side by side; on the right, La Force's advance guard, the main body in the middle, led by Schomberg, and the rearguard under Merillac. In the first line were seven battalions, each with a detachment of 200 *enfants perdus* 100 paces to the front, sufficiently spaced to allow the cavalry of the second line to pass through the intervals. On the wings were two squadrons covered in front and on the flanks by five *carabin* companies. 100 paces behind, in the second line, were seven battalions between which were placed eight squadrons. At 200 paces was the third line, with six battalions in the centre and 12 squadrons on the wings. At 50 paces behind was a reserve of three squadrons. Between the second and third lines was a squadron of 130 *Gendarmes* with the *Maréchal* de Schomberg. A little in front, in the right-hand brigade, *Maréchal* de La Force led the *Maison du Roi*. At the same distance in the left-hand brigade, *Maréchal* de Marillac led his company of *chevaux-légers*. Toiras, in the citadel, was ready to intervene with 600 men and 250 horse.

The army left in France by Marillac had five companies of gendarmes: *Reine Mère, Reine Anne, Elbeuf, Longueville, Matignon,* nine companies of *chevaux-légers: Rouville, Mèche, Vandy, du Hamel, Grandpré, Vaubecourt, la Valette, Crespy, la Bescherelle,* three companies of *carabins: Pré, Salles, Fontenay,* six companies of Liégeois (60 men in each). 11 infantry regiments: *Menillet, Castel Bayart, Sy, Nubécourt, Cignolles, Nettancourt, Atichy, Bettancourt, Renel, Dauphin, Hostel,* and the garrison regiments of *Marillac* in Verdun, *du Kergrist* in Calais, *Nevoy* in Boulogne and Ardres, *Cerny* in La Fère and Saint-Quentin).

Soldiers during the
campaign. Stefano della Bella
(Rijksmuseum, Amsterdam)

The Army of *Maréchal* de La Force, 17 September 1634[3]

4,000 cavalry and 10,000 infantry

Cavalry of the army's vanguard: The *compagnie colonelle*, commanded by Monsieur de Bouchavane, the *Mestre de Camp*'s company, the Scottish company, the company of M. de Blagny colonel, M. de Lorriere's company, the company of M. des Roches-Bariteaut, the company of M. de la Fraizeliere. These seven companies of cavalry were also joined by seven companies of carabins: the company of Monsieur Arnault, Maître de Camp, currently Governor for the King in the town of Philippsburg in Germany, M. d'Arrancourt's company, M. du Prés company, the company of M. de Courval, the company of the Marquis de Villars, the company of M. de Byderan, the company of M. de la Motte.

Infantry of the Vanguard: the regiment of *Picardie*, commanded by the Comte de Barraut, the regiment of *Navarre*, commanded by M. de S. Simon the elder, the regiment *Varenne*, the regiment *Vaubecourt*, the regiment *Rambure*, the regiment *Alincourt*, the regiment *Villeroy*.

Cavalry: The company of the King's chevaux-légers, consisting of 200 gentlemen, commanded by M. de Contenant; the Queen's company; the Prince's company; the company of M. le Cardinal-Duc de Richelieu, commanded by M. de Mouy; the company of M. le *Maréchal* de La Force, commanded by M. le Marquis de Bosse his grandson; the company of the Baron de la Cressonière; the company of M. de La Ferté de Sainneterre; the company of the late Chevalier de Sainneterre; the company of the Marquis de Praslin; the company of M. le Comte de Vattimont; the company of the

---

3   Anon., *L'Ordre du Départ et Acheminement de l'Armée du Roy, vers l'Allemagne, sous la Conduite de Monsieur le Maréchal de La Force, de Vic le 17 de Septembre 1634, Avec le Nombre des Compagnies de Cavalerie, et Régiments d'Infanterie de Ladite Armée* (Lyon: Jean Jacquemeton, 1634).

Count of Vientail; the company of the Marquis de la Valette; the company of the Marquis du Terrail; the company of the count of Pouillé; the company of M. Comte de M. de Beauveau; the company of the Marquis de Fourille; the company of M. le Comte de Dampierre.

Infantry: The regiment of *Normandie*, the regiment of *Piémont*, the regiment of M. de Tonnains, the regiment of M. d'Auquincourt, the Marquis d'Effiat's regiment, the regiment of the Marquis de Mailleraix, the regiment of M. de Aunay, the regiment of M. de Nettencourt, M. du Plessis Joygny's regiment, M. de S. Etienne's regiment, M. de Castelmoron's regiment, M. de Bettencourt's regiment.

Cavalry of the rearguard: The company of M. de la Blocquerie Liégeois, the company of M. de Miches Liégeois, the company of M. le Comte de Guiche, the company of the Marquis de S. Chaumont, the company of the Marquis de Villeroy, the company of M. de Fequiere, present Ambassador for the King in Germany, the company of M. le Premier, the company of M. le Commandeur de la Porte, the company of the Marquis de la Maillerais.

Infantry of the rearguard: Colonel Elbron's regiment (Scots), the regiment of M. de Chasteliers-Barlot, the regiment of Baron de Montozier's, the regiment of Baron de S. Hilaire, the regiment of M. de la Boulley, the regiment of M. le Vicomte de Turenne.

Artillery: 27 large cannon and 34 medium cannon, 800 munitions wagons and carts, 1,600 wagons and carts loaded with food and all the necessaries.

The Battle of Avins, 20 May 1635, Commanded by *Maréchals* Châtillon and Brézé[4]

The Army numbered more than 6,000 to 7,000 cavalry and 20,000 infantry according to Pontis. 6,000 cavalry, excluding officers and valets, and 22,000 infantry in two brigades of 3,000 cavalry and 11,000 infantry, and 24 cannons according to Puysegur. Melchior Tavernier's map shows 30 cavalry squadrons, each of which was usually made up of two cavalry companies, and 22 infantry regiments, each consisting of one battalion. There were exactly 52 companies of cavalry forming 30 squadrons, including one company of the *Gendarmes de Monsieur*, and four companies of *carabins* (*Arnaud, Bideran, Montbuisson* and *Villars*).

The French cavalry and infantry were deployed in three lines, the third line consisting of the reserve of Chastelier-Barlot. The infantry, in the centre, comprised the regiments of *Champagne, Plessis-Praslin, Longueval, Genlis, Lusignan, Maréchal Brézé, La Mothe-Houdencourt, La Meilleraye, Saucourt* and *Piémont* in the front line, and the battalions of *Sy, Chuin, Coursan, Calonge, Bellebrune, Castelnau, Polignac* and *Migneux* in the second line. The infantry reserve, in the third line, comprised the regiments of *Grancey, Menilserran, Monmège* (or *Montmège*) and *Brézé*, totalling around 4,000 men. The cavalry left wing consisted of two lines of five squadrons, while the right wing had 11 squadrons although also in two lines. One cavalry squadron,

---

4   Stéphane Thion, *La Bataille d'Avins, 20 Mai 1635* (Auzielle: LRT Editions, 2011), pp.30–31.

made up of the *Gendarmes de Monsieur* and the *Chevaux-Légers de Monsieur* was in the centre of the second line, while the reserve was composed of eight additional squadrons totalling 800 to 1,000 cavalry.

Only seven artillery pieces are shown on Tavernier's plan, whereas the *Mercure Français* stated that there were 12.

The Army of Piedmont, commanded by *Lieutenant Général* Créquy, June 1635[5]

The *gendarme* companies of Créquy and Alincourt (100 gendarmes each).
The companies of *Chevaux-Légers* of *Boissac, Beauvais, Plésian, Valavoire, la Marcouse, Cornu* and *Saint-Georges*, and a squadron of *Savoie*.
Four companies of the *Dragons de Bouillac*.

The infantry consisted of the regiments of *Sault, Montausier, Bourg-de-l'Espinasse, Aiguebonne, Piles, Mane, Phalsbourg, Ferron* and *Vernatelle, Alincourt* (*Lyonnais*) and *Maugiron* (*Auvergne*).

To this total must be added the Duke of Parma's infantry and cavalry. Créquy was *Lieutenant Général* and Varennes *Maréchal de Camp*.

The Army of Duc de Rohan in the Valtelline, 14 July 1635[6]

(540 cavalry and 13,100 infantry).

Infantry regiments of *Montauzier* (1,200 men), *Canisy* (1,200 men), *Frezelière* (1,200 men), *Dubié* (1,200 men), *Serre* (1,200 men), *Serny* (1,200 men), *Vandy* (1,200 men), *Chauvestin* (1,000 men), *Salis* (1,000 men), *Bruker* (1,000 men), two companies of *Stopa & Genety* (200 men), Swiss (1,500 men); *chevaux-légers* companies of *Miche* (90 men), *Jours* (90 men), *Saint-André* (90 men), *La Vilette* (90 men), *Villeneuve* (90 men), *Canillac* (90 men).

The Army of Duc de Rohan in the Valtelline, August to October 1635

Cavalry: 6 *cornettes* including *Rohan*'s mounted musketeer company and the *Chevaux-Légers* regiments of *Canillac, Montbrun, Miche, Saint-André, Amanty,* and *Villette* companies – 400 men. After this, the Duc de Rohan only mentions three squadrons: *Canillac, Saint-André* and *Villeneuve*.

Infantry: 11 French regiments, *Lèques, Montausier, du Landé, Roquelaure, Serres, Cerny, Vandy, la Frezelière, Canisy, Biès, Neuville le Grand*, 2 Swiss regiments, *Schmidt, Greder,* and 7 Grisons regiments, *Schawenstein, Molina, Salis, Brugger, Jenatsch, Guler, Florin*.

5   Ludovic de Contenson, *Mémoires du Comte de Souvigny, Lieutenant-Général des Armées du Roi* (Paris: Renouard, 1906), tome I (1613–1638), p.289.
6   Richelieu, *Lettres, Instructions Diplomatiques et Papiers d'Etat du Cardinal de Richelieu,* tome V (1635–1637), pp.115–116.

The Army of La Sarre joined the Swedes of Bernhard of Saxe-Weimar in Mentz, September 1635.

On 23 September 1635 (in Saverne), the Army of La Sarre totalled 6,000 infantry and 5,000 cavalry.

Army of La Sarre in October 1635 under *Maréchal* de la Valette

(with two *Maréchals de Camp*, Henri de la Tour d'Auvergne, Vicomte de Turenne and Antoine de Grammont, Comte de Guiche)

1,700 cavalry in 11 regiments: *Cardinal-Duc, Enghien, Sourdis, La Meilleraye, Matignon, Guiche, Sauveboeuf, le Ferron, Nanteuil, Chaulnes, Treillis* plus the cavalry reserve of four companies of *Gendarmes* and *Chevaux-légers* of the King and Cardinal Richelieu.

Infantry Regiments: 12 companies of the *Gardes Françaises, Gardes Suisses, Picardie, Navarre, Normandie, Vaubecourt* (*petit vieux*), *Turenne, Nettancourt* and three German regiments.

The French Army of the Prince de Condé, Siege of Dôle, May 1636[7]

Cavalry regiments of: *La Meilleraye* (Hungarian), *Gassion, Rantzau* (German) and a Swedish regiment.

Infantry regiments of: *Picardie, Navarre, Conti, Enghien, Noailles, Tonneins* and *Nanteuil.*

The Army of Louis de Bourbon, Comte de Soissons, in Champagne, August 1636

Gardes Françaises, Garde Suisses, La Marine, Piémont, Champagne, Vaubecourt, Saintonge, la Roche-Giffart, Charost and *Bellefonds.*

The regiments of *la Trémoille, de Brézé, de Poitou, d'Anjou, d'Avenoux, du Mesnil* and *de Landieu* were in reserve at Senlis.

The Army of *Au Delà des Monts* (Piedmont), commanded by *Maréchal* de Créqui, 1636 (16,000 infantry and 1,300 cavalry)

Includes the *Gendarmes d'Alincourt*, the *chevaux léger* regiments of *Nerestang, Cauvisson, Lorraine, Marolles, Bois David, le Tour, La Ferté, Chamblai, chevaux-légers* companies of *Moissac* and *Palluau Clérambault*; *carabins* companies of *Corvoux, Venterol* and *Saint-Benoît.*

Dragons de Bouillac.

Infantry: the regiments of *Sault, Auvergne* (formerly *Maugiron*), *Lyonnais* (formerly *Alincourt*), *Pierregourde, Florinville, Roquefeuille,* and *Henrichemont.*

---

7   *Mercure François* ès Années 1635, 1636, 1637, vol.21, p.131.

The Army of the Comte d'Harcourt and *Maréchal* de Vitry in Cannes, November 1636 to May 1637[8]

Army assembled to capture the islands of Sainte-Marguerite and Saint-Honorat

Cavalry: two companies of *Gardes* – the compagnies de *Gardes d'Harcourt* and *Vitry*

Infantry: regiments of *Vitry, la Tour, Castreville, Saint-André, Roussillon, Galères, Isles, Vaillac, Cornusson* and *Clermont*.

The Army of the Duc d'Halluin in Languedoc to Relieve Leucate, 24 September 1637

Cavalry, 900 men made up of: *Halluin Garde* (100 horse), *Gendarmes d'Halluin* (100 horse), *Gendarmes de Cramail* (50 horse), *Chevaux-Légers* companies of *Boissac, Espondeilhan, Mirepoix, Montsoulins, Mauléon* (each of 50 *maîtres*), 200 'gentlemen' from the Languedoc.

Dragons de Toulouse and the *carabins* of *Saussan, Sainte-Croix* and *Malves*.

Infantry, seven regiments (*Languedoc, la Tour, Castellan, Serignan, Saint-André, Saint-Aunès, Vitry*), the battalions of *milices* of *Montpellier, Nîmes, Carcassonne, Narbonne, Béziers, Castres, Mirepoix, la Jonquière, Merville* and *Vaillac* for the infantry (10,000 men);

The Army of Champagne of *Maréchal* de Châtillon, 11 April 1637 [9]

(14,000 foot and 5,590 cavalry)

Gendarme companies of *Monsieur* (150 men), *Angoulême* (60 men), *Saint-Geran* (80 men), *Nancé* (60 men), *La Trimouïlle* (100 men), *Tresmes* (60 men), *Roches-Baritaud* (100 men); 39 *chevaux-légers* companies (60 men each), *Monsieur, Mestre de Camp, Taurieres, La Force, Rouville, Brouïlly, La Roque-Massebaut, La Melleraye, La Chapelle-Balou, Bourry, Auzonville, Vatimont, Aubaye, Roches-Baritaud, Viantez, Saint-Germain-Beaupré, Beauveau, Estange, Cressonnière, Pontinière, Montbas, Mazolles, Brezolles, Saint-Aignan, Chemeraut, Pont de Courlay, Coaslin, Rochefort, Plissonières, Gesvres, La Courbe, Dromesnil, Bouflers, Vieupont, Castres, Ambleville, Pibrac, Nonz* (30 men) and *Totrigny* (30 men); foreign cavalry regiments of *Egenfeld* (200 men in two companies), *Gassion* (1,000 in 14 companies), *Carquois* (250 men in five companies), *Treilly* (250 men in five companies), *Grand Maître* or *La Meilleraye* (Hungarian, 150 men in three companies), *Espenan* (Hungarian, 250 men in five companies).

Dragons de Gassion (200 men in two companies); *carabins* companies (50 men each) of *Arnault, Maubuisson, Bouviers, Chaufroy, Belzaise, Monterbaut* and *Saint-Martin*.

---

8   *Mercure François* ès Années 1635, 1636, 1637, vol.21, pp.319–322.
9   Du Bouchet, Jean, *Preuves de l'Histoire de l'Illustre Maison de Coligny* (Paris: Jean Dupuis, 1662), pp.783–784.

Infantry regiments of *Champagne* (1,200 in 20 companies), *Piémont* (1,200 in 20 companies), *Vaubecourt* (1,200 in 20 companies), *Effiat* (1,200 in 20 companies), *Saint-Luc* (1,200 in 20 companies), *Plessis-Praslin* (1,200 in 20 companies), *Bourdonné* (1,200 in 20 companies), *Bellebrune* (1,200 in 20 companies), *Beausse* (1,200 in 20 companies), *Bussy-Lamet* (1,200 in 20 companies), *Escho* (600 in 10 companies), *Nangis* (600 in 10 companies), *La Rochette* (800 in 10 companies).

The Army of Lorraine of *Maréchal* de Châtillon, 22 May 1637 [10]

(10,600 foot and 4,560 cavalry)

Gendarme companies of *Vaubecourt* (80 men) and *Luxembourg* (80 men); 34 *Chevaux-Légers* companies (60 men each), *La Colonelle, Mestre de Camp, Angoulême, Du Hamel, La Blocquerie, Polié, La Pierre, Harambures, Lignon, Saint-Mesgrin, Sirot, Brison, Heilly, Boiorusin, Vignory, Sainte-Maure, La Trousse, Saint-Chamond, Du Tour, De Blin, Orgeru, La Clavière, Arquien, Heucourt, Joüy, La Borde, Ayen, La Lande, La Noüe, Andresi, Roquelaure, Chemeraut & Rozieres*; seven *carabins* companies (of 50 men each); *Carnet, Phenix, La Forêt le Borgne, Mansou, Comble, Viners & Nilly*; four foreign cavalry regiments of *Batilly* (300 men in five companies), *Streff* (420 men in six companies), *Hums* (420 men in six companies) and *Bouillon* (560 men in eight companies) and four companies of *Cravattes* (Croats).

Infantry regiments of *Rambures* (1,200 men in 20 companies), *Cy* (1,200 men in 20 companies), *Turenne* (1,200 men in 20 companies), *Bellebrune* (1,200 men in 20 companies), *Busy-Lamet* (1,200 men in 20 companies), *Beausse* (1,200 men in 20 companies), *Hebron* (1,500 men in 20 companies), *La Bloquerie* (1,500 men in 20 companies), *Vernancourt* (800 men in 12 companies), and *Batilly* (800 men in 12 companies).

The Army of *Maréchal* de Châtillon, 20 April 1638[11]

(20,270 foot and 6,500 cavalry)

Cavalry: *Gendarmes* companies of *Monsieur* (150 men), *Vaubecourt* (80 men) and *Luxembourg* (70 men); *Chevaux-Légers* regiments of *Praslin* (550 men in seven companies including one of *carabins*), *La Ferté-Senneterre* (520 men in seven companies including one of *carabins*), *Aumont* (350 men in six companies including one of *carabins*), *Varimont* (520 men in seven companies including one of *carabins*), *Lignon* (520 men in seven companies including one of *carabins*), *Hecourt* (520 men in seven companies including one of *carabins*), *La Ferté-Imbaud* (520 men in seven companies including one of *carabins*), five foreign cavalry regiments of *Gassion* (1,400 men in 14 companies).

---

10   Du Bouchet, Jean, *Preuves de l'Histoire de l'Illustre Maison de Coligny*, (Paris: Jean Dupuis, 1662), pp.788–789.
11   Du Bouchet, Jean, *Preuves de l'Histoire de l'Illustre Maison de Coligny*, (Paris: Jean Dupuis, 1662), pp.887–888.

Dragoons: *Dragons de Gassion* (200 men in two companies), *Egenfeld* (150 men in two companies), *Hums* (300 men) and *Sillart* (300 men); three *carabins* companies of *Rouvière, Duplu* and *Du Clou* (50 men each).

Infantry regiments of *Gardes Françaises* (1,500 men in 10 companies), *Gardes Suisses* (570 men in three companies), *Navarre* (1,500 men in 20 companies), *Champagne* (1,200 men in 20 companies), *Turenne* (1,500 men in 20 companies), *Douglas Hebron* (2,000 men in 20 companies), *Bellenave* (1,200 men in 20 companies), *Bellefonds* (1,200 men in 20 companies), *Courtaumer*(1,500 men in 20 companies), *Beausse* (1,200 men in 20 companies), *Perigord* (1,200 men in 20 companies), *Langeron* (1,500 men in 20 companies), *Bellebrune* (1,200 men in 20 companies), *Genlis* (1,200 men in 20 companies), *Molondin Suisses* (2,000 men in 25 companies).

The Army of *Maréchal* de Châtillon, 27 May 1639[12]

Gendarmes de Monsieur and *Gendarmes de Guiche; Chevaux-Légers* regiments of *Alais* (11 companies including two companies of *carabins*), *Guiche* (nine companies including two companies of *carabins*), *La Ferté-Imbaut* (eight companies including two companies of *carabins*), *Brouilly* (nine companies including two companies of *carabins*), *Gesvres* (eight companies including two companies of *carabins*), *Cursol* (six companies*), *Baron d'Egenfeld, Fittingost, L'Eschelle, Sirot* (three companies) and *Rucon* and Rucon foreign cavalry regiments, *Recy* and *Monsou carabins* companies.

Infantry regiments of *Gardes Françaises* (10 companies), *Brezé, Genlis, Roncheroles, La Saludie, Verveins, Mignieux, Le Vidame, Aubeterre, Biscaras* and *Longueval*.

The Army of *Maréchal* de Châtillon, 9 June 1639[13]

(8,100 foot and 4,092 cavalry)

Gendarmes de Monsieur (166 gendarmes), *Gendarmes de Guiche; Chevaux-Légers* regiments of *Alais* (699 men in 12 companies including one of *carabins*), *La Ferté-Imbaut* (533 men in eight companies including two companies of *carabins*), *Guiche* (370 men in eight companies including one company of *carabins*), *Cursol* (200 unarmed troopers, the recruits not having arrived), *Brouilly* (267 men in seven companies), *Gesvres* (438 men in eight companies including two companies of *carabins*), *carabins* companies of *Recy* (50 men) and *Monsou* (55 men). Foreign cavalry regiments of *Egenfeld* (208 men in two companies), *Bussy-Helmoru* (294 men in five companies), *L'Eschelle* (250 men in six companies), *Sirot* (167 men in three companies), *Fittingost* (400 men in six companies).

Infantry regiments of *Gardes Françaises* (1,200 men in 10 companies, including 100 musketeers sent to Rocroy), *Gardes Suisses* (400 men in 3

---

12   Du Bouchet, *Preuves de l'Histoire de l'Illustre Maison de Coligny*, (Paris: Jean Dupuis, 1662), pp.979–980.
13   Du Bouchet, *Preuves de l'Histoire de l'Illustre Maison de Coligny*, (Paris: Jean Dupuis, 1662), pp.983–985.

companies), *Brezé* (1,100 men in 20 companies), *La Saludie,* (600 men in 11 companies), *Le Vidame* (700 men in 19 companies), *Longueval* (750 men in 18 companies), *Mignieux* (700 men in 17 companies, including the 50 sent to Rocroy), *Monmège* (250 men), *Verveins* (900 men in 20 companies, including 200 at Cateau and 50 at Rocroy), *Roncheroles* (800 men in 19 companies), *Genlis* (700 men in 19 companies), 150 men of *Molondin*'s companies 'being expected to join this corps.'

Army of Henri de Lorraine, Comte d'Armagnac, Brienne and Harcourt (replacing Cardinal de la Valette), in Piedmont, October 1639 to July 1640

9,500 men (6,000 infantry and 3,500 horses); Plessis-Praslin commanded the infantry, and Turenne the cavalry: Infantry regiments of *Gardes Françaises* (two battalions), *Gardes Suisses* (one battalion), *Auvergne, Lyonnais, Nerestang, Alincourt, Florinville, Villandry, Turenne, Plessis-Praslin, Roussillon, Tavannes, Villandry, La Mothe-Houdencourt, la Valette* and the *Couvonges* regiment (in the citadel of Turin); *gendarme* squadrons of *Beauregard Champoux, Arzillières* and *Condé, chevaux-légers* regiments of *Enghien, Marsin, du Terrail, Beauregard, la Luzerne, la Valette, Souvré, Montpezat, la Rochette, Lesdiguières, Villeneuve, Tavannes, Saint-André,* squadrons of *Ligondès* and *Dizimieux,* the non-regimented company of *Sarroty, carabins* of *Savoie* and dragoons.

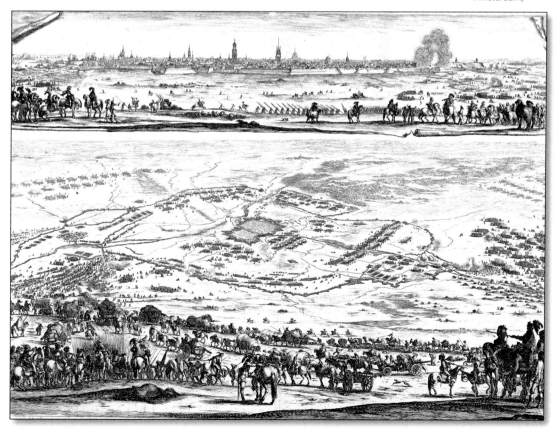

The French Army besieging Spanish-held Arras, 13 June to 9 August 1640. Stefano della Bella (Rijksmuseum, Amsterdam)

Army of Guébriant from 1639 to 1642[14]

The cavalry consisted of Rosen's *Chevaux Léger* and *Dragons* regiments, Streef, Eggenfeld, Batilly, Humes, Lee, Zillard, Boillon, Watronville, Nassau, Muller, Schack, Vaubecourt, Taupadel, Forbus and Trefski regiments.

In addition to Weimarian infantry regiments (*Schmidberg, Forbus, 'Black', 'Yellow', 'Red',* and *'Scottish'* regiments), this Army included four French infantry regiments (*Guébriant, Montausier, Melun* and *Nettancourt).*

The artillery had 12 guns.

The Army at Rocroi, 19 May 1643[15]

Commanded by Louis de Bourbon, Duc d'Enghien with *Maréchal* de l'Hôpital as *Lieutenant Géneral* and three *Maréchals de Camp* (Jean de Gassion, *Mestre de Camp* general of the light cavalry, the Marquis de La Ferté-Senneterre and the Baron de Sirot)

7,000 cavalry in 24 regiments and seven companies, forming 32 squadrons: six *gendarme* companies, *Gardes d'Enghien* company, the *Fusiliers du Roi* regiment (*dragons*), 16 regiments of *chevaux legers: Cardinal-Duc, Mestre de Camp Général, Lenoncourt, Coislin, Sully, Roquelaure, Menneville, La Clavière, La Ferté, Guiche, Marolles, Heudicourt, Gesvres, Aubeterre, Harcourt, Charost*; *Sirot* (Hungarian), the regiment of *Beauveau* (Liège), the regiments *Zillard, Leschelle* and *Von Bergh* (German), regiments *Raab* and *Schack* (Croat).

16,000 infantry in 21 regiments: the *Gardes Ecossaises*, the regiments *Picardie, Piémont* and *La Marine* (vieux corps), the regiments *Rambures* and *Persan* (*petits vieux*), the regiments *Molondin, Watteville* and *Roll* (Swiss), 12 temporary regiments – *Bourdonné, Biscara, Vervins, La Prée, Vidame d'Amiens, Langeron, Brézé, Bussy, Guiche, Harcourt, Aubeterre* and *Gesvres* and eight *Compagnies Royales*.

Artillery: 12 cannon.

The infantry was formed at the centre in 15 battalions in a chequer board pattern in two lines, the Swiss regiment *Molondin* forming two battalions. The 12 pieces of artillery covered the front. The cavalry was formed on the wings, 15 squadrons in two lines on the right, with interspersed musketeer *manches* ('commanded shot') and 13 squadrons in two lines on the left, also with interspersed musketeer *manches*. Behind was a reserve composed of the Hungarian Cavalry regiment, six companies of *Gendarmes*, three infantry regiments and the *Compagnies Royales*.

14   Laboureur, Jean, *Histoire du Mareschal de Guébriant* (Paris: Louis Billaine, 1676), pp.164–165.
15   Stéphane Thion, *Rocroi 1643, La Victoire de la Jeunesse* (Paris: Histoire & Collections, 2013), pp.23–29.

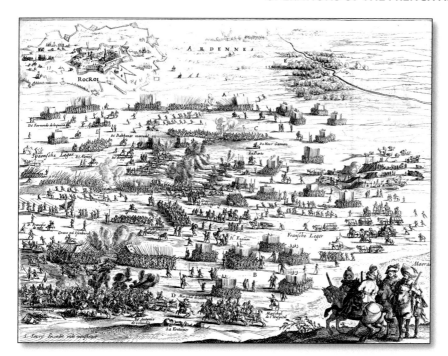

Battle of Rocroi in 1643. Attributed to Salomon Savery (Rijksmuseum, Amsterdam)

French soldiers carrying Spanish colours captured at the Battle of Rocroi in 1643. Nicolas Cochin, 1643 (Rijksmuseum, Amsterdam)

The Army of France commanded by the Duc d'Enghien, including the Army of Turenne, at the Battle of Friburg, 3 and 5 August 1644

The army was formed in three lines, Turenne on the right with the Weimarians, the infantry of the French Army in the centre, and the cavalry of *Maréchal de Grammont* on the left wing. The infantry regiments of the Duc d'Enghien (*Persan, Enghien, Conti, Mazarin Français, Mazarin Italien, Le Havre, Guiche, Desmarets, Fabert*) were formed in three brigades. Turenne's infantry was made up of the French regiments *Montausier, Mézières, La Couronne, Aubeterre, du Tot* and the Weimarian regiments of *Hattstein, Bernhold* and *Schmidtberg.*

The cavalry was composed of the *Gardes d'Enghien* and *Guiche,* the *gendarme* companies of *Enghien, Condé, Conti* and *Guiche,* the cavalry regiments *Enghien, Guiche, Cardinal Mazarin, Mazarin Français, L'Eschelle* and *Beauveau* (both from Liège), *Turenne,* and the Weimarian regiments *Alt Rosen, Fleckenstein, Berg, Baden, Wittgenstein, Russwurm, Neu Rosen, Scharfenstein, Erlach, Tracy, Guébriant, Taupadel* and *Kanoffsky.*

Turenne's German Army, 31 March 1645 (6,000 foot, 5,000 horse and 11 cannon):

French infantry regiments of *Turenne, Mazarin Italien* and *Oysonville,* Weimarian infantry regiments of *Schmidtberg* and *Truchsess.* French cavalry regiments of *Oysonville, Duras, Tracy* and *Turenne,* Liège cavalry regiment of *Beauveau* and Weimarian cavalry regiments of *Betz, Alt Rosen, Öhm, Wittgenstein, Fleckenstein, Taupadel,* and *Baden.*

Count du Plessis's army at the Siege of Rosas, April-May 1645[16] (5,400 infantry and 760 horse).

Generals: M. le Comte du Plessis (who was made a *Maréchal de France* after taking the town); four *Maréchal de Camp*: MM de Vaubecourt, d'Huxelles and de Saint-Mégrin *Maréchal de Bataille*: MM de Saint-Paul, d'Alvimar and Souvigny.

13 Infantry regiments: *Normandie, Sault, Vaubecourt, Plessis-Praslin, Lyonnais, Huxelles, Roussillon, Guyenne, Tavannes, Calvières, Saint-Paul, Chaussoy, Praroman Suisse* – with 415 men per regiment;

3 cavalry regiments: *Boissac, Feuquières,* and *Gault* and two *Gendarmes* companies *la Reine* and *Schonberg.*

The French Army at Alerheim (1645) (Public Domain)

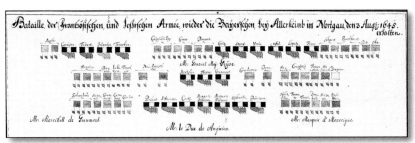

The French Army of d'Enghien and Turenne at Alerheim (or Nördlingen), 3 August 1645:

Right wing: (*Maréchal* de Grammont) 16 French cavalry squadrons: *Gardes de Grammont, Gardes d'Enghien, Carabins,* and *Mazarin, Enghien, Grammont, Chambre, Boury, La Clavière, Marchin, Neu Rosen* regiments, and two infantry regiments, *Wall* (Irish) and *Fabert.*

Centre: (Comte de Marsin) 10 infantry battalions from France, Germany and Liège: *Mazarin Français, Mazarin Italien, Oysonville, Conti, Enghien, Persan, Grammont, Montausier, Le Havre* and *Truchsess* (Weimarian), plus the *Gendarmes* and *Chevaux-Légers* of *la Reine Mère.* 27 pieces of artillery were spread along the front.

Left wing: (Turenne) 12 French and Weimarian regiments: *Cardinal Mazarin, Turenne, Oysonville, Beauveau, Russwurm, Taupadel, Tracy, Neu*

---

16   Ludovic de Contenson, *Mémoires du Comte de Souvigny, Lieutenant-Général des Armées du Roi* (Paris: Renouard, 1906), Tome II (1639–1659), pp.138–139.

Rosen, Alt Rosen, Fleckenstein and *Kanoffsky*. In the second line were six Hessian regiments: *Betz, Rauchaupt, Schwert, Groote, Geiss, Beaucourt*, and two Weimarian regiments: *Öhm* and *Betz,* plus six Hessian battalions: *Franc, Lopetz, Uffel, Vrede, Staufer, Kotz.*

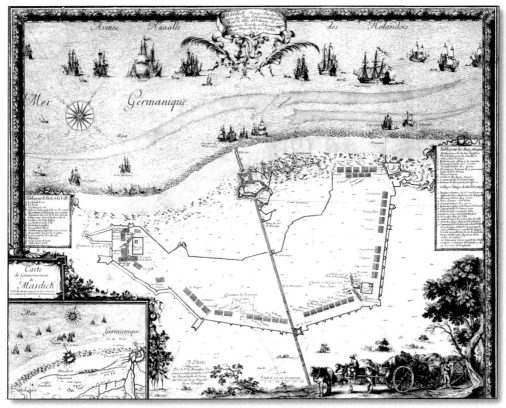

French Army besieging Spanish-held Mardick (Mardyck), 23 June to 10 July 1645. (Riksarkivet, Stockholm)

The Army of the Prince de Condé at the Battle of Lens, 20 August 1648

In Picardie, Condé had 16,000 men and 18 cannon, of which 4,000 Weimarians remained in French service commanded by Erlach. Of the 29 infantry regiments of the army (22 French and seven foreign), 11 were in garrison in different towns and cities. Some infantry regiments, which mustered 1,500 men at the beginning of the campaign, had no more than 300 men. At Lens, the army was composed of 12 infantry battalions and 45 cavalry squadrons.

On the right wing (Condé): 17 squadrons of which nine in the first line from Guards of *M. le Prince, Chappes, Coudray-Montpensier, Salbrick, Vidame d'Amiens, Le Vilette* (formerly *Gassion*), *Ravenel*, commanded by the *Lieutenant Général* Aumont, and eight in the second line, under Claude de la Trémoille from *Orléans, La Meilleraye, Streef, Saint-Simon, Bussy-Almory, Beaujeu.*

In the centre (Gaspard de Coligny): a first line of seven battalions (*Persan, Gardes Suisses, Gardes Françaises, Gardes Ecossaises, Picardie, Orléans,*

Erlach) then a second line of five battalions (*Conti, Condé, la Reine, Dazilly, Mazarin Italien*). Between these two lines were six squadrons of gendarmes (the companies of *Condé, Schomberg, la Reine, Duc d'Orléans, Enghien, Conti, Longueville* and *Marcillac*). 18 cannon were positioned along the front of the infantry, under the command of Timoléon de Cossé-Brissac.

On the left wing (Grammont): 16 squadrons of which nine in the first line (La Ferté-Senneterre): two squadrons from *Les Bains*, two squadrons from *La Ferté-Senneterre*, two squadrons from *Grammont, Mazarin*, and *Arnault carabins*, Grammont's and La Ferté's *Gardes* and seven in the second line (du Plessis-Bellière): *Chémerault, Meille, Lillebonne, Gesvres*.

Behind the centre was the reserve (Comte d'Erlach), six squadrons of Weimarian cavalry from the regiments *Fabry, Erlach, Sirot, Ruvigny*.

The King's Armies in 1648[17]

The *Connétable* (when there is one) is generalissimo of the armies of France, and has as *lieutenants généraux* the *maréchaux de France*, who command in chief in the *Connétable's* absence.

Today, and since the death of the late King, Monsieur le Duc d'Orléans is *Lieutenant Général* of the King throughout the Kingdom and in all his armies. He previously commanded in Army of Flanders. In his absence Monsieur de Rantzau and the late Monsieur de Gassion commanded the same army as *Lieutenant Généraux*.

The army of Flandres was commanded this year by Monsieur le Prince de Condé, whose *Lieutenant Généraux* were *Maréchal* d'Erlach and Monsieur de Villequières, and whose *maréchaux de camp* were Monsieur de La Ferté-Imbaut and others.

The Army of Catalonia is commanded by *Maréchal* de Schomberg, viceroy of this province, with *Maréchal de Camp* Monsieur de Saint-Aulnais, Marquis Saint-Maigrin and others.

The Army of Italy was commanded this year by the Duc de Modena and Principe Thomas, whose *Maréchaux de Camp* were *Maréchal* du Plessis-Praslin, Marquis Ville, who was killed before Cremona, and Marquis de Saint-André and others.

The Army of Germany was commanded by *Maréchal* de Turenne, with Monsieur Taupadel and others as *maréchaux*.

All these armies are made up of *gendarmes, chevaux-légers* and infantry.

The King, the Queen, Monsieur le Duc d'Anjou, Monsieur le Duc d'Orléans, all the Princes of the Blood and the *Maréchaux* de France, each have their own companies of gendarmes, which are independent companies, and whose lieutenants rank equally with all the captains and *Mestres de Camp* of the light cavalry, so that a lieutenant of gendarmes, if he is an older officer than a *Mestre de Camp*, commands him. These *gendarmes* have full armour and are paid for two horses, and are therefore obliged to have a service man with them.

---

17   Anon., *Estat de la France Comme Elle Était Gouvernée en l'an 1648* (Paris: publisher unknown, 1649), p.166.

Chevaux-Légers have only one breastplate. They were also divided into independent companies, and in the absence of the Colonel and the *Mestre de Camp Général* were commanded only by the most senior captain; but since 1636 they have been reduced to regiments commanded by *Mestres de Camp*. The foreigners who then entered the King's service were responsible for this change. The *Colonel Général* of the light cavalry is the Comte d'Alets, son of the Duc d'Angoulême.

The King has at his disposal some two hundred and forty cavalry *cornettes*, distributed in fifty-six regiments, in addition to the foreign regiments, who number 12. Baron de Degenfeld was colonel of the foreign cavalry, but since his retirement there has not been one.

The King has two hundred and ten infantry regiments, under the command of the Duc d'Epernon, who is *Colonel Général*; most of these regiments are made up of thirty companies, and each company pays ninety men, except for the *Gardes Régiments*, whose companies number two hundred men; this regiment has the *Maréchal* de Grammont as *Mestre de Camp*.

In addition, the King has a number of foreign regiments in his service: Germans, Scots, Irish, Italians, Liégeois and others, particularly Swiss, of which there are six to seven thousand in French service. Their *Colonel Général* was formerly Monsieur de Bassompierre, who is now dead, and is now *Monsieur le Maréchal* de Schomberg. There is also a Colonel *Général* of the Corsicans, who is the son of the late *Maréchal* d'Ornano, although there are no Corsicans in the King's service.

The naval army was commanded by the Duc de Richelieu, son of the Baron de Pontcourlay, *Général des Galères* since the death of the Duc de Fronsac, *Amiral de France*. It was made up of around thirty ships and twenty-five galleys.

To pay these soldiers, there are several types of funds: one for those who are maintained every day and paid by the *Trésorier des Guerres Ordinaire*, and the other for those who are paid by the *Trésorier des Guerres Extraordinaire*. The *Gardes Suisses* and the *Gardes Francaises* each have their own treasurers and paymasters, who have other paymasters under them, who pay the role that the commissioners and controllers of the wars provide, sign and verify with their own hands, and according to the review they have made. The naval army and the equipment of the vessels, both of the said naval army and of the coastguard frigates, are paid by the *Trésorier de la Marine*.

7

Accounts of Battles by Eyewitnesses and Contemporaries

The Battle of the Pas de Suse, 6 March 1629

The Battle of the Pas de Suse, recorded by Cardinal Richelieu[1]

That day, the 6th, at eight o'clock in the morning, with the King on horseback and all the troops in battle array, Comminges was sent to those commanding the barricades in order to inform them that the King was present in person and that he wished to know if they would open a passage for him and if M. de Savoie would treat him as a friend or foe in his domain. The Comte de Vérue replied that since we had come so far the affair would have to be settled by force and that we were not dealing with the English. Immediately afterwards, the barricades were attacked; the advance guard of the King, consisting of the *Gardes*, the Swiss, the regiment of *Navarre* and those of *Sault* and of *Estissac* had been placed in battle array between Chaumont and the place which was to be attacked three hours after midnight. The *Gardes*, the Swiss, *Navarre* and *Estissac* were deployed to attack the barricades from the front. *Sault's* regiment, whose officers knew the country better than anyone since most of them came from there, were, with the assistance of good guides, to take a certain path by means of which they could reach the area behind the barricades, in order to attack simultaneously from all sides. The *enfants perdus* were placed in three troops so as to take the said barricades from the middle and the two sides. The troops in the middle were made up of one hundred musketeers, fifty of them guards and the same number of the King's musketeers. Those on the right flank consisted of fifty guards, and those on the left flank, fifty men from the regiment of *Navarre*. These three corps

---

1   Armand du Plessis de Richelieu, *Mémoires du Cardinal de Richelieu*, in *Nouvelle Collection des Mémoires pour servir à l'Histoire de France* (Paris: Michaud et Poujoulat, 1837), Deuxième série, tome VII, p.607.

were supported by three others of one hundred men each from the same regiment as above. There followed a battalion of volunteers commanded by M. de Longueville with nearly three hundred gentlemen, many of whom were of good quality. After, came five hundred of *Navarre's* men. While *Sault's* regiment was ordered to advance on the right in an attempt to take the barricades from behind, that commanded by *d'Estissac* was ordered to climb a hill on the left which dominated the enemy barricades. The enemy, with this in mind, had lined the hill with musketeers, and the five hundred men mentioned above, half-pikes, half muskets, were under orders to clear them so as then to be able to fire on those who were defending behind the barricades, which fortunately, is what took place. Then came a culverin and two *moyennes* along with fifty pioneers to break through the barricade. These were followed by two corps, guards and Swiss, each consisting of five hundred men. The rest of the troops, four thousand men, were in battle array, ready to receive their orders, whether to reinforce the attacks, according to need, or advance further when the passage had been opened.

The attack began at eight o'clock and was soon over, as much because of the violence of the French as because of the enemy, seeing that they were under attack from all sides, took to their heels after their first volley. It can be said in truth that all did well on this occasion; however all the order that had been desirable, and that had been decided upon, was not able to be maintained, as much through the difficulties of the terrain which was harsh and narrow, separated every hundred paces by low dry stone walls, which broke up the battalions, as through the nature of the French, which has always been considered more courageous than wise, and which led each man to march as he wished, which could greatly prejudice the service of the King. In consideration of this, *Maréchals* de Créqui, de Bassompierre and Schomberg, and the *maréchals de camp* were all together at the head of the volunteers, contrary to reason which would have placed them separately in diverse locations, to give orders in all places. *Maréchal* de Schomberg received a musket ball in the side, but in 15 days he was well again; commander de Valençay received another in the thigh, which did not stop him being active throughout the attack, showing courage and bravery, having ordered the Swiss to climb the hill by means of a difficult passage, which was very useful for driving off the enemy.

Before turning to other things, I must mention the perverse effects provoked by the jealousy between the *Maréchal* de Créqui and *Maréchal* de Bassompierre; this unfortunate situation did not prevent the King being victorious and the fighting so intense that M. de Savoie and the Prince de Piémont, who were present on the barricades, were almost captured…

While the front of the Pas de Suse was under attack, the Comte de Sault wasted no time since having encountered Belon's regiment of Milanese, it was cut to pieces to such an extent that he brought to the King nine flags along with ten captains, lieutenants and ensigns. The Marquis de Ville, the Duc's general of cavalry, and one of his best men, was wounded by a musket volley that broke his arm and his shoulder. We lost very few men, five or six officers were wounded and there were no more than thirty dead. Many of our troops entered the town of Suse in pursuit of the enemy, but we ordered

Armand du Plessis de Richelieu (1585–1642). Watercolour by Karl Alexander Wilke (1879–1954) (Public Domain)

them out of the town, because the place was not safe, being difficult to defend and we preferred to accept its surrender twenty-four hours later, peacefully, rather than take it immediately; which could not be done without the risk of pillaging and disorder, inevitable when towns are taken by force. His Majesty strongly recommended this course of action so that his armies should not be denigrated in Italy, where the French were seen as being brave but undisciplined. The town's castle surrendered the following day, but this was not the case with the citadel nor with a fort called Talasse.

The Battle of the Pas de Suse, as recounted by *Maréchal* de Bassompierre[2]

However, M. de Créqui and I, along with the *maréchals de camp* held a meeting to determine the order to be established. The regiments of the *Gardes Françaises* and *Suisses* would take the lead; the regiment of *Navarre* would take the right flank and Estissac the left flank; the two flanks would send two hundred musketeers each up the hills so that they were in a position to dominate and outflank the guards defending the barricades; once that was achieved, at our signal, they would fire a volley from behind the barricade while we attacked it frontally with the two guards regiments; the Comte de Sault with his regiment would proceed below Jalasse, by a roundabout route with local peasants as guides and would then descend on Suse and take the enemy from behind if they were still resisting; at the same time Jallon would be attacked by another regiment, commanded by M. d'Auriac. The orders being given, at eleven o'clock in the evening, we began to move the troops through Chaumont. The weather was very bad and there was two feet of snow under foot.

On Tuesday, 6 March, the King arrived in Chaumont at two o'clock in the morning, with the Comtes de Soissons, de Longueville and de Moret, *Maréchals* de Schomberg, d'Halluin, de la Villette and others. Our troops

---

2   François de Bassopierre, *Mémoires du Maréchal de Bassompierre* (Paris: Jules Renouard, 1877), tome IV, pp.8–15.

followed – seven companies of *Gardes*, six *Suisses*, 19 of *Navarre*, 14 of *Estissac*, 15 of *Sault*, and the King's *Mousquetaires à Cheval*. The Comte de Sault and his regiment left at three o'clock to take up their positions as ordered: the rest remained in battle array five hundred paces from the village of Jalasse. We advanced also six pieces of six-pdrs cannon, pulled along using a hook, to force the barricades. Estissac was ordered to leave one hundred men to guard the ordnance. The order was that each corps would send forward fifty *enfants perdus*, supported by one hundred men, who would be supported by five hundred more. We placed the Princes and the Noblemen at the head of five hundred guards.

At six o'clock in the morning, M. de Créqui and I with de la Vallette, Valençay, Toiras, Canaples and Tavannes placed our troops in the battle array outlined above. The King arrived at the same time with the Comte and the Cardinal: he wanted his musketeers to be mixed up with the *enfants perdus* of the *Gardes*.

On behalf of the King we sent M. de Comminges with a trumpeter to request passage for the army and the King's person from the Duc de Savoie. But as he approached the barricade he was stopped, and the Comte de Verrue came out to speak to him. He said that we did not come as friends, and that, this being so, they would do their utmost to prevent our passage and that if we persisted in the undertaking, we would suffer the consequences.

After Comminges had reported this reply, I went to find the King who was one hundred paces behind our *enfants perdus*, further forward than most of the five hundred *Gardes*, to ask him for permission to begin the festivities and I said to him: "Sire, Sire, the assembly is ready, the violins are in place and the masks are at the door: when it pleases your Majesty the dance can begin." He came up to me and said angrily, 'Do you realise that we only have five pounds of lead for our ordnance?' I replied: "This is a fine time to think of that! Just because one of the masks is not ready, should we cancel the dance? Let us proceed with it, Sire, and all will be well." "Will you pledge that it will be so?" he asked. "It would be very bold of me to guarantee such a hazardous enterprise but I can say we will either be victorious or I shall be dead or captured." "Yes," he said "but if we fail, I will hold you responsible." (…) Then, the Cardinal said: "Sire, judging from the *Maréchal*'s look all will be well: rest assured."

Upon which, I approached M. de Créqui and dismounted to join him, having given the signal for combat to begin. *Maréchal* de Schomberg, who had only just arrived having been obliged to remain behind because of his gout, had come on horseback to see the festivities. We passed the village of Jallasse which the enemy had abandoned. Leaving the village we were welcomed by numerous volleys of musket fire from the enemy who were on the mountainsides and at the great barricade, and many cannonades from the fort at Jallasse. We continued to progress and M. de Schomberg was wounded in the back by musket fire coming from the slopes to the left. Once our men from both flanks had control of these slopes, the enemy began firing from behind the barricade and, charging headlong, we chased them off. We followed them so vigorously that they could not hold any of their positions. Then, fighting at close quarters, the Commander de Valençay took the heights on the left with the Swiss where he was wounded by a volley of musket shot in the knee, but he dispersed the Valaisans led by the Comte de Verrue: his horse was captured. I advanced below with M. de Créqui and the French where the Marquis de Ville was seriously wounded. We followed up our advance so vigorously that had it not been for the resistance offered by a Spanish captain and a few soldiers to our *enfants perdus* enabling the Duc and the Prince to retreat, they would both have been taken. Without interruption, we reached the heights above Suse where we came under heavy cannon fire from the citadel. But we were so delighted to have been victorious that we ignored the cannon fire. I saw something which pleased me concerning the French nobility present that day, as exemplified by, among others M. de Longueville, M. de Moret, M. d'Halluin, the first equerry and more than sixty others. A cannonade fell at our feet and covered all of us with earth; my long familiarity with cannon fire had taught me, more than the others, that once the shot is delivered, there is no longer any danger, so I was able to look at the faces around me and to see what effect the shot had had on them: I did not see one man who gave any sign of astonishment, nor did they even seem to notice. Another cannonade killed one of M. de Créqui's gentlemen and again they took no notice. On approaching the barricade, one of my guards who was supporting me was killed at my side; another, advancing energetically with the enfants perdus was killed on the Suse bridge: one of my gentlemen, the commander of my galiot at La Rochelle named Du Val, received a musket volley on the instep which left him crippled. None of our *enfants perdus* followed the enemy pell-mell into the town and none were made prisoners; and at that moment we could have taken Suse, but we ordered our men to withdraw because we wished to prevent the town from being pillaged, so that it could serve as lodgings for the King…

During the combat at the barricades, the Comte de Sault had gone below Jallon to take the enemy from behind. The enemy, suspecting this, had positioned colonel Belon and his Milanese regiment on the road. But the Comte de Sault surprised the Milanese with a dawn attack and defeated them, took more than 20 officers prisoner, captured nine of the ten regimental standards, and then came to join us at the Cordeliers from where, at around five o'clock in the evening we summoned the town and castle to surrender, which they did. Having given us hostages, we postponed entering the town that day, fearing that there would be disorder and pillaging by our own brave soldiers, enraged by the previous defeat, on entering the town at night.

The Siege of the Islands of Sainte-Marguerite and Saint-Honorat, 1636–1637

This is a collection of interesting letters showing how attacks were planned, based on one or more regiments, and in particular these highlight the role of *enfants perdus*.

Orders given by the *Maréchal* de Vitry for the attack on the island of Sainte-Marguerite, December 1636 and March 1637[3]

The rendezvous was at Cannes, and the naval army had taken up its positions in the same way as it had planned to attack the Isles: that is to say, partly at Gourjean, and partly at Theolé, which are the two extremities of the Levant, and the Couchant: the latter having fallen by lot to the Count of Harcourt, and the other to the Marshal de Vitry, who at the same time sent his orders for the corps of his Regiment, whose *enfants perdus* were to be led by the Sieurs de Lioux, first Captain, Felix Laîné Gentilhomme de Marseille, & the Chevalier de Thorene, also captains of the said Regiment.

[Here is the order for the *Régiment de Vitry*.]

It will be divided into three battalions, the first commanded by Sieur de Vinezac, Lieutenant Colonel, which will be composed of the following companies: la Colonelle, la Maître de Camp, Premont, Lens, Rousser, du Proy, Saint Pol; in the second battalion, the companies of Lioux, d'Allons, Saint-Antoine, Merzellet, Floure, Felix, Bellevue: in the third, those of la Male-Melan, Arnaud, Verclause, les Auverges, & the Chevalier de Thorene; the Sieurs de Lioux Captain, Brosser Lieutenant de Verclause, Guron *Enseigne Colonelle*, will command one hundred men chosen from the whole regiment to make the first descent, after the Guards of the said Sieur *Maréchal*, & will be supported by the Sieur de Vizenac with his battalion.

The said *enfants perdus* will advance & take ground, making a firm stand at the place which can give space behind them to the first battalion to form up in battle, awaiting another order.

Forty armed masters will dismount immediately after the first battalion, who, having dismounted, will divide into two, half to the right and half to the left of the first battalion.

The ladders, twelve in number, will follow the first battalion after 40 gentlemen, and will be led by Caseneuve, Lieutenant of Saint-Antoine, and two sergeants with seventy-two soldiers, who will only have swords, divided, namely four to each carry a ladder, and two others to carry the forks which were to be used to erect and support them.

The *pétardiers* (fireworkers), & those who were to accompany them, to carry the petards, grenades, fire pots, tools and undermining mantles, will go down immediately after the first battalion, the forty masters and the ladders.

Once the above has been done, if each regiment puts a battalion ashore, or at least there are three battalions formed, without a strong jealousy of the approach of the enemies, those who will have been destined to throw grenades and pots of fire will carry it out; whereupon the redoubt at the Pointe de l'Isle will be climbed, namely the Regiment of *Vitry* on the Levant side, & an Islet commonly called the Terre de Lierre [Land of Ivy].

While the orders are being carried out, the second and third battalions of the *Régiment de Vitry* will descend, from which second battalion Felix, Captain, Lieutenant de Merzelet and Ensign d'Allon will command the

---

3   *Mercure François* ès Années 1635, 1636, 1637, Vol.21, pp.306–322

seventy *enfants perdus*, whom Felix will choose from the seven companies of this battalion, who will line up and take their orders on the left and at the same front as the first battalion.

After this second battalion, the nobility with the armed masters.

Then the last battalion will descend in the same order as the other two, with their *enfants perdus* in front, who will be taken from the battalion, & commanded by the Chevalier de Thorene Captain, Roux Lieutenant of the Auverges, & Men Ensign of Mellan.

Given at Cannes on 5 December 1636
signed, Nicolas de l'Hôpital Vitry.
and below, by Monseigneur Charlemagne.

[At this time, French infantry regiment were made of 20 companies to a total strength of 1,200 men. Consequently, each of the two battalions of seven companies were made of 420 men, the third battalion of six companies mustering 360 men. From each battalion, 70 to 100 *enfants perdus* would be drawn, reducing the size of each battalion to between 290 and 320 men.]

[As the attack did not take place that day, here are the arrangements for the following day:]

Here is now the order & particular department for the same *Régiment de Vitry*.

Sieur de Lioux will choose five men from each of the best of the twenty companies of the aforementioned regiment, with the exception of the sergeants, corporals and *anspessades*, namely three musketeers and two arquebusiers, or *pertuisaniers*, making a total of one hundred, and will embark on the small platform with the Guards of the aforementioned Sieur *Maréchal*.

The first battalion will embark on the large platform and will also have the boats of Gabriel Arlac, Pol, Daumas, et cetera. This first battalion will have ten small ladders in this large platform, which it will erect at the edges and entrenchments if there are any, and which will then be used by the rest of the regiment.

Cazeneuve, Lieutenant of Saint-Antoine, will take from the whole regiment three men from each company, strong and robust, with their swords only, to carry and erect twelve ladders, namely four of the said soldiers for each, and two for each fork, who will follow the large platform, from which the battalion having left, they will immediately enter by the stern, in which they will take the ladders and forks, and will take them out by the bow to go and erect them where they are ordered, and will embark on the barques (little boats).

Felix, who was ordered to command the *enfants perdus* of the second battalion, will follow afterwards with the officers who will be destined, namely Lieutenant de Merzollet, & Ensign de d'Allons with two sergeants and seventy men taken and chosen from the seven companies of the second battalion which was commanded by d'Allons, which *enfants perdus* will be embarked on the barques.

The aforementioned Sieur Felix will have his *enfants perdus* carry ten small ladders, which he will use to climb to the edge of the sea, & entrenchments, &

afterwards will be used by the rest of the regiment, if they prefer to go by the great flat, & the rest of this second battalion will embark on boats.

The Chevalier de Thorene, who led the *enfants perdus* of the third and last battalion, will go on boats with the sixty men he will choose to command, & all the rest on *tartanes*.

Given & ordered at Cannes on the sixth of December 1636,
signed Vineat,
Lieutenant Colonel of the *Régiment de Vitry*.

[The attack still failed to take place that day, and these are the orders given for the whole army, for the month of February 1637:]

Everything was therefore ready, and things had got so far, that to remove the jealousies, and contentions which could arise in the course of the command, it was deemed advisable to separate the army into two, so that each would have more care of the quarter where he would be the absolute and independent master: so that in that of the Count Harcourt were the Regiments of *Isles, Cornusson, Clermont, Castreville*, the *Galères* and *Roussillon*; & in that of the *Maréchal* de Vitry, the corps of the Nobility, which truly had rushed there with great honour, the regiments of *Vaillac, la Tour, Vitry* & *Saint-André*.

(…) After that, the orders for the attack were drawn up, and were immediately given by the Sergeant Major of the army, in the following terms, that is to say, that the warships will be placed around the Isle towards the Pointe de Levant, & as close as possible, & that at the first breach made at the Fortin & at Monterey, the army will descend in the following order.

The regiments of *Vaillac, Cornusson*, & *Les Isles* will together form a battalion.[4]

The regiments of *Vitry, la Tour,* de *Castreville*, de *Saint-André, des Galères*, & *Roussillon* another.

Each of the said battalions will detach sixty musketeers & forty pikemen for the *enfants perdus* who will make up a corps of one hundred men commanded by two captains, two lieutenants, & two ensigns, & four sergeants who will go close to the ship which will be ordered to them awaiting the signal to disembark.

When the signal is given, those from *Vaillac* will go down to the port of Pinet. *La Tour* will be a little above them, pulling towards the point, the *Isles* and *les Galères* at the point; *Vitry* & *Roussillon* will have the other point on the side of the port of Saint-Martin, but opposite the descent of Vaillac; *Cornusson* & *Saint-André* on the same side, opposite the descent of *la Tour*.

At the same time, they will beach their boats, erect their ladders, throw down their bridges and climb the cliffs.

If the descent is contested by musketeers from a few distant entrenchments, they will also fire, provided they see that there are no large formations to surprise them and prevent them from taking up their weapons.

---

4   The term 'battalion' is used here by mistake but refers to a brigade (half section of the army)

If the descent is obstinately contested, try to lodge some musketeers behind their entrenchments, in a place where they can see behind.

Musketeers should be placed and left on the bow of the boat, who will not disembark, but will fire constantly to encourage the descent.

The corps that will follow the *enfants perdus* will follow them from a distance that will allow them to attack when the fight begins to heat up, having first withdrawn the boats that will have carried the *enfants perdus* from the lines that will remain to fire continuously and to wait until what they are carrying has been unloaded.

They will use the ladders and bridges where the said *enfants perdus* entered, or else they will erect their own.

The captains and officers who will command the said *enfants perdus*, and support them, will divide up between them, some to be at the head and others to be behind, in order to hasten the descent and prevent disorder.

As the said corps begin to move up, they will form their battalions at the tail of the *enfants perdus*.

All preparations for accommodation will be made quickly on the ground.

There will be unarmed soldiers, who will be ordered to roll barrels, carry picks and shovels to work quickly.

The Regiment of *la Tour* will be housed on the right of the Fortin, and after it on its left the *Isles*, and then *les Galères* on the same side; on the other side of the Fortin will be housed *Vitry, la Tour, Roussillon, Cornusson & Castreville*.

Care must be taken to distribute the tools in advance.

If the Fortin still holds when the raid is made, musketeers will have to be left to fire constantly against the flanks and embrasures.

Monsieur le Comte's Guards will attack on the Monterey side, *Vaillac & Les Isles* will each command twenty-five men who will attack on the side of their descent, *la Tour & Vitry* with as many men on their side, *Roussillon & les Galères* in the same way.

Half of the soldiers who will be commanded for the said attack will make a traverse of barrels, which they will fill with earth to cover those who will be sapping on the Monterey side.

Bridges and ladders will be erected on each side to climb up, and to cover those who will be undermining, having for this purpose provided for the distribution of grenades, fire pots to throw in, petards & finally fire engines.

Finally, the attack on these islands (which were considered to be impregnable) having been scheduled for Tuesday 24 March, the eve of the Annunciation of Our Lady, it was ordered on the morning of the same day; but the rain and bad weather which set in at midday prevented it from being carried out, and caused the ships to be withdrawn to the place from which they had set out.

[The island of Sainte-Marguerite surrendered on 12 May 1637.]

The Battle of Rocroi, 19 May 1643

The Battle of Rocroi as recounted by the Baron de Sirot[5]

The Duc d'Enghien summoned the council of war which consisted of the Prince in person, the *Maréchal* de l'Hôpital, his *Lieutenant Général*; M. d'Espenan, first *Maréchal de Camp*; M. de Gassion, M. de La Ferté-Senneterre, M. de la Vallière, *Maréchal de Bataille*; M. de la Barre, who commanded the artillery, and myself, first *Mestre de Camp* for the cavalry and its commander. The Duc d'Enghien asked whether it would be better to assist Rocroi with the entire army by chancing a battle or whether we could try to achieve the same end by getting men into the town itself. *Maréchal* de l'Hôpital, d'Espenan, de La Ferté, de la Vallière, and de la Barre were of the opinion that it would be better to assist the town by trying to send in men. This would be much safer and less hazardous, in view of the present state of affairs in France, Louis XIII having died only three days before. Given the problems caused by this death, if they lost the battle and were disgraced, the State would, perhaps, be in danger. It was to be feared that quarrels would break out and that some would favour the army of the enemy, embarrassing the King's Council and fostering divisions. But the Duc d'Enghien, M. de Gassion, the Marquis de Persan, the infantry's first *Mestre de Camp* and its commander, and I were of a different opinion (…)

 Maréchal de l'Hôpital and all those who agreed with him insisted. But the Duc d'Enghien stuck to his opinion and he said that we should give battle and even said that that was his wish.

 Thus it was decided that we would give battle if the enemy should resist and if the siege was not lifted at the arrival of our troops. Plans were laid for the battle to come and the battle array and the role of each was determined. M. de Gassion would command the right flank, M. de La Ferté-Senneterre, the left. The Duc d'Enghien, *Maréchal* de l'Hôpital, M. d'Espenan and M. de la Vallière were in the centre, and I was in command of the reserve consisting of two thousand infantry and a thousand cavalry.

 On 13 May, once we had decided upon all the battle arrays and each of us knew what he had to do, the Duc d'Enghien left the place where he was and dispatched all the army's baggage trains to Aubanton and Aubigny, which were only a league and a half apart, and at half past three in the afternoon he arrived within sight of Rocroi. He found it difficult to believe, for he had been told that the enemy would be there to stop him at a certain point. It should be noted that, if they had been captured, it would have prevented our army advancing. With six thousand men they could have defended this position and with the rest of their army take the town which would have surrendered on the evening of our arrival. As soon as the Duc d'Enghien and our generals passed safely through this point, they placed their forces in array, as had

---

5 Claude de Letouf, *Mémoires et la Vie de Messire Claude de Letouf, Chevalier Baron de Sirot* (Paris: Claude Barbin, 1683), pp.36–48.

been decided, and they marched to a certain plateau which was close to the place where the enemy was lined up for battle. The town was behind them within range of cannon fire, and the two armies were only at a distance of two musket ranges from each other, and they remained thus for the entire day; but this was not without large skirmishes, and the cannon made much noise on all sides. Nevertheless, that of the enemy caused much more damage to our army than they received from us; for, besides the fact that it was better placed, it was also much better used, and their gunners were more expert and more skilful than ours. As a result, on that day, more than two thousand of our soldiers were killed or wounded in both the infantry and the cavalry.

Night was more favourable to our army than day; it gave us some respite, and our generals reorganised and strengthened our front line; for the Marquis de La Ferté had separated the left flank, which he commanded, by more than two thousand paces from the battle corps, which could have caused the loss of the battle. If the enemy had charged our troops, as they should have done, they would have defeated them. And neither the battle corps, nor I with the reserve, would have been able to assist them.

However, on 19 May, at daybreak, the enemy's army was still in the same position as ours, and seemed to be prepared for full combat. Indeed, our soldiers having slept in battle order with their weapons, they had only to rise, blow on their fuses, place them on their cannon and fire upon the enemy. And since their intentions were the same as ours, their troops found themselves in the same position. The battle began at four o'clock in the morning, and M. de La Ferté committed the same error that he had made the day before, since he once again, separated the left flank under his command, from the main battle. The enemy charged them, breaking them and putting them to flight. The troops took to their heels without offering any resistance, and only a few officers and the Marquis held firm. They were made prisoner and the latter was wounded in two places. Thus, the entire right flank of the enemy fell upon the reserve under my command. But I was content to resist their assault, and even to beat them back so vigorously that they threw down their weapons and fled back to their reserve, in great confusion, during which time I recaptured seven cannons that they had previously captured. But seeing that their reserve did not budge, I ordered my troops to halt having ensured that they were once more in condition to fight. Hardly had I halted the small corps under my command that the enemy's reserve cavalry charged us. However, seeing that they were not supported and that I had fought off their left flank, that Gassion and the Duc d'Enghien had put their battle corps to flight and that their right flank had folded, they attacked me with apprehension, and they thought more about fleeing than defending themselves when they were charged. So much so, that after defending for a certain time, I pushed them back so vigorously that finally they were forced to yield and to abandon their infantry, consisting of four thousand five hundred Spanish naturals in four regiments, the most experienced in Flanders. One was the *Burgy* regiment which was the strongest; that of the Duc d'Albuquerque, who was cavalry general in the enemy army and the two others were those of *Villade* and of *Villealbois*. Although the infantry saw that they had been abandoned, they held firm, and seeing their cavalry in flight. I straightened up my squadrons and prepared them to charge the enemy infantry.

But as I was leaving, the Chevalier de La Vallière, *Maréchal de Bataille*, arrived bringing an order for the troops that I had rallied on the flank, those commanded by the Marquis de La Ferté-Senneterre and telling them that the battle was lost. These troops were the *Picardie* regiment, the *Piémont*, the *Marine*, *Molodin*'s Swiss and *Persan*'s regiment. These troops, who had been very badly treated, were more than willing to obey the orders of the *maréchal de bataille*. But, seeing that they were about to abandon me, I approached them. I begged them to hold firm. But, seeing that in spite of my remonstrances, they continued to withdraw; I castigated their lack of heart and had very strong words with the Chevalier de La Vallière. I told him that it was not for him to command my troops and that I greatly resented it. These prayers and threats had such an effect on the feelings of the officers that they heeded me and were strengthened in their resolve. But as I led the charge, this same Chevalier de La Vallière halted them a second time and I was followed only by what remained of my reserve corps, that is to say, *Harcourt*'s regiment, and those of *Bretagne* and the *Royaux*, and for the cavalry my own regiment, which had suffered greatly and were much weakened due to the great shock that they had endured and the fierce charges that they had given. Most of them had been killed or wounded and were out of action. Nonetheless, I charged the Spanish troops, but I was not able to crush them because my men were too weak. I therefore ran to these withdrawing regiments which were at more than one hundred paces from me. I called them cowards and men with little heart and honour, for withdrawing without even seeing the enemy. I told them that I would proclaim their shame all over France, and would complain of them to the King and the Duc d'Enghien. They would win the battle if they stayed, because there was only this battalion in front of them that was holding firm and if they listened to me and were prepared to act like brave and honourable men they would defeat them; that they were abandoning me for a man who would lose them their honour and reputation forever, that they should rally my troops and I promised that they would be victorious. Both officers and soldiers listened to these remonstrances and choosing the path of honour rather than follow the orders of the Chevalier de La Vallière, they cried as one: "To the Baron de Sirot, to the Baron de Sirot!" They came to me and I led them to join up with the rest of my troops that were waiting for me. But as I was placing them in battle array to attack these Spanish regiments, the Duc d'Enghien arrived and I informed him of the order that the Chevalier de La Vallière had just transmitted to me and to the troops that were with him. The Prince, seeing that he was being so badly slandered in a matter of such great import, disavowed him and said that he who had said it had lied.

After this disavowal, I asked him to withdraw a little to the side, which he did, and then seeing that the Spanish battalion began to yield, I charged it so vigorously that, unable to withstand the advance of my troops, they were broken and deflated, leaving two thousand dead along with as many made prisoner. Two of their colonels were killed, de Villebois and de Villades. But before this battalion was broken, the Comte de Fontaines, who was a general in the King of Spain's army, and who was in a chair at the head of his battalion since he could not mount his horse because he was suffering greatly from gallstones, was killed. Our troops took possession of his body and carried it to the church in Rocroi. Dom Francisco de Melo who had withdrawn to Marienbourg after the defeat of their army asked for his body back the same day. The Duc d'Enghien returned it to him, after placing it in a shroud and then in a casket. He had it transported in his carriage to Marienbourg, which is only seven leagues from Rocroi, and with it he sent all the chaplains, Jesuits and other clerics in their army whom he had made prisoner.

The Battle of Rocroi as recounted by the Marquis de la Moussaye (dictated to Henri de Bessé, Sieur de la Chappelle Milon, who was employed in the administration of the Royal buildings)[6]

His rank, his affairs, the interests of his house and the advice of his friends called him (Enghien) back to the Court. Nonetheless, on this occasion he preferred the general good to his private advantage, and his thirst for glory meant that he did not hesitate for a moment. He kept secret the news of the King's death and marched towards Rocroi the next day, persuading *Maréchal* de l'Hôpital that he was advancing towards Rocroi only to provide assistance in the form of men and munitions through the surrounding woods (….).

Perhaps believing that the Spanish would defend the narrow pass and that things would end in a fierce skirmish in the woods during which help could be delivered to the town, and that since the army was not engaged beyond the narrow passage it could withdraw easily without risk of a general full scale engagement (…)

De Melo was soon obliged to decide whether he would defend the pass or whether he would wait to be attacked on the plain. Nothing was easier than to defend the pass by pouring his infantry into the woods and supporting them with a large number of cavalry. He could even, by using the advantage of the woods and marshes, tie up the French Army with part of his troops while finishing off the siege of the town with the other part. This seemed the best tactic and there was no one who believed that de Melo would not adopt it. But his ambitions were not limited to the capture of Rocroi. He believed that winning a battle would open the way to the heart of France and his victory at Honnecourt caused him to hope for a similar outcome in front of Rocroi. Besides, in chancing a battle, he believed he was risking at most the smallest part of his army and certain fortifications on the border. The defeat of the Duc d'Enghien, on the other hand, would bring him infinite advantage at the beginning of a Regency which was hardly established.

Reasoning in this way, de Melo who, as is the Spanish temperament, sometimes neglected the present by thinking too much of the future, decided to give battle, and so as to engage the Duc d'Enghien more easily, he waited in the plain and made not the slightest effort to contest the pass; because while he was considering what he should do, there was almost no time left for

---

6   Henri de Bessé, *Relation des Campagnes de Rocroi et de Fribourg* (Paris: Delangle, 1826), pp.12–44.

reflection. The leading troops of the Duc d'Enghien were already appearing, and the French Army would have finished marching through the pass before he had organised his quarters. Nonetheless, if he had wanted to do all he could to prevent our passage early enough, the Duc d'Enghien would have had difficulty in forcing a way through, for there is nothing more difficult in warfare than to emerge from a long path through the woods and marshland within sight of a powerful army posted on a plain. However this may be, it is clear that de Melo wanted a battle since he had taken pains to assemble all his forces and ordered Beck, who was in Palaizeux, to come and join him with all speed.

The Duc d'Enghien marched in two columns, from Bossu to the entrance to the pass. Gassion went ahead with a few cavalry to reconnoitre the enemy and finding the passage defended by no more than fifty horses, he pushed them back and came to report to the Duc d'Enghien the ease with which he had taken the pass.

This was the place where the Prince thought he should speak more openly to *Maréchal* de l'Hôpital because the *Maréchal* saw clearly that in pushing forward onto the plain, it would be impossible to avoid going to battle. Gassion did all he could to gain his acquiescence and the *Maréchal* continued to differ, but the Duc d'Enghien put an end to their dispute and said, in masterly tones, that he assumed full responsibility for the engagement.

The *Maréchal* ceased arguing and placed himself at the head of the troops under his command. The Duc d'Enghien ordered his right flank to advance, placing the infantry in the most difficult places so as to protect the passage of the rest of the army. At the same time, he advanced, with some of the cavalry, as far as a small hill at half range of the Spanish cannon. If de Melo had charged the Duc d'Enghien, he would certainly have defeated him. But the Duc covered the top of the hill so well with the squadrons that he had, that the Spanish could not see what was happening behind him.

De Melo could not believe that such a large number of cavalry could advance without being supported by the infantry. This is why he was content to try by means of skirmishes to see if he could see the area behind the squadrons. But not having been able to win through, he concentrated on placing his troops in battle array.

Thus the two generals had the same ambition: the Prince concentrated on the passage of his troops through the pass and de Melo was only concerned to organise his quarters. The place where the Duc d'Enghien had arranged his battlefield was big enough to deploy his entire army as he had planned. The ground was higher than the surrounding area and sloped down imperceptibly towards the plain. On the left there was a large marsh and, since the woods were not very thick they did not prevent the squadrons from assembling. The Duc d'Enghien occupied these heights and opposite there was another very similar hill where the Spanish were posted facing the French lines, and between these two positions there was a small valley.

It is easy to judge from this situation that neither of the two parties could attack without climbing above the other. Nonetheless, the Spanish had an advantage in that on the slopes of the height that they occupied and in front of their left flank, there was a dense wood which stretched quite a distance down in to the valley, and it was easy for them to position musketeers there so as to harass the Duc d'Enghien as he advanced.

The two generals worked frenziedly to get their troops in to position as they arrived and instead of skirmishing which was the usual custom when two armies approached each other, they both took all the time necessary to arrange themselves in order of battle.

However, the Spanish cannon fire caused much more harm to the French than that of the French to the Spanish, because the latter had more guns, and they were better positioned and better employed. As the Duc d'Enghien extended the flanks of his army, the enemy fired such intense barrages of artillery fire that if it had not been for their extraordinary resistance, the French troops would not have been able to hold the ground that they had occupied. On that day, more than three hundred men were wounded by cannon fire, among them, the Marquis de Persan, *Mestre de Camp* of an infantry regiment, who received a wound in the thigh.

At six o'clock in the evening the French Army had crossed the narrow pass and the reserve were coming out of the woods and taking up their position in the plain. The Duc d'Enghien was keen to begin the combat quickly in order to hinder Spanish preparations. Marching orders were given to the army when an incident occurred that almost handed victory to de Melo.

In the absence of *Maréchal* de l'Hôpital, who was by the Duc d'Enghien's side, La Ferté-Senneterre was alone in commanding the left flank. On that side of the army was marshland through which the Spanish could not attack. In consequence, La Ferté had only to hold his ground and wait for the battle to commence. For his part, the Duc d'Enghien had not left the right flank and while the troops were getting ready for battle he was reconnoitring the Spanish positions and the best places to attack them. At that moment, La Ferté, perhaps following a secret order from the *Maréchal*, or maybe in order to bring himself to Gassion's attention through some extraordinary exploit, ordered his cavalry and five battalions of infantry across the marsh. This detachment meant that the left flank of the army was bereft of cavalry and missing a large part of its infantry. As soon as the Duc d'Enghien was notified, he ordered the army to halt and went to the left flank where the disorder was to be found. At the same moment, the Spanish trumpeted the charge and their army began to march as if de Melo wanted to take advantage of this manoeuvre. But the Prince had filled the void in the frontline with troops of the second and the Spanish halted and gave the impression that their only goal had been to gain some terrain so as to put their second line in place. There are times at war when opportunities pass by like lightening. If the general is not sharp enough to notice them or quick enough to take advantage of them, good fortune rarely comes by again and, more often than not, turns on those who fail to grasp them. The Duc d'Enghien sent word to La Ferté to return to his initial position and before nightfall they had crossed the marsh in the other direction and were back in position. This incident only succeeded in delaying the battle and caused no more inconvenience than allowing the Spanish to better prepare their position than they would otherwise have done.

The night was dark, but due to the proximity of the forest the plain was bright with the great number of fires lit by the soldiers. Woods on all sides surrounded the armies, as if they had to fight a duel. Their guards were so close to each other that it was difficult to distinguish the French fires from those lit by the Spanish. The two camps seemed to be one. No alarm was heard. On the eve of a very bloody battle there seemed to exist a kind of peace between the two camps.

At daybreak, the Duc d'Enghien signalled his army forward. First, he led his cavalry in an attack on one thousand musketeers positioned by the Comte de Fontaines in the woods. Even though they fought on ground that was naturally entrenched and advantageous to them, the attack was so strong that they were all cast down. Fearing that his squadrons be separated from each other as they crossed the remainder of the wood, the Duc d'Enghien and the second line of cavalry turned left and he ordered Gassion to take the first line around the wood to the right. Under the cover of the wood, Gassion stretched out his squadrons and attacked the Spanish cavalry on its flank while the Duc d'Enghien attacked it head on.

Commanding the Spanish left flank was the Duc d'Albuquerque. He knew nothing yet of this first action and had not considered it possible that he could be attacked on two sides simultaneously. Counting on the musketeers posted in the woods to cover his front line, the attack therefore had seriously weakened him and he attempted to pit against Gassion some squadrons of his own. Nothing, however, is more dangerous than to undertake important manoeuvres before a strong enemy on the point of engaging in battle. Already shaken, the squadrons were crushed by the first charge, and all of d'Albuquerque's troops fell one after the other. Seeing them take flight, the Duc d'Enghien ordered Gassion after them, and turned his attention towards the enemy infantry.

For his part, *Maréchal* de l'Hôpital was not as successful since having led his cavalry charge at a gallop his troops tired before reaching the enemy. The Spanish held their ground and smashed de l'Hôpital's cavalry. Having battled with great courage, *Maréchal* de l'Hôpital had his arm broken by a pistol shot and witnessed in an instant his whole flank take flight in confusion. The Spanish pushed them hard, cutting to shreds a number of infantry battalions and capturing the cannon. Their advance was stopped when the reserves came up against them.

While the two flanks fought with mixed fortunes the French infantry marched against the Spanish. Even though several battalions had already come together, d'Espenan, commanding the infantry, having heard of the misfortune that had just beset the left flank, and seeing before him the Spanish infantry waiting with great pride and in good order, made do with slight skirmishes in order to wait and see which cavalry would be victorious.

Meanwhile, the Duc d'Enghien had crushed the German and Walloon infantries, and the Italian infantry had taken to their heels when he realised *Maréchal* de l'Hôpital's rout. The Duc realised that victory depended entirely on the troops he had with him. He immediately suspended his pursuit of the infantry and marched behind the Spanish battalions, against their cavalry, which was attacking the left flank of the French Army. Finding their squadrons scattered, he finished them off with ease.

La Ferté-Senneterre had been caught in the rout of the left flank, having fought with great valour. He was found wounded in several places and was rescued by a charge led by the Duc d'Enghien.

In this way, the Spanish right flank which had been scattered as they chased the French, did not hold the upper hand for long. Those who were chasing took flight themselves and found Gassion in their path, who cut them to pieces.

Only de Melo's infantry was left. They were pressed together as one near their cannon. Their countenance and order indicated that they were prepared to fight to the bitter end. Their commander was the Comte de Fontaines, who, despite having to be carried in a chair because of his infirmity, was one of the best commanders of his generation.

Hearing word that Beck was marching with 6,000 men near the woods, the Duc d'Enghien attacked the Spanish infantry without hesitation, despite having only a small number of cavalrymen with him. The Comte de Fontaines stood his ground and ordered his men to hold their fire until the French were only fifty paces from them. In an instant, his battalion parted and from its ranks a blast from eighteen cannons was fired, followed by a shower of musket shots. The salvo was such that the French could not withstand it. If the Spanish had had cavalry to push forward, the French would never have been able to recover and reorganise themselves.

The Duc d'Enghien swiftly rallied his troops and attacked a second time, with as little success. He attacked a third time without defeating them. The reserves arrived where the Duc d'Enghien was and they were joined by a number of cavalry squadrons that had been engaged in battle with the Spanish cavalry. As a result, the Spanish infantry was surrounded on all sides and were obliged to surrender. The officers thought above all else of their own safety and the ones closest to the front line waved their hats in a plea for mercy.

As the Duc d'Enghien advanced towards them to exchange words, the Spanish foot soldiers thought that the Prince was launching a new attack. This error led them to firing a volley at him – the greatest danger he had had to face that day. Angered by what had just occurred to their general, and believing it to be proof of Spanish dishonesty, the Prince's troops charged at the Spanish from all sides without waiting for the order. The terrible carnage that ensued was vengeance for the danger the Prince had been exposed to.

With their swords drawn, the French attacked the Spanish battalion to the core and despite the efforts of the Duc d'Enghien to stop the violence, the soldiers showed no mercy, especially the Swiss, who are in general more ruthless than the French in such circumstances. The Prince rode to the left and to the right, shouting for mercy to be given, and the Spanish officers, and even some soldiers, sought safety by his side. Don George de Castelui, mestre de camp, was taken by the hand of the Prince himself. All those who were able to escape the soldiers' wrath massed around him to beg for their lives.

As soon as the Prince had given his orders concerning the prisoners, he rallied his troops ready to fight General Beck if ever he attacked Gassion or dared to enter the plain. It was then that Gassion returned from chasing down the runaways and told the Duc d'Enghien that Beck had not left the woods, restricting his actions to rounding up in the pass some remnants of the defeated army. He added that Beck had done so in such confusion and with such little understanding of the advantage that could be gained from the passes in the forest, that it was plain to see that the terror experienced by de Melo's soldiers had been communicated to his. Indeed, having saved some remnants of the Spanish army, he retreated at an incredible pace, even leaving behind two cannon.

Seeing that victory was now assured, the Duc d'Enghien fell to his knees on the battlefield, and ordered all his men to do likewise, to give thanks to God for such a great success. Indeed, France had good reason to thank God because she had not won as important, nor as glorious, a battle for many centuries.

Both sides carried out great actions. The Spanish infantry's valour cannot be praised highly enough. It is almost unheard of that, following the defeat of an army, one corps of infantry, without the aid of a cavalry, could withstand in open field not one, but three attacks without folding. And it is true, that without the support of the reserves, and notwithstanding his victory over the rest of the Spanish army, the Duc d'Enghien would never have broken that brave infantry.

One extraordinary action by *Velandia*'s regiment stood out. During the Duc d'Enghien's first attack, the musketeers and pikemen of this regiment, having been cut to pieces and surrounded by the French cavalry, withstood every charge that was made against them and retreated slowly until they reached the mass of the Spanish infantry.

When the left flank of the French Army had been broken, Sirot was told that the battle was lost and to save his reserves. To this, he replied, "It is not lost because Sirot and his companions have not yet fought." And indeed, his determination played an important role in the victory. But above all else, and the Spanish concurred, nothing was more impressive than the calm and composure shown by the Duc d'Enghien at the height of the battle, and especially when the enemy's left flank was defeated. Indeed, instead of pursuing the scattered remnants of that flank, he turned instead on their infantry. Such restraint meant that he avoided scattering his own troops and retained an attacking advantage against the Spanish cavalry, who thought that victory was theirs. Gassion earned a great deal of honour and the Duc d'Enghien promised to request from the King a marshal's baton in grateful acknowledgement of his actions, a baton that the King granted soon after.

Of the eighteen thousand infantry that made up de Melo's army, over eight thousand were killed and seven thousand taken prisoner. The Comte de Fontaines, general *mestre de camp*, was found dead, by his chair, at the head of his troops. The Spanish regretted his death for a long time and the French praised his courage highly. The Prince himself said that if he had not won he would have wanted to die like de Fontaines. Both Valandia and Vilalua, Spanish *mestres de camp* also, suffered the same fate. All the officers were either killed or taken prisoner. The Spanish lost 18 pieces of field artillery and six batteries. The French captured 200 flags and 60 standards. The pillage was important: added to the booty taken from the baggage train was the silver to be distributed to the Spanish army following the capture of Rocroi. The French lost approximately two thousand men, but very few officers or noblemen.

The Duc d'Enghien, having lodged his army in the enemy encampment and given his orders concerning the wounded, entered Rocroi victorious. He learnt the next day that de Melo had retreated from the battle following the defeat of his army's right flank and had sought to gather the remnants of his army at Philippeville.

It was there that his cavalry rejoined him having suffered few losses. His infantry, on the other hand, was entirely destroyed. The campaigns that followed highlighted the importance of this loss, one that the Spanish have never been able to recover from. A good infantry can never be too carefully maintained, whether in time of war or in time of peace. Indeed, without a great deal of time, it is impossible, even for the greatest of Kings, to rebuild an experienced corps of officers and soldiers used to fighting together and suffering the fatigues of war.

The Battles of Freiburg (or Fribourg), 3 to 9 August 1644

The Battle of Freiburg, attributed to the Marquis de la Moussaye by Ramsay[7]

M. de Turenne had advice at that time, that the Duc d'Enghien had orders to march to Brisach with his army, which consisted of six thousand infantry and three thousand cavalry: this Prince having passed the Rhine, came to M. de Turenne's camp, which was about four or five leagues from Brisach.

After the taking of Freiburg, the enemy's army had continued in their camp: parties were sent out to view it, as also all the roads both through the hills and the woods, in order to get between Freiburg and the Bavarians, and that way to march down into the plain. The Duc d'Enghien resolved to attack with his army some posts where M. de Mercy had three or four regiments of infantry upon a rising ground at the head of his camp, and ordered M. de Turenne to march with the army he commanded through the woods and hills, to endeavour to enter the plain where the enemy were, and attack them in the flank. It was resolved to begin the attack three hours before night.

The Prince having caused the rising ground to be attacked by his infantry, they were at first beaten back, but going thither himself with great resolution, and with a body that sustained those who had been repulsed, he carried those posts, defeated the three or four regiments, consisting of over two thousand

---

7   Paul Marichal (ed.), *Mémoires du Maréchal de Turenne* (Paris: Renouard, 1909), tome I, pp12–25.

men, but lost a great many of his own men, and it growing dark, he halted in the same place.

M. de Turenne at the head of his army entered the defile and advanced towards the plain, where the enemy were in order of battle; first he drove them from a wood, and then from a hedge, and beat them from post to post to the entrance of the plain. The Bavarians lost a great many men, and retired about forty or fifty paces from our infantry, having all their cavalry, and a body of infantry of the second line, to sustain them. The two armies continued thus facing one another, the Bavarians not daring to come to a close engagement again with those regiments that were ready to receive them with their pikes, and the French not daring to enter further into the plain, having no cavalry to sustain them.

In this posture did both armies fight above two hours before night, with great loss on both sides: the King's infantry had behind them the wood, which gave them a fair opportunity to retreat; but they never recoiled, though it was not possible to bring above one squadron of cavalry to sustain them, for want of room to draw up.

The night did not put an end to the fight, but the troops on both sides remained for seven hours continually firing at the distance of forty paces till it was day. In this place, over fifteen hundred of the King's army were killed; and of the enemy upwards of two thousand five hundred: M. de Roqueserviere, *Sergent de Bataille*, was mortally wounded: M. d'Aumont, *lieutenant général*, acted his part there exceeding well.

A little before day the enemy's fire was observed to diminish; the reason was, that they had left only some few men to fire, that their retreat might not be perceived; their army marching to a hill near Freiburg. They had reason to be afraid, that the Prince having been prevented by the night from advancing further, would attack them at break of day in the plain on his side. As soon as anything could be seen at the distance of a hundred paces, we sent some soldiers into the plain, who reported that the enemy were retired; and daylight advancing, M. de Turenne marched down into the plain, and saw the Prince entering it likewise on his side. The armies being joined, the Prince did not think fit to march that day to the hill, where the Bavarians had again encamped and which was not above a league from their former camp: he only went to take a view pretty near the hill, where the enemy having already planted their cannon, fired several shots at those who advanced.

It is certain, had the Prince marched up to them, he would have found them in great confusion; but the infantry of the King's army were so dispirited by fighting the whole night, and by the great number of officers and soldiers killed or wounded, that they were not in a condition to undertake any considerable action. That day was spent in the camp, and it was reported, that the most part of the general officers of the enemy's army were for making use of that opportunity to retire by the hills behind Freiburg, and leave a garrison there; but M. de Mercy carried it against them; he continued there, and caused some trees to be cut down, in order to hinder any approach, and ordered some small works to be made in the most advantageous places.

The next morning early, the army, commanded by M. de Turenne, having the vanguard, he detached seven or eight hundred musketeers, commanded by M. de l'Echelle, *Sergent de Bataille* of the Prince's army, (who did the duty of M. de Roqueserviere, who was wounded in the last action) and eight or ten squadrons of cavalry, under the command of M. Doubatel, *Lieutenant Général*, with four small field pieces, which marched at the head of the said detachment: as they came near the hill where the enemy was, they perceived some musketeers that were guarding some advantageous posts, and who retired to their respective bodies when they were pressed hard, while the enemy fired a great many cannon shot.

The march being very short, when M. de Turenne's army was in this situation, it was but eight o'clock in the morning, so that they had a great deal of time, being the middle of summer. It was resolved, that by opening a great way to the right, they should make room for the Prince's army (which *Maréchal* de Grammont commanded under him) in order to double to the left, and then put themselves in such a disposition, that the hill might be attacked in several places at the same time. All the enemy's troops, both cavalry and infantry, having retired in close order towards the hill, after a very sharp skirmish, the King's army halted: the cannon from the hill did but little mischief, because the French were not in a defile.

In the meanwhile, an officer of *Flextein*, who was detached with fifty cavalry to view the disposition of the enemy from a rising ground near the King's army, came and told M. de Turenne, that he saw a great confusion amongst the Bavarians and that their baggage was marching. M. de Turenne told it to the Prince, who thinking it would be easier to know what there was in that report, and that it might be useful for making the disposition for the attack, he went thither, taking M. de Turenne with him, who told the troops as he passed before them, that he should return immediately, and that it was necessary before the attack, to wait the arrival of the Prince's troops.

There were about two thousand paces from the place where the troops of the right were, to the rising ground where that officer of *Flextein* had been. As we were viewing the disposition of the enemy's army, which seemed to be in great confusion, we heard them make a great volley of small shot, and at the same time a noise of trumpets and kettle-drums. M. d'Espenan, who commanded the Prince's infantry, coming to the hill, and seeing small advanced work, in which the enemy had some musketeers, and by which it had not been thought necessary to begin an attack, sent some infantry to make themselves masters of it, without waiting either the Prince's, or *Maréchal* de Grammont's orders; thinking, as I believe, that the thing would not have had so great a consequence, or, perhaps, to raise his own character in the world by some little action : this was what obliged the enemy to make for great a volley from the hill, upon those troops that were advancing at that time.

The body of M. Doubatel's vanguard, where M. de l'Echelle was, (to whom M. de Turenne had spoken, in going with the Prince, and told them expressly, that they must not stir from their post, and that he would return immediately) began to march towards the hill, and having passed some trees which the enemy had cut down, advanced towards a work, where M. de Mercy was with his whole body of infantry, who, not being attacked but on that side, because the enterprise was without orders, opposed them with his whole force. This was the condition in which the Prince and M. de Turenne found their troops on their return, having galloped full speed upon hearing the noise.

There was not a man of the Prince's army come, but the few musketeers M. d'Espenan had employed to take that work, and M. de Turenne's infantry, which in all made not three thousand men, were not engaged against that fort, but were at a great distance from it, without having orders for what they were to do. The Prince stayed with that first body, which was already beaten back, close to the enemy's redoubt, and so, as may easily be judged, very much exposed, there being no cavalry to sustain them but *Flextein's* regiment, which continued under the fire of the enemy's whole infantry with wonderful resolution, and lost the half of the men.

M. de Turenne went to his own body of infantry that were not engaged, in order to help the retreat of those who had attacked, or in case they were not quite repulsed, and there was room for doing it, to make an attack : as he was advancing, the situation of the affair showed, that all that he had to do, was to halt a little out of musket shot, and wait for the Prince's infantry.

We continued in this posture a pretty while, it requiring a long time to make the disposition for an attack, in rugged and hilly ground. Then the Prince thought fit that M. de Turenne should march with his infantry, *Maréchal* de Grammont was to have charged the enemy in the flank, or to have sustained with the cavalry, if the attack had succeeded. We marched straight to the fall of trees which was in the middle of the hill, and opposite to the left of the Prince's army. The regiments of cavalry of M. de *Turenne* and *Tracy*, sustained the Prince's infantry, who were repulsed after a very obstinate fight, where this cavalry performed wonders, in bearing the fire without moving.

M. de Turenne, who had M. Tournon with him, sent word several times to the Prince, that whatever his troops might suffer, he would endeavour not to retire altogether till it was night. It is certain, could the enemy have made a right judgement of the confusion of the King's troops, the whole army had been ruined, at least all the infantry. Those of M. de Turenne were also led on to that hill at the time that those of the Prince were attacking, but the soldiers were so disheartened, that they advanced very little towards the enemy.

This battle lasted two full hours, and ended with the day, the enemy not stirring from their posts. The Bavarians lost a great many men, and among the rest, Gaspard de Mercy, major general, the count's brother; but their loss was not so great as that of the King's armies, whereof the root were almost entirely ruined: nevertheless, as the enemy had lost almost the half of their infantry two days before, and had suffered pretty much on this occasion, they had but a small number of infantry left. Had it not been for that accident of M. d'Espenan's attacking contrary to orders, which put all in confusion, and if the infantry of the King's two armies had attacked the hill abreast, according to the disposition that was going to be made, the enemy's army would have been undone, and unable to resist. In the French Army there were a great many officers killed; M. de l'Echelle and M. de Mauvilli, *Sergent de Bataille*, with almost all the commanders of the different bodies of the cavalry, and some of those who commanded the infantry.

Night having parted the two armies, which were but fifty paces from each other (the most advanced bodies, at least), that of the King returned to its former camp. A vast number of wounded were sent to Brisach, and provisions ordered from thence, and a day or two after, there came an account, that the enemy's army having decamped from that hill, and left a garrison in Freiburg, was marching into the Schwartz-Welt, which is the Black Forest, in order to get into the country of Württemberg. As the country, through which they were obliged to pass, is full of very narrow ways, where it is with great difficulty that baggage can follow, it was resolved to march with the whole army in order to surprise the enemy; and for that end, M. Rosen was detached with eight squadrons, and set out three or four hours before the army. As he was an excellent officer, and of great experience, he had orders either to attack some troops which the enemy had detached to make their march easier, or to stop the body of the army by harassing it, and thereby give time for the King's army to come up.

The King's army marched at the break of day, leaving the baggage with a guard, and followed M. de Rosen's route, who had set out about midnight. After a march of five or six hours in a rugged country, and where the troopers were often obliged to dismount and file off; the army got upon a little rising ground. The Prince was with the main body, and M. de Turenne's army had the vanguard. We saw M. de Rosen's troops in a valley, about a quarter of a league off; and upon the top of a hill, (which M. de Rosen could not see, because he was in the bottom) five or six thousand men at most, which was the enemy's whole army, that were retiring. A little after, M. de Rosen with his eight squadrons, consisting of full six hundred cavalry, began to follow the enemy, and get up that hill, which was pretty long. M. de Turenne, by order of the Prince sent immediately a gentleman, called la Berge, to tell M. de Rosen, that it was the enemy's whole army that were marching upon the hill: before he got to M. de Rosen, who saw only some troops of the rearguard, Rosen was advanced so near, that M. de Mercy perceiving he was not sustained, and that the foremost troops of the King's army were a quarter of a league from him, and were filing off one by one, to form the first squadron, (which takes up a great deal of time) faced about upon M. de Rosen with the whole body of his troops; but some of the enemy's squadrons advancing before their infantry, M. de Rosen beat them back and following them in order, three or four battalions fired upon him, which stopped his detachment, however, without putting them in confusion: seeing himself very near the enemy's main body, and their front very much larger than his own, he began to retire. Two or three squadrons of the second line sustained those of the first, that were very little moved by so great a fire, and after having lost four or five standards, they retired very slowly in good order.

The enemy's cavalry dare not pursue them briskly, for fear going too far from their infantry; or else, because being as yet stunned with the battles of the preceding days, their main design was to retire without fighting. Rosen's foremost squadrons being sustained by those of the second line, and the whole body of the enemy's cavalry and infantry continuing to march against them, and being between forty and fifty paces from one another, they retired five or six hundred paces, mixed with the enemy, who made more use of the fire of their infantry than of their cavalry. It was one of the most remarkable actions I ever saw, for the intrepidity of troops in the midst of so much danger; a degree of bravery to which none but those who have been in many battles, and have had both good and bad success, can arrive. The enemy who saw that there were already two squadrons of the vanguard of the King's army formed upon the rising ground, where I said they were filing off, began to halt, and a little after, to retire.

Rosen's cavalry that had been repulsed, not being in a condition to pursue the enemy, because there was not a body of the King's army that had passed the defile strong enough to sustain them, made a halt, and M. de Mercy retired to a wood about twelve or fifteen hundred paces from the place of action, from whence he directed his march through the hills towards the country of Württemberg.

The battle of Freiburg as recounted by *Maréchal* de Gramont[8]

We advanced without a plan for battle. Having attacked Gravelines, the King's army, commanded by the Duc d'Orléans was focused entirely on making this attack succeed. But because the Duc d'Enghien and *Maréchal* de Guiche (de Gramont) had entered Luxembourg where they had captured a few small castles, they were soon in a position to use His Majesty's army to glorious ends. Cardinal Mazarin sent a letter to inform them that the Bavarian Army, led by Mercy, had attacked Freiburg and that it was of the utmost importance that the King's army currently in Luxembourg should join the army led by *Maréchal* de Turenne in Germany; and that the two armies joined together under the Duc d'Enghien's command would be strong enough to come to save Freiburg and lift the siege. But to be able to do that great speed would be needed and he promised that they would neither lack the money nor any other necessities in the pursuit of this objective. And, if the truth be told, they were amply supplied. We marched with nothing but the lightest amount of food and cannon, leaving behind the heaviest equipment. When we came to Benfeld, the Marquis d'Aumont arrived, sent by de Turenne, to bring news that Freiburg had fallen. He believed, however, that if we quickened our advance we could still engage the enemy in battle if they held their positions, or, if they abandoned them, attack the town itself. This led to the decision to cross the Rhine immediately at Brisach where *Maréchal* de Turenne was to be found.

The Duc d'Enghien, the two *Maréchals* and M. Erlach, the Governor of Brisach held a war council on the spot. Erlach's opinion was not to attack the enemy where they were positioned, but instead to circle them by way of Langhenzeling and the San Peter valley, and in so doing cut off their supply lines forcing them to either die of hunger or engage a battle which would no longer be as advantageous for them as currently, entrenched and waiting as they were.

---

8   Antoine de Gramont, 'Mémoires du *Maréchal* de Gramont', in *Nouvelle Collection des Mémoires Pour Servir à l'Histoire de France* (Paris: Michaud et Poujoulat, 1839), Troisième série, tome VII, pp.256–258

Maréchal de Guiche was of a similar opinion, but *Maréchal* de Turenne said that he had reconnoitred a valley which was not protected by the enemy and that his troops could attack them by that route while the Duc d'Enghien's troops attacked the entrenchments directly. His plan was accepted. The advance was very orderly and since the attack needed to be at night, the troops arrived in position at exactly the time we had decided.

The command of the Duc d'Enghien's flank was given to d'Espenan. The Duc d'Enghien wanted *Maréchal* de Guiche to stay at his side, but de Guiche, having advanced and seen that the enemy's fire stretched all along their position and was not fixed in one place, realised at once that d'Espenan's troops were having no effect and warned the Duc d'Enghien that things were not going well, and that since it was already engaged, there was no going back. He added that there were two regiments – *Conti* and *Mazarin* – that were good and strong, and that he would lead them in an attack of the positions in front of him. To do so he put foot to ground and marched straight towards the position. On seeing this, the Duc d'Enghien did the same. And when one of the *Maréchal's* officers tried to dissuade him he very nearly received a sword in his stomach for his trouble. To bring the telling of this episode to a close, the Duc d'Enghien and *Maréchal* de Guiche marched together towards the enemy position and won a vigorous fight with such audacity that it is hard to imagine. The enemy, the Emperor's elite infantry, defended to the bitter end and were spared no quarter. It is no exaggeration to say that they lost more than three thousand men in the field.

Meanwhile, *Maréchal* de Turenne was fighting hard on his flank and attacked vigorously, but with little success as his enemies could not be undone. Nonetheless, General Mercy, commanding the Bavarian Army, seeing that the position was won, pulled back his troops and cannon with such order that cannot be overly admired and positioned them on the Black Mountain near Freiburg. Not having the time to entrench his troops he built a fortification with felled trees certain that he would be attacked a second time. He was not mistaken: at daybreak we marched against him believing, with reason, that since the night before he had been forced from a good position and having retreated to a place which he had had little time to fortify, that he would be undone with ease.

That day, Hesse's army was the vanguard of the attack. The wide area between the town and the mountain meant that the enemy could attack our rearguard with its numerous and seasoned cavalry, leading *Maréchal* de Guiche to position his army in the plain to rebuff such an attack. In addition, he beseeched the Duc d'Enghien (who had proved his ardour the night before) to be careful not to over commit himself to the battle.

The second attack decided, command was given to de Roqueserviere and de l'Echelle, both *Sergents de Bataille*. D'Espenan, buoyed by having initially captured a tricky redoubt guarded by some dragoons below the enemy's main position, thought that he needed simply to march on them to undo them. He was, however, badly mistaken since they held their ground with peerless resolve, and d'Espenan was unable to take them. A very large number of soldiers and officers were killed there, including the two *sergents de bataille*.

Seeing that the enemy cavalry in front of him was showing no sign of wanting to engage in battle and that the fight was raging on the crest of the hill, *Maréchal* de Guiche was certain that the Duc d'Enghien would not fail to enter the fray himself. And so, de Guiche decided to leave his troops under the command of the Comte de Palluau and join the battle that was being fought elsewhere.

On being told by numerous wounded officers and soldiers returning from the battle that the Duc d'Enghien was personally at the head of his infantry leading the charge under heavy fire from the enemy, de Guiche stepped up his pace to be at his side. When he arrived in the Freiburg vineyard, not twenty paces from the enemy position, his horse was killed stone dead by a musket shot to the head and he was thrown to the ground. As he was being lifted to his feet he saw the Duc d'Enghien retreating with only a small number of his men (the rest having been killed fighting by his side), having had two horses killed under him and numerous holes shot through his clothes by muskets.

The Duc d'Enghien ran to embrace *Maréchal* de Guiche and told him that his troops had been undone by their own fervour and that the attack had not been carried out as they had decided it should. M. d'Espenan proposed another line of attack by which the enemy would certainly be overcome since a number of infantry regiments had not yet taken part in the battle.

It needed the bravery and boldness of the Duc d'Enghien to consider starting afresh after having endured what he had just experienced and having most of his troops either killed or demoralised. But he was of a unique breed of man: one whose courage increases proportionally to the danger he faces. There are very few like him.

Maréchal de Guiche was very pleased to hear him speak in such a manner and admired the noble-mindedness of the young Prince. But since he loved him tenderly and that what he proposed did not seem feasible, de Guiche advised him with respect that what d'Espenan had done today and the night before should not strengthen His Highness' resolve in thinking that the action being proposed was wise. *Maréchal* de Guiche added that he was convinced that as many soldiers as took the field would be lost during the attack. The Duc d'Enghien accepted this reasoning.

At that moment, a messenger came to warn *Maréchal* de Guiche that, on seeing the lack of success of our infantry, the Bavarian cavalry was advancing. De Guiche quickly returned to his troops. When he arrived he saw that the Bavarian cavalry did not distance itself very far from the walls surrounding Freiburg meaning that an attack on them would require excessive boldness and complete madness in equal measure.

Then, a new infantry attack, led by M. de Mauvilliers, was launched without *Maréchal* de Guiche's knowledge. Like his two predecessors, de Mauvilliers, a *Sergent de Bataille*, was killed at once. This attack was as successful as the first: *Maréchal* de Guiche had to abandon his position for a second time and rushed to where the action was taking place. There, he found the infantry in appalling disorder, reduced to fending off volleys of musket fire by pressing up as close to the field fortifications built by the enemy.

Seeing this unfortunate state of affairs, *Maréchal* de Guiche made his way swiftly to join the Duc d'Enghien, who was with *Maréchal* de Turenne, supporting the infantry with a large number of men. De Guiche painted a vivid picture of the situation he had just witnessed explaining that it would be inhumane to leave an infantry, which instead of defending itself could only run for cover, be killed. The Duc d'Enghien agreed with him, but was also worried that if he ordered them to retreat before nightfall then the enemy cavalry would cut them to pieces as they retreated. Having seen the situation at first hand (and come under heavy fire at close quarters), and concluding that the field fortifications in place would stop the enemy cavalry from passing that way, *Maréchal* de Guiche assured the Duc d'Enghien of the contrary. And concerning the plain, de Guiche added that he would make sure that the enemy would not dare an attack through there. His advice was heeded and orders were immediately given to pull back the troops, and this was achieved without consequence. The losses suffered in soldiers and officers are difficult to number. Those of the enemy equally so: the general's brother, Baron de Mercy, was killed as well as many other officers of rank.

We stayed three days in our encampment and spent them transporting back to Brisach all the officers and soldiers wounded during the two great attacks. It was a terrible time because of all the dead bodies causing such infection that many men died of it. But it was inevitable: there was no other course of action possible.

Once the wagons sent with the wounded had returned from Brisach, and with the enemy still posted in their positions, the option rejected at Brisach was chosen and *Maréchal* de Guiche marched the vanguard towards Langhendhentzeling.

Having to expose our flank so close to the enemy, the manoeuvre proved quite bold and hazardous, but the enemy took no action and let the two armies pass without hindrance. However, guessing that the plan was to cut off their supply lines, the enemy marched swiftly, but with some difficulty (due to the amount of equipment and large cannon they took with them), towards the San Peter Valley.

Early the next morning we left Langhendhentzeling to march on San Peter. That day the vanguard was led by *Maréchal* de Turenne accompanied by the Duc d'Enghien. They found the enemy above the abbey at San Peter. On seeing the advance, the enemy had abandoned the wagons, cannon, munitions and equipment that they could not take with them on the horses that they had beforehand unhitched from the wagons.

At first, the enemy's flight led the Duc d'Enghien and *Maréchal* de Turenne to believe that they would be able to charge and engage the enemy's rearguard in combat while waiting for *Maréchal* de Guiche to reach them as he could only march in line. But things did not go according to plan: Mercy, who without a doubt was one of the greatest commanders of the century, charged them so violently that they were obliged to retreat swiftly before him in some disorder. He captured several standards from colonel Rosen, whom he beat soundly, and took many prisoners. Once he had the advantage, and seeing the King's army arriving, he lost no time and marched towards Philingen to avoid a battle he did not want to wage. Once all of our troops had arrived, we marched together so as not to repeat the same mistake as had just occurred. This gave Mercy two hours start on us and it did not prove possible, however hard we tried, to catch up with him. We returned to the abbey at San Peter to camp and the soldiers were able to recover from their exertions by plundering with great satisfaction the food that they found in the wagons that the enemy had left behind.

The Battle of Alerheim or Nördlingen, 3 August 1645

The Battle of Alerheim by Ramsay[9]

M. de Mercy retired farther into the country towards Dinkefpuhel, where he left three or four hundred men, and encamped three or four leagues from thence behind the woods. A few days after, the King's army arrived near Dinkefpuhel, and formed a design to attack it; a detachment of musketeers was ordered to advance among the ruins of some houses, where they opened some trenches: but before midnight, an officer that had been prisoner and had made his escape from the Bavarian Army, came and told M. de Turenne, that M. de Mercy thinking that the King's army would be intent upon the siege of Dinkefpuhel, was marching by night, and was but two leagues off, behind the woods. M. de Turenne went immediately to acquaint M. d'Enghien with the news, who resolved to leave all the baggage with two or three regiments of cavalry, and to march presently with the whole army in quest of M. de Mercy.

We set out an hour after midnight. M. de Turenne had the vanguard and we crossed a wood. M. d'Enghien was there, and had left *Maréchal* de Grammont with his army in the rearguard. As we were going out of the wood we saw, for by this time there was daylight enough, a small troop of Bavarians; and a little after, as we were driving them back, we discovered some of the enemy's squadrons, who having seen the head of our vanguard,

Antoine de Gramont (1604–1678). Watercolour by Karl Alexander Wilke (1879–1954) (Public Domain)

---

9   Paul Marichal, (ed.), *Mémoires du Maréchal de Turenne* (Paris: Renouard, 1909), tome I, pp.57–69.

retired in all haste towards the body of their army, whereof these squadrons were the vanguard: so that if we had not set out too soon, we had found the enemy on their march, and consequently in a very bad posture. They halted behind several ponds, and presently drew up in order of battle, and having planted their cannon, began to make some works on their front, and entrench themselves.

The King's army, as they went out of the wood drew up likewise in order of battle; but could not march up to the enemy but through defiles. We brought up our cannon, which galled them pretty much; but theirs that were already planted, did us a great deal more mischief. The whole day was spent in gunning one another, with great loss on both sides. The next morning, two hours before daylight, the King's army retired by the same road it had come, which was by a defile in the wood. The enemy pursued only with some horse, and there happened but one skirmish, though they had once an opportunity to have defeated a part of our rearguard. We repassed the wood, and went to join the baggage near Dinkefpuhel, where we encamped : but not judging it advisable to stop at so inconsiderable a place, we resolved to march to Nördlingen, and get there before the enemy; which was very easy to be done. The next day the army decamped early in the morning, and after a two or three hours march, arrived about nine o'clock in the plain near Nördlingen: no enemy appearing there, we resolved to halt, and had some thoughts of encamping, but no orders were yet given for unloading the baggage, or pitching the tents. As M. de Turenne was advancing into the plain with a small guard, and while the Prince was out not far off with another, he fell upon a German party that were marauding, and brought away two or three prisoners, who reported that the enemy's army was passing a rivulet a league from thence in order to draw near to Nördlingen. M. de Turenne immediately joined the Prince, and having learnt that there was no rivulet between the place where the enemy was passing and that where we were, orders were sent to the army that no man should stir from his post. The Prince and M. de Turenne advanced still with a few men, in order to reconnoitre and have a greater certainty of what the enemy were a doing, and whether they continued their march. The plain is so open, and stretches so far, that there was no danger in advancing with a few men.

M. de Mercy, who commanded the Bavarian Army, to which a body of six or seven thousand Imperialists, commanded by General Gleen, had joined, being come to the banks of a rivulet about nine o'clock in the morning; and judging, as it was true, that the King's army was encamped near Nördlingen, and that we intended to besiege it, thought that by passing that rivulet without baggage, he might with safety draw near Nördlingen, because of the hills and some advantages he might take with his army: he likewise imagined that we would not attack him that day, and so he should have time to entrench himself , which he was wont to do very expeditiously, having commonly following his army no other carriages but the ammunition wagons, and those in which were the tools and implements. He continued his march, and posted himself three or four hundred paces from the rivulet upon a hill (called Vineberg), which, at the place he stopped, was pretty high, but sloped insensibly towards a village (called Allerheim). In order to make the best use of the place, according to the strength of his army and the situation of the ground, he began to draw up his right wing, composed of a body of Imperialists and some of his own troops, from that part of the hill which was nearest the rivulet, to the village, having two regiments of cavalry and his cannon in the place where his right wing began. From the place where the right wing terminated, the infantry extended in order of battle behind the village, and in the action almost all of them fought, in order to defend it; but at first it was possessed only by a detachment of musketeers in the church and upon the steeple. Next to the infantry, which was in two lines, as was the cavalry, the left wing, composed of the Bavarian cavalry, and commanded by M. John de Wert, ended at a little castle (Pufendorf), situated upon a rising ground (the hill of Allerheim), round which there was some infantry that closed the left of the army, as the two regiments of infantry abovementioned closed the right. The space between the village and the castle was a plain which might well contain twelve or thirteen squadrons. This was the disposition that M. de Mercy made, as well for fighting, as for encamping, if we had not attacked him.

The Prince having perceived that the enemy's army was passing the rivulet, sent orders to the troops to get themselves ready to march, and being confirmed by the scouts, and by what he himself saw, that the enemy was not unwilling to fight, he passed the place, behind which he would have had a great advantage, and sent orders for the whole army to march. About twelve o'clock the army advanced into the great plain, and about four o'clock the two armies came in sight of one another. It took up a good deal of time to extend and put ourselves in a posture of fighting. That village, which was before the enemy's army, justly made it doubtful, whether it were better to attack it, or march towards the two wings with the cavalry only: but as it is not very safe to attack wings, without at the same time charging the infantry posted in the centre, it was not judged proper, whatever difficulty there might be in attacking the village, to charge with the cavalry, without the infantry marching in the same front; and as the village was above four hundred paces more advanced than the place where the enemy's army was, it was thought best to halt with the two wings, while the infantry should attack and make themselves masters of the nearest houses of that village, or at least of some of them. For that end, our cannon were brought up, that we might not be annoyed by those of the enemy, without annoying them with ours: but as cannon that are planted have a great advantage over those that march, because the horses must always be put to the carriages in order to advance, whereby a great deal of time is lost, those of the enemy did a great deal more damage than ours.

In this disposition the infantry of the King's army marched straight to the village; the right wing being opposite to the enemy's left wing in the plain, and the left wing to the enemy's right, which was upon that hill, from which there was an insensible descent to the village. Our infantry found but little resistance at the nearest houses, but as they advanced farther, three or four regiments of the enemy (one, part of which possessed the churchyard, and the other had made holes for firing out of the houses) gave so great a fire, that they halted all of a sudden, and began to give way. We sent some regiments to their assistance; and M. de Mercy, who was behind the village, caused his men to be sustained by other troops. Thus the fight became very obstinate, with great loss on both sides; but less on that of the enemy, because they were lodged in the houses; and even while their first line was fighting in the village, the second was not idle upon the hill. These expedients did not succeed; but they showed a great deal of skill and presence of mind in the general. The Prince came often into the village; he received a great many shots in his clothes, and had two horses wounded under him. He left *Maréchal* de Grammont on the right wing of his cavalry. M. de Turenne also did what he could to make the infantry that were in the village near his wing to advance. M. de Bellenave, major-general of his army was killed there. M. de Castelaun, quartermaster general of that of the Prince, was very dangerously wounded, as well as a great number of officers. In the heat, and about the end of this battle, M. de Mercy, general of the Bavarian Army, received a musket shot, of which he died on the spot; and I imagine, that when the enemy's left wing, commanded by John de Wert, advanced against the Prince's cavalry, they knew nothing of his death: the battle having lasted above an hour in the village, where some squadrons were employed to sustain the infantry, the enemy's left wing began to march.

It has often been said, that there was a fault committed in passing a few ditches that were between the two wings, but I don't think there was any great matter in that; for the whole right wing of the King's army was in order of battle, and saw before it the left of the enemy, which advanced at a slow pace to engage and found but small resistance. Although *Maréchal* de Grammont did all that could be done, he was taken prisoner, not having been able to get either the first or second line to do their duty.

The Prince, who was very near the village, went to the wing where M. de Turenne commanded, who seeing that the attack of the village did not succeed, and that the cavalry of the enemy's left wing were marching up to the French cavalry, advanced with his wing towards the hill, and having discoursed a moment with the Prince, told him, that if he would be pleased to sustain him with some squadrons of the second line and with the Hessians, he would go and charge the enemy: the Prince having consented, M. de Turenne continued his march up the hill at the head of *Flextein's* regiment. Being within a hundred paces of the enemy, and turning about, he saw that all the French cavalry – of the right wing – and the infantry that had been beaten out of the village, were entirely broke and scattered in the plain.

As M. de Turenne was continuing his march up the hill with eight or nine squadrons abreast, the infantry, which the enemy had at the two extremities of the wing, gave a fire, and the cannon had time to give three or four discharges, the first with ball, and the last with cartridge-shot, with which M. de Turenne's horse was wounded, and he himself received a shot in his cuirass, and the colonel and some of the other officers of *Flextein's* regiment were wounded before it attacked a regiment of cavalry that faced it. Notwithstanding this, the whole wing having marched abreast, broke the whole first line of the enemy, some squadrons making more, some less, resistance; and the enemy's second line sustaining the first that was broke, the fight was very obstinate. We had only one or two squadrons in the second line; and the Hessians, who made the body of reserve, were a little too far off: for which reason we were driven back a little, but without being routed; for our squadrons continued still in good order, and some of them had even the advantage of those of the enemy; but their numbers made them too strong for us.

The Hessians came up, and the Prince at their head acted with no less courage than conduct. When the Weimarian cavalry saw the Hessians approach, they rallied, and we all at once charged the whole body of the enemy's cavalry, who had formed themselves into one line; we broke it; all the cannon upon the hill were taken; the regiments of infantry that were with the right wing were defeated, and Gleen, the general of the Emperor's army, was made prisoner.

On the other hand, all the Prince's cavalry, both of the first and second line, and even his reserve, commanded by the Chevalier de Chabot, and all the infantry, who being beaten out of the village, had fled to the plain, were entirely routed: John de Wert leaving the victory on that side to be pursued by two regiments, who drove our troops two leagues even to the baggage, returned to sustain his right wing, or to stop their flight. If, instead of returning by the place where he had been first posted, and leaving the village on the left-hand, he had marched into the plain against the Weimarian and Hessian cavalry, we should not have been in a condition to have made the least resistance, and our left wing, thus hemmed in, would have been very easily put into confusion.

The sun was already set when M. de Wert's cavalry began to return behind the village; and night coming on presently, the two wings that had beaten what was before them, stood in order of battle facing each other; and as the cavalry of the King's army was a little farther advanced than the village, some of the enemy's regiments that were in the churchyard and the church, surrendered to M. de Turenne, and came forth without arms at twilight, not knowing that their own troops were not five hundred paces off.

The cavalry of both armies continued a part of the night very near one another in the plain, their advance guards being not fifty paces from each other. About an hour after midnight, the enemy's army began to retire, without having any more reason for it than that of the King, except that they had lost their general. We heard no great noise, for they had no baggage. I believe they carried away but four small pieces of cannon; all the rest, which were twelve or fifteen, remained upon the field of battle. At break of day not one of the enemy was to be seen; we understood that they had retired towards Donawert, a small town (four leagues off) where there is a bridge upon the Danube. M. de Turenne pursued them within sight of Donawert, with two or three thousand cavalry.

The whole right wing of the King's army was beaten, and all the infantry were put entirely into confusion, except three Hessian battalions that made the reserve, and I believe there were at least three or four thousand infantry killed upon the spot. Of the enemy's army, the whole right wing was beaten, three or four regiments of infantry, that were mixed with it, were routed, two surrendered in the church; a great many men were killed in the village, and almost all their cannon was taken. As for the loss of men, I believe, the King's army lost more than the enemy. On the one side, *Maréchal* de Grammont was taken, and on the other General Gleen, and a very great number of officers, and many standards. Our German cavalry of the old corps behaved exceedingly well, as also the regiments of *Duras* and *Tracy*.

It was some days before we could draw together above twelve or fifteen hundred of all the French infantry. After having stayed a day or two near Nördlingen, the Prince knowing that the citizens were the strongest there, and that the garrison consisted but of four hundred men, resolved to attack it: the citizens desired to capitulate the very first night, and the garrison was sent to the enemy's army; but I think their arms were taken from them. We stayed seven or eight days at Nördlingen, which is a pretty large and fine town, where we greatly refreshed ourselves; we found there some arms, harness, abundance of horses for the baggage, and plenty of medicine for the wounded.'

The Battle of Alerheim by the *Maréchal* de Gramont[10]

But, as the generals ate, we saw arriving at full gallop a Swedish reiter who came to announce that the enemy were no more than half a league away: this appeared so improbable, and so unlikely, that the company broke into laughter, and the Duc d'Enghien jokingly said: 'You will at least agree, my friend, that if these men were as wise and skilled as you tell us, they would have taken a position that puts the Vernitz river between us.'

"I'faith, Monseigneur," replied the horseman, "Your Highness may believe whatever you wish; but if Your Highness would come with me five hundred paces from here, on this small rising that is here on the left, I shall show him that I am neither blind nor poltroon; and Your Highness would agree with me that the army of Mercy is separated from his own only by a riverless plain as flat as the hand."

The reiter spoke so positively and with such assurance that we began to fear that he spoke truly. The Duc d'Enghien, the two *Maréchals* de France and the general officers mounted their horses with a few squadrons to appraise the situation for themselves, and the truth of such circumstantial news; and as they advanced they discovered the enemy arraying for battle and that they, having the higher ground, saw all the movements of our army. It was at this moment that Mercy and Gleen made a grave misjudgement; for if they had detached a large cavalry corps led by soldiers in open order to reach eight or ten plum-trees where the Duc d'Enghien and all the generals were placed to better observe the movement of the enemy, these would have found themselves engaged so far forward and so distanced from the rest of their troops, that they would inevitably have been taken or killed. But as it is impossible for a man to think of everything, this did not enter the heads of Mercy nor of Gleen; and they did not think, seeing that they were going to give battle, of anything other than taking the most advantageous position:

---

10 *Maréchal* Antoine de Gramont, 'Mémoires du *Maréchal* de Gramont', in *Nouvelle Collection des Mémoires Pour Servir à l'Histoire de France* (Paris: Michaud et Poujoulat, 1839), Troisième série, tome VII, pp.261–263

which they succeeded to perfection, as there was none better than that which they chose.

There was a village in the middle of the plain, in which they filled the houses and church with the infantry; and to defend it they raised a sort of entrenchment, where they placed their large infantry corps on the right and on the left. There were two small hillocks, on each of which was an old ruined château where their cannon was positioned: their first cavalry wing, composed of cuirassiers of the Emperor, held the right side of the village up to just below the hillock on which the cannon was positioned; the left wing, composed of Bavarian troops, stretched up to the other hillock; and the second line was in the necessary distance. These positions of strong defence did not hinder the resolution to fight: and as it was a little late, the troops were urged strongly to form rank, realising that if they waited until the following day, the affair would become more difficult, especially as the enemy would finish the entrenchment that they had already begun, and that it would then be unassailable.

Maréchal de Gramont had the right wing opposite that of Bavaria: and as it was believed to be impossible to attack their cavalry, which was flanked by the infantry from the village and the cannon of the two hillocks, without taking over the village, it was resolved to attack, although this appeared hard and difficult. Marsin and Castelnau were given this expedition. An officer of confidence had the order, with a few others, to reconnoitre a place which from a distance appeared to be a gulley between the left wing of the enemy and our right; but this passage was poorly observed by these gentlemen, who, without having seen it (the peril of approaching too close being manifest), reported that it was of considerable size, over which the squadrons could not pass: this was the source of much distress; and nearly caused the Duc d'Enghien to call a counsel of war, which the situation certainly merited.

In the meantime the attack of the village became terrible, and the Duc d'Enghien constantly pulled troops from the right wing to defend his infantry, which suffered greatly and which was nearly broken from time to time: *Maréchal* de Gramont, seeing this with distress, galloped as hard as he could to join the Duc and to inform him of the greatest inconvenience which could occur; for on returning to his position, he saw that the enemy had brought down infantry from the hillock on which their cannon was placed, which had already begun to cause much damage to the squadrons of our right; wishing to remedy this, he advanced the second line, the regiments of *Fabert* and the Irish *Wal.* During this lively skirmish, he received a musket shot to the middle of his helmet, by which he was so concussed that he fell on the neck of his horse as if dead; but he came to himself a little time after, and as the shot had not pierced him, he suffered only a serious contusion, which nevertheless did not prevent him from acting during the rest of the action, or from being wherever his presence was necessary.

At the same time, the two infantry regiments of *Fabert* and *Wal* pursued that of the enemy, which was troubling our cavalry; but at that moment, disorder and confusion began to appear in the village, and Baron de Marsin and the Marquis de Castelnau had been seriously injured and obliged to withdraw. The Duc d'Enghien, seeing that the affair of the village was not going well, and that the situation was nearly irremediable, passed to the left wing, which was composed of Hessian troops and commanded by *Maréchal* de Turenne, and found upon arriving that this general was impatient to sound the charge: and it was at this time that were made the impressive cavalry charges that made so much noise and of which so much has been spoken.

At that moment, the Bavarian left wing charged our right, and, in battle array, they crossed the place that had been reported to be a nearly impracticable gulley; which caused such surprise and fright to all our French cavalry, that it fled two leagues ahead, without waiting for the enemy to be within pistol range, an event which one would not have believed possible.

All *Maréchal* de Gramont was able to do was to place himself at the head of the two regiments of *Fabert* and *Wal*, which did not waver in the slightest from their positions, and when they were at point-blank range they fired with such fury onto the enemy cavalry that it opened the charging squadrons, and *Maréchal* de Gramont took this opportunity to enter within, along with those men remaining around him: which did not serve him overmuch, as he found himself surrounded on all sides, and with four cavalry who were going to kill him, arguing together over who would do so. His captain of the guard killed one, and Hemon, his aide-de-camp, killed another, which gave him a little respite. He survived by good fortune: a captain of the *La Pierre* regiment, named Sponheim, heard him named as *Maréchal* de Gramont, and rallied two or three officers from his friends, who diverted the company, pulled him from the intrigue and saved his life. The captain of his guards died there, the lieutenant was injured and taken prisoner with him, the cornette and the quartermaster were killed, and all the company of his guards, who were a hundred maîtres, with the exception of twelve who were also taken; four aides-de-camp were killed, three of his pages, and all his servants who had followed him were also killed at his side. Such is the result of affection for a much-loved master.

Another extraordinary occurrence happened to him: for the leading captain, wishing still to take him to General Mercy, unaware of his fate and not yet knowing that he had been killed by the first commanded musketeers upon the attack of the village, found a small Lorraine page of the Baron de Mercy, aged fifteen years; upon hearing that the general of the French had been captured, he wished to avenge upon him the death of his master: and as he had no pistols and *Maréchal* de Gramont was being led with the reins of his horse pulled back, he seized one of the *Maréchal's* pistols and shot him in the head; but by good fortune it had been fired in the battle, and could not do harm. The Germans wished to inflict a serious punishment for such an evil action; but de Gramont said that he was a child whom he wished to forgive, and prevented him from being shot then and there, the Germans being without pity in such situations.

While these things were happening on our right wing, the same could not be said for our enemy's, who, after a furious battle, were entirely defeated by the Duc d'Enghien and *Maréchal* de Turenne, who were on the left. General Gleen, who was in command, was injured and taken prisoner, as were a great number of senior officers and soldiers, as well as many cannon and standards. The battlefield was ours, with all marks of victory: upon seeing this, and with Mercy dead, Jean de Werth, who commanded the Bavarian Army, thought only of withdrawing in the best possible order to a mountain near Donauwörth, named Schellenberg, which had been fortified since the time of the King of Sweden.

The Battle of Lens, 20 August 1648

The Battle of Lens by the *Maréchal* de Gramont[11]

In the evening, we halted the battle array and we gave three most important recommendations to all the troops: the first, to watch each other as they marched, so that the cavalry and the infantry would remain on the same line, and so that they could keep their distances and intervals; the second, to charge only at a walking pace; the third, to allow the enemy to fire first.

This was the arrangement of the army: the Prince de Condé took the right wing of the cavalry, which consisted of nine squadrons: one from his guards, two from his *Altesse Royale*, one from the *Grand Maître*, one from *Saint-Simon*, one from *Bussy*, one from *Streiff*, one from *Harcourt le Vieux*, and one from *Beaujeu*; Villequier was *Lieutenant Général* under him; the *Maréchals de Camp* were Noirmoutier and La Moussaye; the Marquis de Fort was the *Sergent de Bataille*, and Beaujeu was commander of the cavalry of this brigade.

The left wing was commanded by *Maréchal* de Gramont with the same number of squadrons: one *carabin* squadron, that of the guards; two from *La Ferté-Senneterre*, two from *Mazarin*, two from *Gramont*, and one from La Ferté's guards; La Ferté was *Lieutenant Général*; Saint-Maigrin was *Maréchal de Camp*; Linville was *maréchal de bataille*, and the Comte de Lillebonne was the commander of the cavalry of this brigade.

The first line of infantry between the two wings was composed of two battalions of the *Gardes Françaises*, the *Gardes Suisses* and *Ecossaises*, the regiments of *Picardie* and his *Altesse Royale*, and those of *Persan* and *Erlach*. The cannon marched at the head of the infantry.

Six *gendarme* squadrons protected the infantry: one each from the companies of the King, the Queen, the Prince de Condé, the Duc de Longueville, the Prince de Conti, the *Chevau-Légers* of his Royal Highness, and one from the Duc d'Enghien; this corps and the first line was under the orders of Châtillon, *Lieutenant Général*, and the *Sergents de Bataille*, who were Villemesle and Beauregard.

The second line of cavalry, commanded by *Maréchal de Camp* Arnault, was composed of eight squadrons: one from *Arnault*, two from *Chappes*, one from *Coudray*, one from *Salbrich*, one from *Vidame* and two from *Villette*.

---

11   *Maréchal* Antoine de Gramont, 'Mémoires du *Maréchal* de Gramont', in *Nouvelle Collection des Mémoires Pour Servir à l'Histoire de France* (Paris: Michaud et Poujoulat, 1839), Troisième série, tome VII, pp.279–281.

The second line of the left wing was commanded by Le Plessis-Bellière, *Maréchal de Camp*, and composed of seven squadrons: one from *Roquelaure*, one from *Gesvres*, one from *Lillebonne*, two from *Noirlieu*, one from *Meille* and one from *Chémerault*.

The second line of infantry was composed of five battalions: one from *la Reine* with three hundred commanded men of the garrison of La Bassée, one from *Erlach Français* and *Rasilly*, one from *Mazarin Italien*, one from *Condé* and one from *Conti*.

The reserve corps was composed of six squadrons: one from *Ruvigny*, one from *Sirot*, three from *Erlach* and one from *Fabri*. It was commanded by Erlach, the *Lieutenant Général*, and Rasilly, *Maréchal de Camp*.

We marched at dawn on the 19th, in the same order, expecting to encounter the enemy at the position in which they had shown themselves the previous day with forty squadrons: but the surprise was extreme when, having passed beyond the said position, we saw the entire army arrayed for battle and positioned as thus: the right wing composed of Spanish troops, beneath Lens, of which they had taken control the previous night, having before them a number of ravines and ditches, and the infantry were in the brush, which provided natural entrenchment; and the left wing, composed of the Duc de Lorraine's cavalry, on a hill before which there were also a number of gullies.

The King's army being presented before that of the enemy, and the Prince de Condé, having recognised that if he wished to fight with a joyful heart it was unthinkable to attack the advantageous position the enemy occupied, contented to place himself before it; and the entire day passed with light skirmishes and a number of cannon shots fired from both sides.

The next day, the Prince saw that in the place where they were there was neither forage nor water, and so he decided to march to Neus, a village two leagues from the place where he was encamped, in order to obtain supplies and victuals at Béthune, and in this way be in condition to follow the enemy wherever they went: and as he wished to show them his desire to fight, and that he did not fear them, he decamped from his position in front of them in broad daylight.

The reserve corps began the march, followed by the advance guard; the second line followed by the first, in the same order and the same distance that had been observed the day before; but as the Price de Condé left ten squadrons for the rearguard a little too far from his line, led by Villequier and Noirmoutier, General Bec made use of this opportunity as the skilled captain he was, and charged them so vigorously with the cavalry of Lorraine that he broke them and put them in great disarray. Brancas, the mestre de camp, had his arm broken and was made prisoner, and many junior officers and cavalry were either taken or killed. And the Prince de Condé had great fortune not to be so; for he wished to remedy by his presence the disorder that he saw, but so great was the terror of his troops he was unable to do so, and he was pursued for a long time; and it was well that he had taken a good horse, for without it he would have suffered the same fate as his page, who was injured and taken behind him.

General Bec, proud of this success, and his natural pride increased by the success he had just won, together with the German braggery which made him despise our troops, ordered the Archduke and the Comte de Fuensaldagne to march at all haste, and gave his word that the French Army would be defeated as soon as battle was engaged.

While our troops were being routed, *Maréchal* de Gramont's Captain of the Guard came to inform him that he saw the wing of the Prince de Condé in great confusion and making movement that did not bode well; which obliged *Maréchal* de Gramont to turn around all his troops whom he marched in battle array, leaving only small troops of thirty maîtres behind the squadrons marching alongside the battalions for skirmishing, in the event that the enemy wished to follow. This done, he went at full gallop to the wing of the Prince de Condé, who embraced him and told him with much pain that his own regiment, which he had led, had abandoned him most shamefully, and that it would not have required much for him to have been killed or taken. The conversation they had together was of the shortest length; for seeing that the enemy was assembling and that they were already positioning their infantry and their cannon, they resolved to give battle then and there, knowing full well that on such occasions long discussion is neither prudent nor wise. The Prince de Condé said only to *Maréchal* de Gramont that he asked for time to put the second line into the position of the first, because he found this line so terrified that it would certainly be defeated if he led it once more into the charge. And it was indeed his presence of mind and this perfect knowledge he had of men that put him always above the others in the most perilous and the greatest occasions; for everything he had to do came to him in an instant. Such men are a rare genius of warfare, a species of which there are only one in a hundred thousand.

Maréchal de Gramont left the Prince de Condé and returned to his wing; and passing to the head of the troops, he told them that battle had just been decided; he asked them to remember their valour, and what they owed the King, and also to observe well the orders they had been given; he said that this action was of such importance given the current state of affairs, that it was either victory or death, and that he was going to show them the example by entering first into the enemy squadron that would be opposite his own. This short and moving speech was infinitely pleasing to the soldiers; all the infantry shouted for joy and threw their hats in the air; the cavalry took their sword in hand and all the trumpets sounded fanfares with an inexpressible joy. The Prince de Condé and *Maréchal* de Gramont embraced warmly, and each thought of their own business.

Close to the wing commanded by *Maréchal* de Gramont was a small village, which broke nearly all his battle order: to allow the Prince de Condé to array for battle, this obliged him three times to withdraw a little to the left and for his troops to make a quarter turn, then march along the high ground; after which he turned to the right and re-arrayed for battle. This manoeuvre was troublesome, and most dangerous in the presence of an alert enemy; but it was not possible to do otherwise. Finally, as he saw there was enough ground, he marched straight on the enemy at a slow pace, with such silence (most unusual for the French) that in his wing the only person that could be heard speaking was himself.

Maréchal de Gramont had the troops of Spain to fight; for as they had the right and he the left, they were opposite each other: the Comte de Bucquoy was at the head of the first line, and the Prince de Ligne at the second. They were positioned on a small hillock; and it can be said that it was a duel rather than a battle, as each squadron and battalion had their counterpart to fight.

The enemy held firm with the advantage of their higher ground. They were five or six paces behind the crest, so that if they were charged, the enemy cavalry would fall on them in disarray, while our cavalry would be able to counter-attack in order. They had no sword in hand; but like all the Spanish cuirassiers in Flanders, they carried *mousquetons*, which they held on the thigh when not fighting, the same as if they were lances. At twenty paces from them, *Maréchal* de Gramont sounded the charge, and informed the troops that they would have to withstand a furious discharge; but after this he promised them that they would easily have the advantage of their enemy. This discharge was so close and so terrible that one would have said Hell opened: there were hardly any officers at the head of the corps that they commanded that were not killed or injured; but it can be said that the return from the charge was worthy of Matins; for our squadrons entered theirs, and resistance was practically nonexistent. We had little mercy, and many were killed.

The second line came to defend the first; but they were so violently charged by ours that they hardly held at all and were broken. Our infantry had the same advantage over theirs; and we lost few men, except in the regiment of the guards who had been charged on the flank by a number of squadrons, and lost six captains and many officers.

The reserve corps commanded by Erlach defended marvellously the wing of the Prince de Condé, who broke the first and second enemy lines, after having charged ten times in person, and carried out actions worthy of this valour and capacity that are so well known.

Never has there been a victory more complete; General Bec was fatally injured and taken prisoner, as were the Prince de Ligne, general of the cavalry, all principal German officers, all Spanish and Italian mestres de camp, thirty-eight pieces of cannon, their pontoons and all the baggage train.

The battle was well and truly won, but, as *Maréchal* de Gramont reformed his squadrons which found itself a little in disorder having charged many times, one of the enemy squadrons which was fleeing as fast as possible fell on him at the moment he expected the least; and he would have been taken or killed had they not been in such a hurry to flee, for he found himself in the middle of them. Nevertheless, they fired a discharge as they passed, which killed one of his aides-de-camp at his side: a most strange episode.

The two wings continued to pursue victory, and the Prince and the *Maréchal* met beyond the gulley of Lens; and with sword in hand, the Prince came to the *Maréchal* to embrace him and congratulate him on what he had achieved; but there was such a furious fight between their two horses, which before had been as gentle as mules, that they nearly ate each other, and they nearly endangered the lives of their masters more than the battle itself.

The number of prisoners increased to five thousand; and as they needed to be sent to France under an escort sufficient to lead such a large number, the order was given to Villequier, with two cavalry regiments and one infantry regiment; in consequence, the army was obliged to remain close to the battlefield for seven or eight days to await the return of the troops and for our horses to lead all the captured soldiers to Arras and La Bassée, which required a number of journeys.

The Battle of Lens by La Peyrère[12]

The Prince was delighted by the presence of the Archduke. His plan had succeeded; it seemed that his retreat had simply been a feint to engage the enemy in battle. This was indeed a subtle trap for the greatest captains of Spain, for which the Archduke fell. The illusion which confused him was bizarre; he raced to victory and did not have time to take breath for the battle. The Prince was ready, the Archduke was not; the French hastened to array themselves for battle, to surprise the Spanish in their disorder. (…)

It was around eight o'clock in the morning when the army began to march in excellent array to the sound of trumpets, drums and cannon. The Prince called a halt from time to time to redress the lines and to maintain distances, and the cannon of the Comte de Cossé was so well and so diligently used that it fired while marching, which is a significant feat; they had the advantage that, by firing from the plain onto the hillock of the enemy position, all shots reached either the squadrons, or the battalions, and created great confusion for them to array themselves for battle. Their cannon, which fired from the top of the hill to the foot, did not have the same effect as ours, although the numbers were unequal, with the Archduke having 38 and the Prince 18.

The enemy was impatient to fight; they looked brave and marched resolutely towards us. However they were attempting two things at the same time, marching and arraying for combat, which is a hindrance when marching to a decisive battle (…)

The two armies were at 30 paces from each other when three shots were fired from the left wing of the enemy into our right wing. Condé, who feared the precipitation of his soldiers, halted them and forbade the musketeers from opening fire before the enemy had fired; fire should not begin until at point-blank range. This halt had three good effects; it tempered the ardour of our troops, readjusted the battle array and confirmed the soldier in the resolution to withstand the enemy discharge.

The Prince of Salm advanced at a trot with his first line of Walloon and Lorraine soldiers against Condé's first line, who advanced at a walk to receive them. The two lines met horse to horse, pistol to pistol, and remained in this position for a fairly long time, awaiting who would fire first, with neither side wavering.

---

12   Isaac de la Peyrère, 'La Bataille de Lens, donnée le 21 août 1648', Victor Cousin, *La Société Française au XVIIe Siècle* (Paris: Didier et Cie, 1858), Vol.1, pp.405–407.

The enemy was more impatient and opened fire; it was as though the gates of Hell had opened! All our front line officers were killed, injured or unseated. Condé gave the signal to fire, then, leading the Gassion regiment with his sword held high, he crushed the squadron facing him. His six other squadrons followed him, and, on his example, charged the first enemy line so violently that it was overwhelmed.

Account of the Battle of Lens, on 20 August 1648, by one of Condé's officers[13]

After the Prince de Condé took Ypres, he led his army back to Béthune, where he set up camp. Between Lillers and this town he summoned Erlach to join him, to repair by the junction of their troops the great loss of his cavalry (…) who had been greatly inconvenienced during the siege of Ypres by the hindrance caused to convoys and foraging parties.

Archduke Leopold during this time had taken Courtrai, and marched to Lillers: one of our parties took a company of Croats in the war with the commanding captain who was garrisoned in Gère; the Prince generously sent him back to the Archduke with his corps trumpeter, and ordered him to pay his respects to the Archduke. He did so while General Beck was in the tent of the Archduke. But this Prince received this honour with a stupid arrogance and responded with such words that it would be shameful to repeat what the trumpeter reported, and Beck, to go further than the impoliteness of the Prince, said such idiotic things that he revealed the character of the low gentlemen that he was, calling the Prince de Condé a young leveret that he threatened to take by the ears to Luxembourg. As the trumpeter replied in a similar style, he was threatened with prison, and finally was dismissed, very poorly satisfied. The man who told us this was in the suite of the Prince who, awaiting the return of his trumpeter, read Dante in Italian and interpreted to a few assistants a word that many did not know, which was *vespaio*, meaning a swarm of wasps; M. de la Moussaye brought the gazette from Brussels, in which the enemy, proud of their success in the seizing of Ypres, had published a rather uninspired gibe, saying that his Imperial Highness sought everywhere the army of the Prince de Condé and that he would give wine to the man who could find this army and bring him news of it; as the Prince turned the affair to mockery, the trumpeter arrived and related the content of his embassy to Condé so heatedly that his master who, out of all the heroes of his century is the most sensitive to glory, changed his tone and swore that he would spare him the trouble of searching if he was hardy enough to leave the woodland where he had entrenched his army.

In the meantime, this army arrived at Estaires.

There was a château on the Lys where we had forty or fifty men garrisoned. The Archduke took it the same night and from there, covered all the way by the river, he marched on Lens.

---

13   Archives du Château de Chantilly, Manuscrit MS933, *Relation de la Bataille de Lens, le 20 août 1648, par un officier de Condé.*

Lens is outside the marsh that this river makes, which is called Watergangs. There is on the plain which goes to Arras a small stream, which has its source near to this town and it was occupied by the Spanish army who camped there at the top of the Rideau of Lens and positioned its cannon in two small spinneys on the Rideau.

And brave as they were in their gazette, the Spaniards entrenched without reflecting that they had thirty-five thousand men. Hearing the cannon fire to the south of Lens, the Prince de Condé rejoiced to see his enemies on a plain and that same hour commanded *Maréchal* de Châtillon to prepare a guard corps positioned on a bridge they had won. He had woodcuts brought, and charged those facing him with his guards and the guards he found there so brusquely that the enemy abandoned the passage (…) to their army which was only two leagues from there.

The Prince crossed the Lys and left the baggage train beneath Béthune; I have never seen anyone cross with such impetuosity; one hour before dawn we arrived at the edge of the gullies. This great Prince was naturally content when the artillery was advanced.

The narrator of this account found himself in an orchard of fruit trees, on the edge of which was our hero, who saw the pieces of cannon go by which increased as they passed. Our hero cut a switch from which he made an implement to throw apples, and began to throw against the Marquis of Normanville; the Prince found this entertainment pleasing, and he took one also.

This pleasant prelude to battle continued, with each man taking part until M. de Cossé passed with the last piece of artillery under his command.

Then *Maréchal* d'Erlach came to greet the Prince, to whom he had brought eight thousand good men (author's note: in fact he brought less than four thousand). The sun was already high in the sky, and the enemy generals came with twelve hundred horses to see if it was all of our army or a part that was already downstream of the river; to remove their doubt, His Highness marched his artillery at the first line; they saw it clearly and returned to their entrenchments, leaving the entire plain free for us.

While marching, His Highness formed his troops into three lines, which together made at the most twenty thousand men and at least eighteen thousand; he placed the *Gardes*, *Picardie* and the regiments of the army of Erlach in the first line, and for the cavalry, all the gendarmes of both the King and the Princes and all the companies of the guards of the generals; the second line was arrayed in the same way and our light cavalry commanded by Guiche; M. d'Erlach was the third line and the reserve corps; M. de Cossé led a band of artillery. At the first line he marched them as fast as the troops; in this array we went to show our army to the Archduke, who was well covered by his lines, in front of which we halted a stone's throw away, and remained there all day (…)

It is to be noted that the Prince had spoken so much of the German troops that never fired first and obliged their enemies to discharge their weapons then flee before them that each officer had this in mind, and while this was said only with regard to the cavalry, nevertheless nearly the entire infantry made it a point of honour not to fire at all.

Night came and the army had not eaten; they could not fast until the following day when they would have to fight, particularly the horses. The Prince resolved that at daybreak they would withdraw to a village named Loo which our rearguard touched in order for the soldiers to fill their stomachs, and said aloud that he was ready to fight the Archduke whenever he desired, and this public remark contributed to the beginning of battle the following day.

That night, the enemy brought out of their entrenchment the regiment of Croats, but they were much astonished when they encountered our artillery, and they returned in haste.

Dawn came, and to show the enemy that they would not emerge covertly, His Highness waited until the sun had risen, and then he ordered a volley from six pieces by Monsieur de Cossé, and then marched without breaking his battle array, but sending only to the right the companies of gendarmes and *chevau-légers* and those of the guards of the generals retreating in the same order that they were to make the advance guard.

The Lorraine troops of the Spanish army and a few other squadrons, seeing the small number of unregimented companies, fell on them with their entire cavalry wing, broke them easily and pressed them so closely that they were only able to rally with the support of the regiment of Picardie that had the right wing of the first line.

This happy commencement caused Lorraine to cry victory. Beck, who thought he could gain precious time, led the Archduke out of the lines and showed him our infantry dispossessed of cavalry in the middle of one of the largest plains in the world; the Archduke said that he had given the express order that no risks should be taken. Beck insisted and said that there was no more risk, and he offered his head in answer to their (oath?) of the battle; the Spanish reproaching him that he gave up an opportunity to redress their affairs and to rewrite the history of Rocroi, jumped the entrenchment, arrayed their regiments for battle and ran to us.

This was the master stroke of our hero (…)

He did nothing but fill the place of the fallen by the cavalry which was in the second line to defend it. And he sent the troops towards the left, marching straight on the enemy, where each soldier was ready for battle and the columns were formed, but were not yet in battle array.

The regiment of the *Gardes* that had been the first to fire its volley was cut to pieces, and the regiment of *Picardie* which did not wish to fire broke seven regiments, among which was that which had killed the regiment of the guards; the regiments that Erlach had led which were *Nettancourt*, *Vaubecourt* and others did not fire either.

Our cavalry suffered greatly, for the enemy still had three squadrons against one, but when they were broken, they always came to rally behind *Picardie*; [author's note: three names of unidentified officers are listed here], after having charged twenty times and breaking the corps that they fought, came here to refresh themselves, and Streif came here to die.

Your gazetteer found *Maréchal* d'Aumont here, whom the Spanish brought as prisoner after having … to kill him in cold blood with a pistol shot in his order, while he was prisoner.

History shall tell the rest … suffice to say that we took more than six thousand prisoners and did not kill one hundred … men; all their cavalry fled. Beck was injured and captured by a lieutenant of the Aumont regiment; M. d'Arnault wished to reproach him for something relating to the death of Monsieur de Feuquières, and Beck responded very brutally. We took him as a prisoner to Arras, where he died as brutally as he had lived; the Prince, far from taking his revenge on him, lent him his carriage to take him there.

Through the account of a Jesuit reverend father of the group … which followed the Archduke, we learnt that as soon as he had given the generals and the three Spaniards the permission to join the battle under their insistence, he armed himself, confessed, and fled.

Conclusion

The transformation of a military force during times of war is an intricate subject. The evolution of the French army from the late sixteenth to the end of the seventeenth century serves as a compelling case study. This book aims to illustrate the process of this transformation, particularly when guided by capable leadership, exemplified by ministers Richelieu and Mazarin, supported by figures like Servien or Le Tellier. Their efforts culminated in the development of an exceptionally effective army, instrumental in Louis XIV's dominance of Europe in the latter half of the seventeenth century.

Summarizing the insights gleaned from this book, we find that the experience of warfare, especially notable victories, often spurred scholarly and practical reflections. Figures like Machiavelli, Du Bellay, Montgommery, Du Praissac, and Billon contributed theoretical frameworks, although these were seldom directly implemented due to the rapid evolution of military practices and weaponry. Nonetheless, they occasionally provided guiding principles. For instance, the works of Billon and Walhausen exerted influence on certain military leaders. However, the application of theories often lagged behind the exigencies of war and the realities of the battlefield.

The evolution of the French army underscores the cyclical nature of military theory, regulation, and practical experience. This unique evolution was shaped by diverse influences, including religious factors and the legacy of the Wars of Religion. For instance, commanders such as Rohan, Guébriant, and Turenne from Protestant backgrounds, and Châtillon, Brézé, and Condé from Catholic backgrounds, exhibited distinct strategies and resource management approaches. The Protestant generals, in particular, demonstrated adeptness in resource allocation. The amalgamation of these differing perspectives resulted in an innovative military force, ultimately establishing one of the premier European armies.

Colour Plate Commentaries

A. An ensign of the *Gardes Françaises* between 1620 and 1630 from Jacques Callot and K. A. Wilke. In 1629, each company had an ensign and a colour. Article 265 of the *Michaud Code* of 1629 ordered, 'that in quarters, a part of the regiment shall stand guard in front of the *mestre de camp*'s lodgings, if all the colours are carried there, otherwise with the colour of each company.' Article 260 of the aforementioned code stipulates that, 'all troops going to and from the Kingdom march in corps and in order, and that no soldier has to leave his rank or lose sight of his colour.'

B. Musketeer, *c.* 1628–1635 from K.A. Wilke and re-enactor clothing (Association La Courbière). In France, the musket definitively replaced the arquebus from 1622.

C. Pikeman, 1646–1647 from *Soldiers at Rest in an Inn* by Jean Michelin (Musée du Louvres) and *Le Maréchal de Bataille* by Lostelneau. In the 1640s, only the pikemen of the old regiments seem to have kept the helmet and armour.

D. Musketeer, 1646–1647 from Lostelneau's *Le Maréchal de Bataille*. Musketeers were armed with a musket with 12 charges of powder, and a sword.

E. *Chevau-léger* Officer *c.* 1640–1643 from the painting *Halt of Bohemians and Soldiers*, by Sebastien Bourdon in the Musée Fabre, Montpellier, and a model in the collection of the Musée de l'Armée in Paris. French officers wore a scarf, generally white, to distinguish themselves and proclaim their alleigance.

F. *Chevau-léger* wearing a *chapeau d'arme c.*1640–48, from a model in the Musée de l'Armée in Paris. From the 1630s onwards, the *chevau-léger* equipment became much lighter: they no longer wore tassets, brassards or *genouillères*. The ordinances, from 1636, regularly repeat that trooperss must be armoured, and the pot was the most common type of helmet. However, the *chapeau d'arme* helmet seems to have been fairly common in the French cavalry, the breastplate was not always worn.

G. *Gendarme de la Maison du Roi,* from a model in the collection of the Musée de l'Armée in Paris and studies by K. A. Wilke. Like the *chevau-légers,* some *gendarmes* wore the *chapeau d'arme.*

H. *Mousquetaire du Roi c.* 1636, from a XVII century engraving *Louis XIII, King of France, at the Battle of Corbie in 1636,* and a watercolour by Henri Boisselier (1881–1959).

Bibliography

Archives, Unpublished Sources

Archives du Service Historique de l'Armée de Terre *(SHAT)*
SHAT 1642 A71-158
SHAT 1643 A79-159

Archives du Château de Chantilly
Manuscrit MS933, *Relation de la Bataille de Lens, le 20 août 1648, par un officier de Condé*

Primary sources

Many of the titles listed here may not appear to be primary sources (e.g. Duc d'Aumale, *Histoire des Princes de Condé*; Caron, *Michel Le Tellier, son administration comme intendant d'Armée en Piémont*; Vicomte de Noailles, *Episodes de la Guerre de Trente Ans…*). The reason for this, however, is that only the proofs, *relations* or *état des armées*, documents produced at the time of the events and included as appendices in these works, have been used as references.

Anon., *Estat de la France Comme Elle Était Gouvernée en l'an 1648* (Paris: publisher unknown, 1649)
Anon., *Institution de la Discipline Militaire au Royaume de France, A Treshault & Trespuissant Prince Antoine Roy de Navarre* (Lyon: Macé Bonhomme, 1559)
Anon., *La Défaite des Troupes de Monsieur de Favas, La Nouë, & Bellay, au Bourg de Saint Benoît en Bas Poitou, par Messieurs les Maréchal de Praslin, Duc d'Elbeuf & Comte de La Rochefoucault* (Lyon: Abraham Saugrain, 1621)
Anon., *L'Ordre du Départ et Acheminement de l'Armée Du Roy, Vers l'Allemagne, Sous la Conduite de Monsieur le Maréchal de La Force, de Vic le 17 De Septembre 1634, Avec le Nombre des Compagnies de Cavalerie, et Régiments d'Infanterie de Ladite Armée* (Lyon: Jean Jacquemeton, 1634)

Anon., *Mercure François ès Années 1635, 1636, 1637*, ou *Suite de l'Histoire de Notre Temps, Sous le Règne du Très-Chrétien Roi de France et de Navarre, Louis XIII* (Paris: Olivier de Varennes, 1639), Vol.21

Anon., *Mercure François ès Années 1639 &1640*, ou *Suite de l'Histoire de Notre Temps, Sous le Règne du Très-Chrétien Roi de France et de Navarre, Louis XIII* (Paris: Olivier de Varennes, 1646), Vol.23

Aumale, Henri d'Orléans (Duc de), *Histoire des Princes de Condé Pendant les XVIe et XVIIe Siècles* (Paris: Calmann Lévy, 1886), tomes 3 and 4

Bassompierre, François (de), *Mémoires du Maréchal de Bassompierre* (Paris: Jules Renouard, 1877), tome IV

Bessé, Henri (de), *Relation des Campagnes de Rocroi et de Fribourg* (Paris: Delangle, 1826)

Billon, Jean (de), *Les Principes de l'Art Militaire* (Rouen: Berthelin, 1641)

Brantôme, Pierre de Bourdeilles (dit), *Œuvres Complètes du Seigneur de Brantôme. Vies des Hommes Illustres et Capitaines Français* (Paris: Foucault, 1823), tome IV

Campion, Henri (de), *Mémoires de Henri de Campion* (Paris: P. Jannet, 1867)

Caron, Narcisse L., *Michel Le Tellier, Son Administration Comme Intendant d'Armée en Piémont 1640–1643* (Paris: Pedone-Lauriel, 1880)

Castelnau, Michel (de), *Mémoires de Messire Michel de Castelnau*, in *Collection Complète des Mémoires Relatifs à l'Histoire de France* (Paris: Petitot, 1823), Tome 33

Chastenet, Jacques (de), *Les Mémoires de Messire Jacques de Castenet, Chevalier, Seigneur de Puysegur, Colonel du Régiment de Piedmont, & Lieutenant Général des Armées du Roy* (Amsterdam: Abraham Wolfgang, 1690)

Courtilz de Sandras, Gatien (de), *Mémoires de Mr d'Artagnan, Capitaine Lieutenant de la Première Compagnie des Mousquetaires du Roi* (Cologne: Pierre Marteau, 1701), tome I

Contenson, Ludovic (de), *Mémoires du Comte de Souvigny, Lieutenant-Général des Armées du Roi* (Paris: Renouard, 1906), tome I (1613–1638) and tome II (1639–1659)

Daniel, Gabriel (Révérend Père), *Histoire de la Milice Française* (Paris: Jean-Baptiste Coignard, 1721), tome II

Du Bouchet, Jean, *Preuves de l'Histoire de l'Illustre Maison de Coligny* (Paris: Jean Dupuis, 1662)

Du Praissac (Sieur de), *Les Discours Militaires Dédiez à sa Majesté* (Paris: Guillemot & Thiboust, 1614)

Du Val, François, *Mémoires de Messire du Val, Marquis de Fontenay-Mareuil*, in *Collection Complète des Mémoires Relatifs à l'Histoire de France*, (Paris: Petitot, 1826), vol. 1

Gramont, Antoine (de), *Mémoires du Maréchal de Gramont*, in *Nouvelle Collection des Mémoires Pour Servir à l'Histoire de France* (Paris: Michaud et Poujoulat, 1839), Troisième série, tome VII

Henri III, *Code du Roy Henri III, Roy de France et de Pologne* (Lyon: Publisher unknown, 1593)

Isambert, Decrusy and Armet, *Recueil Général des Anciennes lois Françaises Depuis l'an 420, jusqu'à la révolution de 1789* (Paris: Belin-Leprieur, 1828), tome XIII and tome XVI

Laboureur, Jean, *Histoire du Mareschal de Guébriant* (Paris: Louis Billaine, 1676)

La Nouë, François (de), *Discours Politiques et Militaires du Seigneur de La Nouë* (Bâle: Publisher unknown, 1587)

La Valière, François (de), *Pratiques et Maximes de la Guerre* (Paris: Jean-Baptiste Loyson, 1666)

Letouf, Claude (de), *Mémoires et la Vie de Messire Claude de Letouf, Chevalier Baron de Sirot* (Paris: Claude Barbin, 1683)

Lostelneau, Colbert (de), *Le Mareschal de Bataille Contenant le Maniement des Armes, Les Évolutions, Plusieurs Bataillons Tant Contre l'Infanterie que Contre la Cavalerie, Divers Ordres De Bataille* (Paris: Estienne Migon, 1647)

Machiavel, Nicolas, *Oeuvres Complètes* (Paris: Gallimard, 1952)

Marichal, Paul (ed.), *Mémoires du Maréchal de Turenne* (Paris: Renouard, 1909), tome I

Montluc, Blaise (de), *Commentaires de Messire Blaise de Montluc, Mareschal de France*, in *Nouvelle Collection des Mémoires Pour Servir à l'Histoire de France, Depuis le XIIIe Siècle Jusqu'à La Fin Du XVIIIe* (Paris: L'Editeur du Commentaire Analytique du Code Civil, 1838), tome 7

Noailles, Amblard (Vicomte de), *Episodes de la Guerre de Trente Ans, le Cardinal de la Valette, Lieutenant Général des Armées du Roi, 1635 à 1639* (Paris: Perrin, 1906)

Peyrère, Isaac (de la), 'La Bataille de Lens, donnée le 21 août 1648', in Cousin, Victor, *La Société Française au XVIIe Siècle* (Paris: Didier et Cie, 1858), tome 1

Plessis-Praslin, César de Choiseul (Comte de), *Mémoires du Maréchal du Plessis*, in *Collection des Mémoires Relatifs à l'Histoire de France* (Paris: Petitot et Monmerqué, 1827), tome LVII

Pluvinel, Antoine (de), *L'Instruction du Roy en l'Exercice de Monter à Cheval* (Paris: Michel Nivelle, 1625)

Rabutin, Roger (de), *Les Mémoires de Messire Roger de Rabutin Comte de Bussy, Lieutenant Général des Armées du Roi, et Mestre de Camp Général de la Cavalerie Légère* (Amsterdam: Zacharie Chatelain, 1731)

Ramsay, James II, *Histoire du Vicomte de Turenne, Maréchal-Général des Armées du Roi* (La Haye: Jean Neaulme, 1736)

Richelieu, Armand du Plessis (de), *Mémoires du Cardinal de Richelieu*, in *Nouvelle Collection des Mémoires pour Servir à l'Histoire de France*, (Paris: Michaud et Poujoulat, 1837), Deuxième Série, tome VII

Richelieu, Armand du Plessis (de), *Mémoires du Cardinal de Richelieu*, in *Nouvelle Collection des Mémoires pour Servir à l'Histoire de France*, (Paris: Michaud et Poujoulat, 1838), Deuxième Série, tome VIII

Richelieu, Armand du Plessis (de), *Mémoires pour l'Histoire du Cardinal Duc de Richelieu, Recueillis par le Sieur Aubery* (Cologne: Pierre Marteau, 1667), tome II

Richelieu, Armand du Plessis (de), *Testament politique d'Armand du Plessis, Cardinal Duc de Richelieu* (Amsterdam: Henri Desbordes, 1688)

Richelieu, Armand du Plessis (de), *Lettres, Instructions Diplomatiques et Papiers d'Etat du Cardinal de Richelieu, recueillis et publiés par Mr Avenel,* in *Collection de Documents Inédits sur l'Histoire de France,* (Paris: Imprimerie Impériale, 1861), Tome IV (1630–1635)

Richelieu, Armand du Plessis (de), *Lettres, Instructions Diplomatiques et Papiers d'Etat du Cardinal de Richelieu, Recueillis et Publiés par Mr Avenel,* in *Collection de Documents Inédits sur l'Histoire de France,* (Paris: Imprimerie Impériale, 1863), Tome V (1635–1637)

Richelieu, Armand du Plessis (de), *Œuvres du Cardinal de Richelieu* (Paris: Plon, 1933)

Rohan, Henri II (de), *Le Parfait Capitaine; Traité de la Guerre* (Paris: Jean Houze, 1636)

Rohan, Henri II (de), *Mémoires du Duc de Rohan, sur les Choses Advenues en France Depuis la Mort de Henri-le-Grand Jusques à la Paix Faite par les Réformés au Mois de Juin 1629,* in *Nouvelle Collection des Mémoires pour servir à l'Histoire de France* (Paris: Michaud et Poujoulat, 1837), tome 5

Saulx, Guillaume (de), *Mémoires de Guillaume de Saulx, Seigneur de Tavannes,* in *Collection Universelle des Mémoires Particuliers Relatifs à l'Histoire de France,* tome XLIX (London: Publisher unknown, 1789)

Scepeaux, François (de), *Mémoires de la vie de François de Scepeaux, Sire de Vielleville et Comte de Durestal,* in *Nouvelle Collection des Mémoires pour Servir à l'Histoire de France, depuis le XIIIe siècle jusqu'à la fin du XVIIIe* (Paris: Michaud et Poujoulat, 1838), tome 9

Walhausen, Jean-Jacques (de), *L'Art Militaire pour l'Infanterie* (Publisher unknown, 1615)

Zur-Lauben, Béat F.P. (baron de), *Mémoires et Lettres de Henri Duc de Rohan, sur la Guerre de la Valteline* (Genève: Vincent, 1758), tome I

Secondary Sources (published)

Belhomme, Victor L., *Histoire de l'Infanterie en France* (Paris: Lavauzelle, 1893), tomes 1 and 2

Bonaparte, Napoléon, *Précis des Guerres du Maréchal de Turenne* (Paris: Hachette, 1872)

Danskin, Neil, *The French Army in the Thirty years' War,* (Tonbridge: Pallas Armata, 1995)

Gerrer, Bernard, Petit, Patrice, and Sanchez Martin Juan L., *Rocroy 1643, Vérités et Controverses sur une Bataille de Légende* (Publisher unknown, 2007)

Lucht, Antje and Jürgen, *Fahnen & Standarten aus der Zeit des Dreissigjährigen Krieges 1618–1648, Band III* (Freiburg: Edition Peterstor, 2015)

Suzane, Louis A.V., *Histoire de l'Histoire de l'Ancienne Infanterie Française* (Paris: Librairie Militaire, Maritime et Polytechnique de J. Corréard, 1853)

Thion, Stéphane, *La Bataille d'Avins, 20 mai 1635* (Auzielle: LRT Editions, 2011)

Thion, Stéphane, *Rocroi 1643, la Victoire de la Jeunesse* (Paris: Histoire & Collections, 2013)

Journals

Anon., 'Relation de la Bataille de Lens en Flandre, Gagnée par l'Armée Française, Commandée par le Prince de Condé', in *Recueil des Gazettes Nouvelles Ordinaires et Extraordinaires*, 129, (1649), pp.1127–28

Anon., 'Un Récit Inédit de la Bataille de Rocroy', in *Revue Historique du Plateau de Rocroi*, nos 18 and 19 (1924)

About the Author

Stéphane Thion has a PhD in Human Sciences from the Université Toulouse Capitole. Passionate about history and strategy, and well-versed in research methods (he is currently Director of the Doctorate of Business Administration programme), he has been conducting research in the field of military history for over 15 years. He is the author of several historical works on the 17th century: *French Armies of Thirty Years War; La bataille d'Avins 1635; La bataille de Rocroi.* He is also the author of the book *Le Soldat Lagide de Ptolémée Ier Sôter à Cléopâtre* and numerous articles in French magazines.

About the Artist

Giorgio Albertini was born in 1968 in Milan where he still lives. After studying Medieval History at the University of Milan, he become involved in archaeology and has been involved in several excavations for European institutions. He was responsible for the graphic depiction of archaeological sites and finds. He also works as a historical and scientific illustrator for many institutions, museums, and magazines such as *National Geographic Magazine, BBC History*, and *Medieval Warfare*. He has always been interested in military history and is one of the founders of *Focus Wars* magazine.

Other titles in the Century of the Soldier series

For the complete range of Century of the Soldier titles please go to
www.helion.co.uk/series/century-of-the-soldier-1618-1721.php